True North

Alternative and Off-Beat Destinations In and Around Duluth, Superior, and the Shores of Lake Superior

Tony Dierckins & Kerry Elliott

X communication

X-communication
1002 North Thirteenth Avenue East
Duluth, Minnesota 55805
(218) 724-2095
www.x-communication.org

True North: alternative and off-beat destinations in and around Duluth, Superior, and the shores of Lake Superior

Text by Tony Dierckins & Kerry Elliott
Layout & Design by Tony Dierckins
Copy editing by Scott Pearson

Please see page 238 for complete photo and illustration credits.

Library of Congress Control Number: 2002100704

ISBN: 1-887317-00- 0

02   03   04   05   06   10   9   8   7   6   5   4   3   2   1

The authors would like to thank:

Kent Aldrich, Dan Amell, David "Drew" Anderson, Sally Anderson, Ted Anderson, Tim Anderson, Guy Evans, Simon Gray, Adam Guggemos, Susan Gustafson, Chris Hazelton, Jim "Senator" Held, George Kessler, C. Patrick Labadie, Grady Larimper, Mark Lindquist, Suzi Ludwig, Paul Lundgren, Scott Lunt, Tim & Toni MacEvoy, Jack & Hank MacEvoy, Lynette Maki, Julie & Joe Maiolo, Brad Nelson, Maryanne Norton, Tim Nyberg, Bob Olson & Julie Louise Zimmerman, Scott Pearson, "Dr." Dan Proctor, Carlene Sippola, Jean Sramek, Bob Swanfeld, Jon Swanson, Joe Taatjes, Sean Taylor, Mark "Sporty" Voigt, Tom Wigstrom & Lisa Spencer, and the Thursday Night Brewhouse/Starfire Lounge Brain Trust...

...Pat Maus of the Northeast Minnesota Historical Center...

...The great staff of Duluth's St. Louis County Public Library...

...Bob Berg and the Duluth Preservation Alliance...

...Gerri & Gordon Slabaugh and the wonderful folks at Adventure Publications...

...and everyone else whose assistance and suggestions helped shape this book.

Contents

Introduction

Outside the entrance to Duluth's Greysolon Plaza (the former Hotel Duluth), you'll find a compass embedded in the sidewalk. The compass arrow pointing north does not, as one would expect, point straight ahead, but rather at a 45 degree angle to the right—what most people would consider northeast. Duluth, you see, doesn't follow the traditional north-south-east-west layout of most towns. Instead, Duluth hugs the shore of Lake Superior, just as its residents—and those of Superior and the towns along the North and South Shores—embrace the lake.

And so in these parts you won't find true north simply by following the main streets, just as you can't get a true appreciation of this region simply by sticking to the beaten paths that lead to the more typical "touristy" stops along the trail.

Not that those destinations aren't popular for good reason. There are many wonderful places that tourists and local residents regularly visit: Superior's Fairlawn Mansion (Pattison estate) and Barker's Island, Duluth's Canal Park shops, the Aerial Lift Bridge, the Lakewalk, Leif Erickson Park, the Rose Garden, the beach on Park Point, Great Lakes Aquarium, Glensheen Mansion (Congdon estate), Betty's Pies, Gooseberry Falls, Split Rock Light House, Bayfield's quaint shops, etc. We could fill a book describing all the great "touristy" things to see and do in the Twin Ports and along Lake Superior's shores. But of course, many others already have.

You see, we're proud that we're not like other places. We like being a little off center. We like the idea that Duluth's Eighth Street Video is located on Ninth Street, that the Chester Park Laundry doubles as a tropical bird aviary, that the sign on the House of Donuts proclaims "Open 24 Hours. Sunday 'til 5," that Duluth's annual "Christmas City of the North" parade is held before Thanksgiving.

But this region isn't all about Duluth any more than Gooseberry Falls represents the North Shore. And so we we'd like to introduce you to places in this great area you may not know about. We think you'll find that most of the places featured in our book prove to be much more interesting than some of the, shall we say, homogenized establishments that cater to their expectations of your taste.

This project started out to be just about Duluth, but as we shared our idea with others, they told us of more places we simply had to include, many of which are found along Lake Superior's North and South Shores. And so while the book remains centered on Duluth, it has reached up both shores along Minnesota Highway 61 and Wisconsin Highway 13.

We've done our best to omit chain franchises or businesses that are not locally owned. In Duluth we decided to concentrate on places found below Skyline Parkway, not to imply that there is little worth seeing up in the 'Heights, only that there is little to distinguish the Central Entrance strip and the Miller Hill Mall shopping corridor from any suburban shopping center. We've also left out all of Duluth's Canal Park, as the establishments located there have no problem finding customers.

Not all the entries in the book would normally qualify as "alternative" or "off-beat"—a few are probably well-known to visitors. We've included them here because of some unique feature they offer, such as their history, location, or product (like the handcrafted beer at Fitger's Brewhouse). Essentially, everything we've included illustrates the fact that there's more to this region than most visitors—and many local residents—ever experience.

We hope you find the book useful and that it helps you find true north.

– The Authors.

Tips for Travelers

(maps, getting around, unusual laws,
radio stations, etc.)

Tips for Travelers

One of our goals for this book is to show visitors that there's more to Duluth than Canal Park, more to Superior than Barker's Island, more to the South Shore than Bayfield, and more to the North Shore than Gooseberry Falls—all wonderful places, but not a true representation of all that the area has to offer.

And so we created this section to help you find your way around once you leave paths worn smooth by visitors. We've included maps—one showing the North and South Shores as well as individual maps of Duluth and Superior—featuring major thoroughfares to help you get to the places we've highlighted in other chapters. We've also included a page filled with tips on driving in Duluth, from negotiating hills in the winter to figuring out which side of the street to park on. And since you'll be in the car, we've listed all the stations your radio will pick up so you can find your favorite format without messing with the "scan" button.

This section also gave us an opportunity to have some fun, as you'll discover when you read our reasons to go to Superior and our list of some rather obscure and outdated Minnesota and Wisconsin laws.

We've even added a page that attempts to explain the area's weather and—to make every last moment of your visit more interesting—we've included some ideas to make even the ride home something different, at least for those who live south of the Twin Ports in Minnesota (and who make up the vast majority of visitors to this area).

Lake Superior

Lake Superior's
Minnesota North Shore &
Wisconsin South Shore

Driving Duluth

- For the most part, streets (Superior Street, 1st Street, etc.) run relatively east and west (or "across"); avenues run relatively north and south (or "up and down"). Lake Avenue and Superior Street is the "zero" intersection: numbered avenues start from Lake Avenue (1st Avenue East is the first avenue east of Lake Avenue, and 1st Avenue West is the first avenue west of Lake Avenue) and numbered streets start from Superior Street (1st Street is the first street above Superior Street).

- Because of the numerous creek ravines that run through the city, many of Duluth's streets and avenues come to sudden dead ends where it would be impractical to build bridges.

- Several streets in and around downtown are one-ways from Mesaba Avenue to 24th Avenue East, including Michigan Street (heading east, it ends at 4th Avenue East), 1st Street (heading west), 2nd Street (heading east), and 3rd Street (heading west, beginning one way at 22nd Avenue East). Also, 14th Avenue East is a one-way heading up the hill, and 12th Avenue East heads one way down the hill.

- When driving east on 2nd Avenue between Mesaba Avenue and 6th Avenue East, drive at a steady 30 mph and you should find the traffic lights lit green the whole stretch.

- Due to its narrow streets, alternate-side parking is enforced year round throughout most of Duluth. The "parking side" switches each Sunday, and residents must move their cars between 4 P.M. and 8 P.M.

- The steepest hill in Duluth is 5th Avenue West above 5th Street—a 26 percent grade.

- Winter driving on slippery hillside roads can be tricky, particularly if you don't have a four- or front-wheel drive vehicle. Fortunately, the plow crews move quickly in Duluth. If you do find yourself driving Duluth when the streets are thick with snow or ice, try this: stick to main thoroughfares, especially when you have to go uphill, and approach your destination from above (it's easier to go down a hill in poor conditions than to go up).

Getting from Duluth's Canal Park to Downtown Duluth without Driving

Too many Duluth visitors miss out on the wonderful downtown shops and restaurants because they don't want to drive from their hotels in Canal Park and park or are uncomfortable crossing I-35 on Lake Avenue on foot.

You can get to "Old" Downtown (between Lake Avenue and 4th Avenue East) using the Lakewalk. Find the stairs near the bathroom facilities just past Endion Station and follow them up. You'll find a small park that covers the highway, complete with benches and statuary and intersected with sidewalks. The sidewalks lead to boardwalks near Michigan Street. These boardwalks will lead you to three different intersections in "Old" Downtown: Second Avenue East and Superior Street, First Avenue East and Superior Street, and Lake Avenue and Superior Street.

Another way to get downtown is through the Skywalk. Cross the blue drawbridge to the Duluth Entertainment & Convention Center (DECC). The DECC connects to the Skywalk system and leads directly to the Wells Fargo Building at Third Avenue West and Superior Street.

What you'll find in "Old" Downtown (and in this book): Electric Fetus, Lizzard's Gallery, Chinese Dragon, Last Place on Earth, Carlson Books, Lester River Fly Shop, Lake Superior Smokin' Brews, First Oriental Grocery, Hacienda Del Sol, Romano Grocery, Chinese Garden, NorShor Theatre, Green Mercantile, Round About Records, Browser's N'eTc., Original Coney Island, Greysolon Plaza, and the Old City Hall and Jail.

What you'll find Downtown (and in this book): Fragments of History, Tony's Trading Post, Global Village, Jitters, Explorations, Toys for Keeps, Mr. Nick's, India Palace, Coco's to Geaux, Duluth Tobacco & Gift, Cantonese House, Sammy's Pizza, Coney Island Deluxe, Thai Krathong, Dirtygirlz Cooperative, Chef Yee's, Exchange Deli, Angela's Bella Flora, Duluth Civic Center, Duluth Union Depot, Board of Trade Building, Alworth Building, and Wirth Building.

Duluth, Minnesota (main thoroughfares)

Town of Proctor ★

Where is West Duluth?
West Duluth was once a city separate from Duluth. It is now the area west of Lincoln Park containing the following neighborhoods: Fairmont, Irving, Cody, Spirit Valley, Denfeld, Oneota, and Bayview Heights.

0   .5   1
scale in miles

Becks Rd.

Skyline

Parkway

Boundary Ave.

Bayview Heights

Skyline

Parkway

Haines Rd.

Piedmont Ave.

Piedmont Heights

Skyline

♦ Spirit Mountain Ski Hill

Lake Superior Zoological Gardens

Cody

Spirit Valley

Central Ave.

Denfeld

Lincoln Park (aka. West End)

40th Ave. W.

Norton Park ♦

Fairmont

Grand Ave.

Carlton Ave.

Superior St.

Smithville

Riverside

Irving

Oneota

Wade Stadium ♦

Michigan St.

Fond du Lac

Grand Ave (Hwy 23)

Arbor St.

Morgan Park

Becks Rd.

Commonwealth Ave.

New Duluth

Gary

To Oliver

Richard I. Bong Bridge (To Superior)

St. Louis River

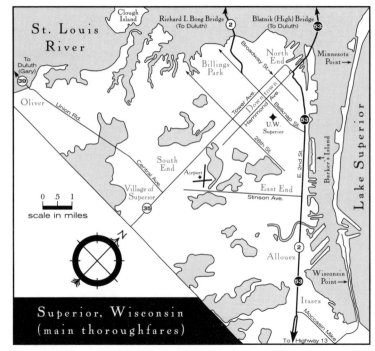

Superior, Wisconsin
(main thoroughfares)

Visit Superior

Too few visitors to Duluth ever cross the river to Superior, and that's a shame. Superior is home to museums, historic sites, and many taverns and restaurants. Many before you have found it a great place to visit or make their home:

Gangster Al Capone once suggested to a friend that she'd find Superior a hospitable place to live (see next page).

Movie star Arnold Schwarzenegger lived in Superior while attending his alma mater, UW-Superior (rumor has it that's his cabin atop Silver Cliff on Minnesota Highway 61 past Two Harbors).

And Superior is home to Raymond "Bud" Somerville, the first inductee into the United States Curling Association's Hall of Fame.

By the way, in Superior, Highways 2 and 53 are the same as East 2nd Street when they pass through town.

Ten Reasons to Go to Superior

Why do so few visitors to Duluth ever make the short drive to Superior? Maybe it's because of the whole Minnesota vs. Wisconsin issue, the Packers vs. Vikings rivalry, or the slew of bad driver jokes tossed in both directions. But whatever the reason, if you don't head "O.T.B." (over the bridge) as local residents like to say, you're not getting a true north experience. If you can't find your own reason to go or aren't satisfied with those mentioned on page 8, we've listed a few more for you below. The list contains ten reasons, but not necessarily the top ten.

- Twenty-six bars operate along one ten-block strip of Tower Avenue, plus nine more a block or less off Tower.

- Bars stay open until 2 A.M. on weeknights, 2:30 A.M. on weekends (in Minnesota, bars always close at 1 A.M.).

- Superior has more places to eat at 2 A.M.

- Liquor stores are open on Sundays (liquor stores are closed in Minnesota on Sundays).

- You can smoke in restaurants (Duluth has banned smoking in its restaurants).

- Lower cigarette taxes = cheaper cigarettes (please, for your own good, don't smoke!).

- As Al Capone once told a friend, Superior "is full of speakeasies and brothels...the law won't give you any trouble there" (of course, that was during Prohibition).

- Two bridges cross between Duluth and Superior: The Richard I. Bong Bridge and the Blatnik Bridge, also known as the High Bridge. So, technically, you can go to Superior on a bong and come back on a high (we have no idea what this means).

- Closet Green Bay Packer fans from Minnesota can cheer the Pack in relative safety.

- You can't get to the South Shore from Duluth without driving through Superior!

Obscure Minnesota Laws

Not many of these laws are still on the books, but we want you to be prepared. Remember, ignorance of the law is no excuse.

In Minnesota…

- A person may not cross state lines with a duck atop his or her head (also, citizens may not enter Wisconsin with chickens on their heads).
- It is illegal to sleep naked.
- All men driving motorcycles must wear shirts (there was no mention whether women must wear shirts).
- It is unlawful to tease or torment skunks or polecats.

In Duluth…

- All bathtubs must have feet.
- Dogs may not nap in barber shops or beauty salons. The law also makes it illegal to let a dog, horse, or any other animal sleep in a bakery.

Further up the map…

- If you visit Hibbing, keep close tabs on your cat, for "If any cat is found running at large, or is found in any street, alley, or public place, it shall be the duty of any policeman or other officer of the city to kill such cat."
- If you travel to International Falls, keep in mind that cats are not allowed to chase dogs up telephone poles.
- And if you stop by Virginia, remember that you're not allowed to park your elephant on Main Street.

Obscure Wisconsin Laws

When visiting the Dairy State, keep a close watch on your activities surrounding dairy and faux-dairy products, for in Wisconsin...

- At one time, margarine was illegal.
- Butter substitutes are not allowed to be served in state prisons.
- All yellow butter substitutes were banned after people began smuggling them in from Illinois.
- It was once illegal to serve apple pie in public restaurants without cheese.
- While all cheese making requires a cheese maker's license, making Limburger cheese requires a *master* cheese maker's license.

Furthermore...

- You must manually flush all urinals in a building.
- Citizens may not murder their enemies.
- It was once illegal to kiss on a train.
- It was once illegal to cut a woman's hair.
- Car dealerships cannot sell cars on Sunday.

And to clear things up...

- "...Whenever two trains meet at an intersection of said tracks, neither shall proceed until the other has."

Radio Stations

Commercial-Free & Public Radio

KUMD • 103.3 FM • Duluth • "Duluth Public Radio"
A member-supported, independent public radio station broadcasting from the University of Minnesota Duluth campus. Eclectic mix. "World Café" weekday afternoons from 2-5 P.M. and Sunday morning. Blues Saturday afternoons. Music by women Sunday afternoons. "This Way Out" (gay-lesbian-bisexual-transgender news and entertainment) late Sunday afternoons. Jazz Sunday evenings.

WTIP • 90.7 FM • Grand Marais • "Public Radio for the North Shore"
An eclectic mix of folk, bluegrass, singer/songwriter, acoustic, classical, American Indian, Celtic—you name it— along with some programming from KUMD (including the "World Café").

WSCN-FM • 100.5 FM • Duluth • Minnesota Public Radio & NPR / Talk *(WLSN 89.7 on the North Shore)*
NPR, news, information, and entertainment: "Talk of the Nation," "All Things Considered," "Fresh Air," "This American Life," "A Prairie Home Companion" (Saturdays at 5 P.M. and Sundays at noon). Jazz with Leigh Kammam on Saturday nights.

WSCD-FM • 92.9 FM • Duluth • MPR & NPR / Classical music *(WMLS 88.7 on the North Shore)*
Classical music along with some WSCN programming (e.g., "A Prairie Home Companion").

KUWS • 91.3 FM • Superior • Wisconsin Public Radio & NPR
NPR, news, and a great mix of music broadcasting from the campus of the University of Wisconsin, Superior.

Radio Stations, continued

KDAL
610 AM • Duluth
Talk with News, Weather, & Sports

KDAL "96 Lite"
95.7 FM • Duluth
Adult Contemporary

KDNW
97.3 FM • Duluth
Christian

KKCB "B-105"
105 FM • Duluth
Country

KLDJ "KOOL 101.7"
101.7 FM • Duluth
Oldies

KQDS
94.9 FM • Duluth
Classic and New Rock

KQDS AM "Sunny"
1490 AM • Duluth
Big Band

KRBR "The Bear"
102.5 FM • Duluth
New Rock

KTCO
98.9 FM • Duluth
New Country

KUSZ "USA Radio"
99.9 FM • Duluth
Country

KXTP "Radio Disney"
970 AM • Duluth
Disney Programming

KZIO
104.3 FM and 106.3 • Duluth
"Hot Oldies"

WEBC Radio
560 AM • Duluth
Talk

WDSM
710 AM • Duluth
Sports

WNCB
89.3 FM • Duluth
Christian hits

WNXR
107.3 FM • Superior
Oldies & Brewers' baseball

WWAX "Kiss 92"
92.1 FM • Duluth
Top 40

WWJC Radio
850 AM • Duluth
Christian Information

WXXZ
95.3 FM • Grand Marais
Classic and New Rock

KUSZ "The Point"
107.7 FM • Duluth
"Today's Hits and Yesterday's
Favorites"

Informative Websites

If you're looking for more information about Duluth, Superior, or places to go or things to do up and down the Lake Superior shores, try these websites:

Local Press:

www.ripsawnews.com (the *Ripsaw*, local arts and entertainment weekly)

www.duluthnews.com (*Duluth News-Tribune*, Duluth's daily paper, a member of the Knight-Ridder chain)

www.duluthshippingnews.com (daily reports and schedules of arrivals and departures from the Duluth harbor)

General/Visitor Info:

www.duluthsuperior.com

www.digital.myareaguide.com

www.duluthmn.dgn.myareaguide.com

www.duluthnews.com/justgo

www.visitduluth.com

www.ohwycom/mn/d/duluth.htm

www.duluthpreservation.org/index.html

www.dnr.state.mn.us/parks_and_recreation/state_parks

www.northshore.hypermart.net/events.htm

www.northshorevisitor.com

www.exploreminnesota.com

www.visitsuperior.com

www.superior-wi.com

www.travelwisconsin.com

Colder by the Lake?

Most out-of-towners have a pretty bad impression about the weather "up north," especially about Duluth's weather. "How can you live up there?" they ask. "With all that snow and it gets so ding-dang cold?" Well, they may not say "ding-dang," but they do think it's rather cold in these parts. And they're right. Kinda.

The oft-repeated refrain from TV weathercasters is "colder by the lake." This refers to the fact that there is often a great deal of difference in temperature from the harbor to "over the hill" in the 'Heights and further up at the airport, where the official temperature is measured. In the summer, "colder by the lake" is generally the rule, as the cold waters of Lake Superior act as an air conditioner, keeping the average summer temperature at 62 degrees (Duluth is the coldest major urban center in the contiguous United States). Meteorologists have reported as much as a 40-degree difference between the airport and harbor on a summer's day. In the winter, however, it is often warmer by the lake, as residents below the hill are protected from icy northwest winds.

But don't take anything for granted—even the forecast. The Lake Superior region is one of those places that lays claim to the old adage "If you don't like the weather, wait five minutes." The lake makes weather predicting rather unpredictable and keeps the jobs of area meteorologists very interesting.

The Twin Ports don't get as much snowfall as one might expect, but the North Shore does get more snow than any other place in Minnesota. The real dumping ground is the South Shore, also known as the snow belt, which receives more than its fair share of lake-effect snow. Common from November to February, lake-effect snow is any snow—from flurries to squalls—that the presence of the Great Lakes cause or help to develop.

Lake Superior is also susceptible to great blasts of wind many have mistakenly called Nor'Easters (a similar phenomenon found along the eastern seaboard) that make sailing treacherous. Some call these winds "the gales of November" after the reference in Gordon Lightfoot's famous ballad, "The Wreck of the Edmund Fitzgerald."

Take the Long Way Home

If you're from the Twin Cities and have visited before, you know what a pain traffic can be on a Sunday evening when it seems that everyone is trying to get back from mowing the lawn at the cabin with enough time to mow the lawn in the suburbs. Next time, make extra time so you can take your time and enjoy the time. Here are some ideas:

Take the Scenic Route
Instead of I-35, follow Grand Avenue south until it becomes Commonwealth Avenue and, eventually, Scenic Highway 23 and enjoy a leisurely drive until the highway connects with I-35 near Askov.

Take Skyline out of Town
Heading west on Skyline Parkway will eventually bring you to the on-ramp of I-35 at Boundary Avenue. If you stay on Skyline to the end, you'll find yourself at Becks Road. A right will take you to I-35, a left to Scenic 23.

Go through Wisconsin
Wisconsin's Highway 35 out of Superior will take you all the way to Stillwater, Minnesota, or Hudson, Wisconsin, so if you're from the eastern suburbs, this is a fun way to go. You'll have to jump on Highway 8 at St. Croix Falls and head west to stay on 35.

Treat Your Tank & Tummy
Stop in Cloquet and fill your tummy at Gordy's Hi-Hat, a classic drive-in restaurant open during the summer. You'll find good old-fashioned burgers and fries and thick malts to chase them down. When you're full, top off the tank with a taste of architectural history at the Phillips 66 service station at the corner of Route 45 and Route 33—it was designed by Frank Lloyd Wright.

Outdoor Adventures

(day trips and some stunning views)

Outdoor Adventures

Obviously you can't have a chapter titled "Outdoor Adventures" in a book that covers the North and South Shores without mentioning Lake Superior itself. We thought you'd like to know a little something about that big body of water that dominates—and has shaped—the landscape that surrounds it. Lake Superior was formed about 10,000 years ago, near the end of the most recent ice age. As the giant glaciers melted, they formed lakes, including Glacial Lake Duluth, Superior's predecessor (Skyline Parkway runs along what was once its beach). With its surface 602 feet above sea level, Superior has the highest elevation of all the Great Lakes. It is also largest in area with 31,280 square miles (an area equal to Connecticut, New Hampshire, Massachusetts, Rhode Island, and Vermont combined), and the cleanest and coldest as well (average temperature, 40 degrees Fahrenheit). It contains three quadrillion gallons of water, or about ten percent of the world's fresh water. From east to west Lake Superior extends 383 miles; it stretches 160 miles across at its widest and reaches depths of 1,279 feet.

There's a lot to do along Superior's shores (2,700 miles of shoreline surround the lake), but far too many visitors limit their adventures to a drive along the highway and a stop at Gooseberry Falls or the Split Rock Lighthouse. We want you to see more of it. At the same time, we realize that not everyone is an outdoor enthusiast who packs plenty of gear and is ready to kayak or rock climb at a moment's notice. Most of us are lucky to remember to pack a decent pair of athletic shoes.

If you did, you're in luck. The following 38 pages are filled with adventures you can experience without gear—we did them all with nothing more than a beat-up pair of hiking boots, and most often even those weren't required. Almost all of the adventures are found less than a mile from shore (most even closer than that) and many are found inside the Duluth city limits (only Eagle Mountain on page 45 takes you more than three miles from the shore). You can get to all of them in a car, and none of them require even as much as a state park pass.

Bring a camera.

Amity Creek: Seven Bridges & The Deeps

Amity Creek is a western feeding branch of the Lester River that converges with the larger waterway just above Superior Street within the boundaries of Lester Park. On its way downstream toward the Lester and Lake Superior, Amity winds through gorges of rhyolite and over basalt ledges, forming many waterfalls along the way.

One of the more popular spots along the Amity is The Deeps, a large pool formed by erosion at the base of a waterfall just upstream from the Lester near Occidental Boulevard (which becomes Seven Bridges Road). A foot-bridge above the waterfall connects to hiking trails. What do folks do at The Deeps? They jump in.

While most of the Amity is quite shallow, some areas in The Deeps reach forty feet down. Local adrenaline junkies like to leap from nearby cliffs, and have been doing so for years. Launching spots such as "Stumpy," "The Tower," and "The Pine" offer jumpers a challenge. (Cliff jumping is extremely dangerous; jumpers do so at their own risk.)

The Amity is also the creek over which the seven stone arched bridges of Seven Bridges Road cross. The road is the result of efforts by former mayor Sam Snively, who donated 60 acres of his own property and convinced other land owners to donate the property on which the road was built and some of the necessary funds to build it (see pages 30 and 31 for more details).

"The Deeps" of Amity Creek, a popular cliff jumping site.

Chester Park

Chester Park is one of Duluth's original three parks (along with Lincoln and Zenith) and a popular trail system among UMD and St. Scholastica students and East Hillside residents—especially dog lovers. The park takes its

name not from Chester Congdon, as many believe, but from Charles Chester, who homesteaded a property along the creek near what is now 5th Street, just east of 13th Avenue East, on May 31, 1856 (ruins of his home remain).

The park's 108 acres include 2.5 miles of hiking trail along Lower Chester (the area below Skyline Boulevard), which is home to a pair of footbridges, several waterfalls, and a cauldron known as Devil's Hole. Four miles of cross country ski/hiking trails can be found in Upper Chester (also known as Chester Bowl). Upper Chester also contains soccer fields (flooded in the winter for ice skating), a small ski hill, and some ski jumps. The Chester Bowl ski jumps were the training grounds for several national champions and members of the U.S. Olympic Ski Jumping Team. Many of the park's stone walls and stairways were constructed by the WPA in the 1930s. Mountain bikers, please take note: The trails are very fragile; bikes are *not* allowed.

You'll find ample parking in the lot at Skyline Boulevard and Chester Parkway, which runs along the east side of the creek starting at the 8th Avenue East Bridge. You can also park along the bridge at 4th Street between 13th and 14th Avenues East.

One of Chester Creek's waterfalls near Skyline Boulevard.

Congdon Park & Tischer Creek

The 38 acres along Tischer Creek that make up Congdon Park were donated to the city in 1908 by Chester A. Congdon, who along with his wife Clara built a family mansion, Glensheen, at the site where the creek empties into Lake Superior. In 1925 Mayor Sam Snively saw to it that the park was developed, establishing gravel-covered trails, stone stairways, and wooden bridges—even a bridle path once graced the park. The park fell into disrepair over the years, but in 1972 the Duluth Junior League, along with the Department of Parks and Recreation, restored the park as a nature trail with the help of local Boy Scouts and UMD students.

The park rests between Superior Street and Vermillion Road and winds along the creek near 32nd Avenue East. A stairway leads down to trails within the deep walls that form the park's boundaries. High cliffs of red rock, produced by lava roughly one billion years ago, show how much the creek has eroded the stone over the eons. White cedars appear to grow straight out of the cliffs (a trick of erosion), and Norway pines and a variety of hardwoods line the creek. Several waterfalls grace Tischer Creek; one forms a large swimmin' hole.

You can enter Congdon Park at 32nd Avenue East and Superior Street. Look for stairs leading down into the creek gorge near the park's sign, on the uphill side of Superior Street just west of the bridge. You can park along 32nd Avenue East near Congdon School.

Steep red rock cliffs line portions of Congdon Park's Tischer Creek.

Enger Park & Twin Ponds

Most people know Enger Park for its six-story, bluestone tower, but there's a lot more to the greenspace than a great view. The park contains a gazebo, pavilion, gardens, and the Peace Bell.

The Peace Bell is a replica of a cherished temple bell in Ohara, Japan. The Japanese government took the original bell from Ohara in 1940 to be melted down as part of the war effort, but for some reason the bell never met the furnace. After the war, American sailors aboard the *U.S.S. Duluth* took the bell as a spoil of war and sent it to their ship's namesake city. The bell was returned to Ohara in the 1950s. Years later, the town of Ohara had a replica of the bell made for its sister city, Duluth, and the new bell was dedicated at Enger Park in 1994. It was then dubbed the Peace Bell.

In keeping with the Japanese theme, beautiful gardens with a trickling fountain/stream and winding footpaths make up most of Enger Park. The groomed areas are surrounded by rock outcroppings that lead to thick stands of trees. A gazebo to the east provides a view without climbing the tower's six stories of stairways, and a stone pavilion complete with a fireplace, picnic tables, and restrooms provides visitors with a comfortable spot for an outdoor meal.

Just east of the park along Skyline Parkway you'll find Twin Ponds. As Lake Superior is often too cold to take a dip, many Duluthians use the ponds as a swimmin' hole.

Enger Park's Peace Bell, donated by its Japanese sister city, Ohara.

Kitchi Gammi Park (a.k.a. Brighton Beach)

Most people who haven't been there in a while still call Kitchi Gammi Park "Brighton Beach." In fact, Brighton Beach is just part of the park (and the road that goes through it is named for the beach). Found along the Lake Superior shore just a quarter mile from Lester River where London Road converges with Scenic Highway 61, Kitchi Gammi Park provides visitors with various picnicking and outdoor-cooking spots, restrooms in the summer, and a quaint gazebo overlooking the lake. It even has some swingsets and a sandbox for the kids to play on and in.

But Brighton Beach remains Kitchi Gammi's central attraction. This stretch of shore isn't what most people think of when they think about going to the beach. It's sort of a compromise between the craggy rocks of Stoney Point and the sandy shores of Minnesota Point. In other words, it's covered in rocks—big ones for climbing over and sunning upon and small ones perfect for skipping upon the water. You can swim here, but no lifeguards patrol the area.

Some of these rocks are often formed into circles for driftwood fires on cool fall and summer nights, as the park provides a view of the city lights of Duluth and Superior. If you're an early riser, take a drive out to the park and watch the sunrise over the unbroken horizon.

The rocky "beach" at Kitchi Gammi Park, with Wisconsin in the distance.

Hartley Park (a.k.a. Hartley Nature Center)

Hartley Park (sometimes called "Hartley Nature Center") is made up of 660 acres of diverse natural habitat, including streams, ponds, forests, and wetlands, on the site that was once a farm owned by Guilford and Caroline E. Hartley, who left many landmarks throughout Duluth (see pages 228 and 234).

The park contains about five miles of trails—three of which are maintained for cross-country skiing—that are popular among runners, hikers, and dog owners. It's also home to a 50-acre wetland, streams, and an abundance of wildlife such as bears, white-tailed deer, mink, fox, owls, and a variety of other birds.

The view of Duluth and Lake Superior from Hartley Park's Rock Knob.

Perhaps the most obvious natural landmark in Hartley Park is Rock Knob, a 100-foot stone hill that many park visitors use as a vantage point to view the park and its surroundings. On a clear day, you can see Lake Superior while Duluth's houses and buildings remain hidden by trees.

Ruins of some of the outbuildings and other remnants of the Hartley family farm can be found throughout the park.

Hartley Park is open until dark during winter and until 10 P.M. in the summer. To get there, take Woodland Avenue north past Minneapolis Street and look for the sign on your left. For more information on the park, call (218) 724-6735.

Lester Park

Lester Park is located a few blocks upstream from the mouth of Lester River at the edge of Duluth's Lakeside neighborhood. Its eastern border runs along Lester River Road, and it's bordered on the west by Amity Creek and Seven Bridges Road (see page 19). The park includes miles of hiking and cross-country ski trails and a central park area near the parking lot that has picnic tables, grills, fields, shelters, and playground equipment.

The hiking and ski trails lead along both Lester River and Amity Creek. Portions of the river run through a fairly deep gorge in parts of the park, and hikers can either stroll on the smoother trails above the river or along rougher trails next to the water. For the view, get close to the river, where you'll find steep cliff walls, waterfalls, and swimming holes below the cascades.

Just downstream from the point where the Lester and Amity merge, cliff jumpers will find another spot to test their nerves. Old bridge footings and natural cliff walls form platforms for jumps as high as 60 feet, but most range from 20 to 30 feet. (Cliff jumping is extremely dangerous; jumpers do so at their own risk.)

To get to Lester Park, take Superior Street past 60th Avenue East to Lester River Road and turn left. You'll find a parking lot on your left less than a quarter mile up the road.

In September, Lester River runs shallow as it approaches Lake Superior.

Minnesota Point (a.k.a. Park Point)

Minnesota Point, a.k.a. Park Point, is the northern half of the largest freshwater sandbar in the world (Wisconsin Point, of course, is the southern half). Most of Minnesota Point is a residential area, but the entire stretch of shore on the lakeside—all of it sandy beach—is open to the public. Most visitors stop where the road ends, at the recreation center just shy of Sky Harbor Airport. But for others, this is where the adventure begins.

Wildflowers grace the beach near the Minnesota Point Hiking Trail.

Behind the airport you'll find the entrance to the Minnesota Point Hiking Trail. An old-growth forest of naturally regenerating red and white pines (some about 200 years old) begins shortly thereafter and continues almost to the end of the point at the Superior Entry. The sandy soil is often a challenge to hike, and bicyclists would be ill-advised to try these trails (besides, they'll also damage a delicate ecosystem). Stay on the trail: much of the ground cover is thick with poison ivy.

Along the trail, hikers will encounter the ruins of the oldest standing lighthouse on Lake Superior. Built in 1858, the Minnesota Point Lighthouse operated for 20 years. The ruin of the U.S. Lighthouse Station Depot rests nearby (see page 55).

To get to the hiking trail, simply cross the Aerial Lift Bridge and drive along Minnesota Avenue until you run out of road (about four miles).

Mission Creek Trail

Mission Creek Trail is perhaps the most historically significant trail in Duluth. It is named for the Ely Mission, which was founded on the current site of the Fond du Lac Community Church in 1834. Fond du Lac was home to the first mail route in the area; established in 1857, carriers used dogsleds to bring mail as far away as Canada, and the route started on what is now the Mission Creek Trail. A brownstone quarry run by C.A. Krause operated on the creek in the 1880s, and much of the rock (Fond du Lac sandstone) was used in such historic Duluth buildings as Old Central High School (see page 71). A portion of the trail was once a road, built by the WPA, that connected with Skyline Drive. Mission Creek was also a popular recreation area and included Ojibway Lodge, an ice skating rink, a ski hill, and even ski jumps.

The 3.25-mile trail follows a path created by American Indians long before the area was settled by Europeans. Half of the trail criss-crosses the creek over several footbridges while the other half takes hikers through a heavily wooded area filled with birches, maples, and a variety of other trees. It starts next to a holding dam near the site of the old quarry and at one point connects with the Willard Munger Trail.

To get to the trail, go south on Grand Avenue (Highway 23) to 131st Avenue West, turn right at Fond du Lac Park and follow the road until it ends at a gate. If the gate is open, follow the dirt road until you reach the trailhead (if the gate is locked, you will have to walk in).

Mission Creek Trail: thick with hardwoods that explode in fall colors.

Oneota Cemetery

The tree stump marker of H.A. Michelson.

Most people don't think of cemeteries as spots for outdoor adventures, but if you've ever taken the time to look around while you remember your lost loved ones, you've probably noticed what beautiful places they can be. If you don't find cemeteries morbid, you're in for a natural and architectural treat.

Take Duluth's Oneota Cemetery, for instance. Established in 1895 in what was then Oneota Township, the cemetery includes some wonderful old markers, and because of its location next to Skyline Parkway, it also has a great view of St. Louis Bay.

Among the notables buried here are George Stuntz (and his dog Kayuga), the surveyor who mapped out most of Duluth and Superior, and environmental politician Willard Munger (for whom the Munger Trail is named).

To get to Oneota, take Central Avenue north from I-35 to Highland Street and turn left—Highland runs right past the cemetery before connecting with Skyline Parkway.

An eroding marker set in 1890.

Forest Hill & Park Hill Cemeteries

Forest Hill Cemetery, which can be accessed through the gate at Woodland and Carlisle Avenues, is the final resting place for many Duluthians. It is also a sprawling park filled with trees, ponds, nesting geese during the summer, and some very interesting grave markers.

The names on the markers in the older portion of the cemetery read like a who's who of Duluth and Northeastern Minnesota history. You'll find markers and mausoleums for Congdons, Alworths, Denfelds, Hibbings, Chisolms, and enough Hartleys to fill the Kitchi Gammi Club (some with last names such as Munger-Hartley and Hartley-Congdon, reflecting the past social circles of Duluth's elite). The resting place of Captain Charles S. Barker, for whom Superior's Barker's Island is named, is marked by a large stone cube graced with a round, bronze relief of the Captain's profile.

Some of the markers even reflect the region itself, such as the Walbank mausoleum laid in 1890, made of Lake Superior Brownstone. A stone obelisk dedicated to those of Scottish descent who have passed stands near a cannon memorializing those Duluthians who died in the Civil War.

Park Hill Cemetery, located behind Forest Hill on Vermillion Road, also contains some historic grave sites, most notably those of lynching victims Isaac McGhie, Elmer Jackson, and Elias Clayton (see page 212), who were originally buried in unmarked graves. A few rows away lies Olli Kinkkonen, a Finnish immigrant lynched for his political views in 1918 (see page 213).

One of Forest Hill's striking markers.

Skyline Parkway: a car or bike tour

The 28 mile roadway known as Skyline Parkway sits almost 500 feet above Lake Superior and stretches along a ridge of what millions of years ago was the beach of Glacial Lake Duluth. The road once reached from Occidental Boulevard (Seven Bridges Road) along Amity Creek near the Lester River all the way into Jay Cooke State Park. It can still be accessed at Occidental and East Superior Street, but now ends where it intersects with Becks Road near Gary-New Duluth.

The parkway was first imagined by William K. Rogers, president of Duluth's first park board, and was presented to the Duluth City Council in 1888. By 1900 it was only five miles long. During the 1920s, Mayor Sam Snively—dedicated to making Duluth "the most beautiful city in the Northwest"—saw to it that the roadway was extended. The mayor had already built Seven Bridges Road with private funds. By 1927 the parkway ran to Jay Cooke State Park and in 1927 was named

Duluth's Skyline Parkway

Skyline Parkway, continued

Skyline Parkway. (Before that, the road had been named Carriage Drive, Rogers Boulevard, and Terrace Parkway.) In 1935 Snively began work to connect Skyline to Seven Bridges Road, a task that would not be completed until 1939, two years after he left office.

Today, much of the parkway is interrupted by larger thoroughfares that took priority over a leisure route. Starting at Spirit Mountain and heading west, the road remains unpaved. One of its original stone bridges can be seen along this stretch, which features a stunning view from Bardon's Peak.

Today, Seven Bridges Road consists of eight bridges (there were originally nine; two were abandoned when Skyline Parkway was completed; a newer bridge near Superior Street is not considered part of Seven Bridges Road). To learn more about Skyline Parkway and Seven Bridges Road, see Mark Ryan's website at www.geocities.com/SoHo/Lofts/4839/SevenBridges/.

Western Waterfront Trail

The 2.5-mile Western Waterfront Trail winds along the St. Louis River valley and was designed to allow users to get as close as possible to the water and wetlands that surround it.

One leg of the crushed limestone trail follows a path along the river that takes hikers around two of its bays, ending up at a parking lot at 63rd Avenue West. Another crosses Kingsbury Creek and traverses the perimeter of Indian Point Campground before stretching along the St. Louis until it reaches the Riverside neighborhood. The scenery on the Western Waterfront Trail is very different from that of most other Duluth parks. It includes expansive wetlands that are home to a variety of waterfowl, wildflowers, and other plant life. Rather than looking down toward the lake, hikers can gaze up toward Spirit Mountain—a great spot to watch the fall colors.

Wetlands of the St. Louis River valley along the Western Waterfront Trail.

The trail has two access points: a parking lot at Grand Avenue and 71st Avenue West (next to the Tappa Keg Inn and across from the Lake Superior Zoo) and another at Grand Avenue and Pulaski Street (take a left just past the Willard Munger Inn). Both access points also provide a gateway to the Willard Munger Trail, a paved bicycle/inline skating trail that rolls all the way to Hinkley, Minnesota. If you're from out of town and wish to give the Munger Trail a try, you can rent bicycles and other gear at the Willard Munger Inn.

Wisconsin Point

While Wisconsin Point together with Minnesota Point make up the world's largest sandbar, the Points differ greatly from one another. Minnesota Point is highly developed with homes, community buildings, businesses, and even an airport. Wisconsin Point has been left almost completely natural. This may well be because it is considerably more narrow than its Minnesota counterpart.

All the better for its recreational users. Most of the Point is covered by pine forest and a vast stretch of beach. The beach is a popular spot for late-night summer parties, when the shoreline is likely to be dotted with bonfires and revelers. Hikers and bikers will enjoy the Osaugie Recreation Trail, a 5.5-mile trek running between the Nemadji River to Moccasin Mike Road and on to the end of the Point, where a lighthouse stands at the end of a long stone pier.

The Point is also home to the site of a traditional Fond du Lac Chippewa burial ground that dates from the 17th century. The graves were moved to Superior's St. Francis Cemetery in 1918, but the site is well marked and many visitors still leave offerings of respect, such as tobacco, dream catchers, and other less traditional gifts.

To get to Wisconsin Point, take Highway 53 southeast to the outskirts of Superior and turn left onto Moccasin Mike Road—the road will take you all the way to the end of the point (see the map on page 8).

The lighthouse at the end of Wisconsin Point.

Snow Sliding on Duluth's Hills

In a city built on a hillside with winter weather conditions from late October to early May, it's an easy bet that Duluth has seen its share of snow sliding. In the 1880s, the Duluth Snowshoe and Toboggan Association was all the rage, and members included former Mayor H.B. Moore and financier W.H. Alworth. Members often marched en masse from their unofficial headquarters at the St. Louis Hotel to a sledding hill somewhere near downtown off Superior Street (newspapers accounts are vague about the exact location). In other days gone by, local residents braved traffic by sliding down Duluth's steep streets.

Jack and Hank MacEvoy sliding behind Holy Rosary School.

The DSTA is long gone, and street sliding has become extremely dangerous, but that doesn't keep local residents from sliding. One popular hill can be found off Seven Bridges Road near the Lester Park Junior Hockey Association's rink. Another is located behind the parking lot next to Holy Rosary school at 2802 East 4th Street (you have to climb over the fence). Brave souls use the ski hills at Chester Park when the runs aren't open to skiers, and the city's golf courses provide some great runs for toboggans, sleds, and saucers.

Snow sliding hasn't always been just for fun. The Finnish called it *luskiainin*, and sliding was an important part of their agrarian culture. It was thought that sliding helped the flax grow: the further you went down the hill (and out onto the lake when there was one), the higher the flax would grow. Falling off was considered bad luck.

Stoney Point & the Buchanan Wayside

North Shore • Lakeside at Mileposts 15 & 16 on Scenic 61

Stoney Point is a stretch of rocky shoreline along a loop of road off Scenic Highway 61. The western point of Stoney Point Road connects to Highway 61 at Milepost 15, just across the road from Tom's Logging Camp. The waves can be particularly dramatic at Stoney Point, forcing spray high into the air when they meet the rocks. Kayakers and even surfers take advantages of the waves along this stretch of 61 to play in the lake. Since the 1990s Stoney Point has become increasingly popular among shorecasters and picnickers. In fact, many local residents asked us to not mention it, but it's way too late to put that genie back in its bottle. Visitors should be aware that many people live nearby, so be careful to respect their property and privacy. We also ask that you respect Stoney Point and pick up after yourselves when you leave.

Less than a half mile from Stoney Point, the Buchanan Wayside marks the spot of an abandoned town named for President James Buchanan. The town, laid out in 1856, was the seat of the land office for Northeastern Minnesota. After the office relocated, the settlement disappeared. The wayside is made of stone walls that enclose a small picnic area and historic marker. It also provides access to a stretch of shoreline very much like that of Stoney Point, making it a great alternative if Stoney's crowded.

The rocky shore adjacent to the Buchanan Wayside along Scenic 61.

Split Rock River Loop

North Shore • Inland at Milepost 43 on Highway 61

Split Rock's split rock?

The Lake Superior Hiking Trail runs up and down the North Shore inland from Highway 61, providing hikers with days and days of adventure and camping spots, but gearless day trippers can enjoy it as well. One of the most spectacular legs of the trail is Split Rock River Loop, a five-mile hike that gently rises along Split Rock River.

From the wayside parking area, take the trail up the west side of the river, but pay attention to the map at the trail's entrance, or you could find yourself on the path to Gooseberry Falls State Park instead of Split Rock. A few waterfalls and sheer red rock walls make up just some of the river's beauty. About 1.5 miles up the road you'll find a large rock column that has been split in two—many consider this the source of the river's name. About another mile up, a bridge crosses to the river's east bank. The trail follows the river from above and eventually leads hikers to a high peak that overlooks the river valley—a great spot to see fall colors. However, after following the trail down to the highway, you will find yourself almost half a mile from your car and must walk along the highway to reach it.

Split Rock's name may have come from its landmark rock formation or from fishermen who saw two large cliffs a mile east of the river's mouth "split apart" as they approached from the lake. The Ojibwe called the river Gin-On-Wab-Iko-Zibi or "Eagle Iron River."

Palisade Head

North Shore • Lakeside at Milepost 57 on Highway 61

About four miles up the shore from Silver Bay, you'll find Palisade Head, a cliff that climbs 320 feet above Lake Superior near the mouth of Palisade Creek. A winding road brings you to the summit of Palisade, and trails among rock outcroppings provide opportunities for exploration and picnicking. Keep the kids and dogs close: it's a long way down.

The reason most folks come to Palisade Head is the view. The Apostle Islands, 30 miles away off Wisconsin's South Shore, can be seen on clear days, as can the Sawtooth Mountains (actually lava deposits) up along the shore, and Shovel Point (sometimes called "Little Palisades") in Tetteguche State Park.

In recent years, Palisade Head and Shovel Point have become a magnet for rock climbers looking for a challenge. The sheer face of Palisade—igneous rhyolite overlaying soft basalt that has been undercut by Lake Superior's waves—provides just what they're looking for. Kayakers can also be found playing among the waves below.

Don't bother stopping by in the winter—the road isn't plowed.

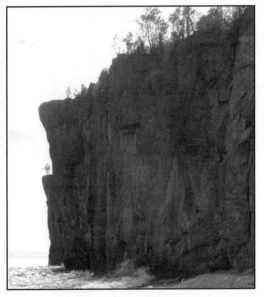

Baptism River's Waterfalls

North Shore • Lakeside at Milepost 58 on Highway 61 • Park free at wayside next to Tetteguche State Park.

The Baptism River's 70-foot High Falls in Tetteguche State Park.

The North Shore's Baptism River is home to several waterfalls, but the most spectacular is High Falls, a 70-foot drop a mile or so up easily hiked trails. Only at the 130-foot waterfall on the Pigeon River at the Canadian border will you find a higher falls in Minnesota. The river also contains Two-Step Falls downstream from High Falls. Though not as tall, Two-Step spills over some spectacular rock formations and is well worth the hike down a steep stairway.

Day trippers can park in the lot adjacent to the Tetteguche State Park headquarters (the Baptism is actually part of the park). Well-groomed trails lead hikers to both falls and, further inland, climb to the Lake Superior overlook, which provides a view of the river valley leading into Lake Superior.

Tetteguche is also home to Palisade Head and Shovel Point. A trail near the park headquarters leads to an overlook at Shovel Point, providing another great view of the lake.

The park, by the way, takes its name from an old logging camp established near Mic Mak Lake by eastern Canadians (Mic Mak is the name of a New Brunswick Indian tribe).

Crystal Beach Sea Cave

North Shore · Lakeside at Milepost 60 on Highway 61 (at the junction with Highway 1)

Without a kayak, the Crystal Beach sea cave is a pretty tricky place to get to, but it's well worth the time and trouble. The cave—more of an arch, really—is one of the largest on Lake Superior, carved from the rock by the lake's relentless waves. You can't get in the cave from the beach without a kayak or canoe, but you can see it fairly close up. It lies to the east of a horseshoe-shaped beach surrounded by cliffs where Crystal Creek empties into Lake Superior. Ruins of abandoned structures indicate that this area was once used for some kind of commercial enterprise.

Gaining access to beach is the tricky park. First, there's no place to park (Superior Outlook Bar & Grill is across the highway where 61 meets with Highway 1; ask if you can park in its lot and make sure to patronize it if you do—the owner is a friendly gent and knows how to get to the trail). On foot, cross to the lake side of the highway and over Crystal Creek—be very careful. You'll find a rocky trail leading down just past the guardrails and the "Crystal Creek" sign. Follow the trail down and you'll find yourself at the beach.

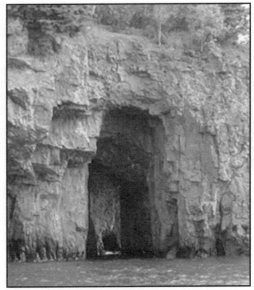

Caribou River Falls

North Shore • Inland at Milepost 70 on Highway 61

You won't find caribou anywhere near the Caribou River—they've been gone for more than 100 years—but you will find one of the best waterfalls along the North Shore, especially if you go during the spring thaw or after a good hard rain when the swollen river practically leaps off the cliffs on its way to the big lake.

The river and its falls are part of Caribou Falls State Park, which is little more than a parking lot, some outdoor toilets, and a hiking trail that leads to the falls and, eventually, to the Manitou River and Crosby Manitou State Park (about six miles away). The trail starts at the parking lot, and you need only hike half a mile up before you get to the falls. When you reach the falls, the trail gets a bit tricky as it descends to the base of the falls on a path of loose rock. But it's well worth the maneuvering, as the trail brings you very close to the falls for an incredible look at the descending cascade. Amazingly, trees grow from the sides of the sheer cliffs that surround the cascade's cauldron.

The trail continues to the top of the falls, where a small bridge traverses the Manitou and hooks up with the Lake Superior Hiking Trail.

Father Baraga's Landing at Cross River

North Shore • Lakeside at Milepost 79 on Highway 61

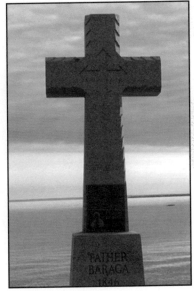

Missionary Frederic R. Baraga, born in Yugoslavia in 1797, came to America in 1830 to devote his life to the American Indians of the Upper Great Lakes and was named bishop of Upper Michigan in 1853. But before that, he had a little trouble in a canoe. Crossing 30 miles of open Lake Superior waters from La Pointe on Madeline Island ten years before he became bishop, he and some native guides encountered a storm that almost took their lives. But they eventually found harbor at the mouth of a gently flowing river, and Baraga nailed a wooden cross to a stump and wrote upon it: "In commemoration of the goodness of almighty God in granting to the Reverend F.R. Baraga safe passage from La Pointe to this place, August, 1843." The river became Cross River, and the wooden cross has since been replaced by one made of concrete.

You can visit the cross and enjoy the scenic beauty surrounding the mouth of the Cross River without hardly walking a step. A short road off Highway 61 leads to a small parking lot (and boat landing) practically next to the cross itself (a short path leads to the cross). Outcroppings of igneous rock provide great spots for picnicking or just playing around on the rocks. The area also has picnic tables, but no camping is allowed. Pick up some food to go from the Cross River Café and enjoy a meal outside.

People live nearby, so drive carefully and respect all private property.

Temperance River's Hidden Falls

North Shore • Inland at Milepost 80 on Highway 61

A mile up the road from Cross River is Temperance River State Park, home to the dangerous beauty of Hidden Falls (the name Temperance comes from the lack of a "bar" at the river's mouth). You can park along the highway waysides on either side of the Highway 61 bridge that crosses the river, then follow the maps to the more

than six miles of trails that traverse the park. But watch your step and hang on to the kids and dogs—you get dangerously close to steep drops.

Within the park, a series of cascades brings the river down 162 feet through a rocky gorge within the space of only half a mile. The last cascade is found only 100 feet from the river's mouth. Along this span, the river has carved deep cauldrons into the rock.

The park's six miles of foot trails (and eight miles of cross-country ski trails) allows visitors to take long or short hikes at their discretion. It's just a 10-minute round trip to the lower footbridge and 30 minutes to the upper footbridge and back. A series of seven scenic overlooks can be found in less than an hour's round-trip hike from the parking areas.

Heartbreak Ridge (a great drive for fall colors)

North Shore · Inland at Milepost 82 on Highway 61

No tragic story of lost love inspired the name Heartbreak Ridge. It comes from a time when draft horses were used in the timber industry to pull logs out of the forest. The steepness of the ridge was too much for the sturdy horses in the winter, when it was sleek with ice and snow. Consequently, loggers could not move logs up and down the rise. Bypassing the ridge caused them extra work, breaking their hearts.

Call it Breathtaking Ridge if you want, because this spot is home to thousands of sugar maples, which explode into reds, oranges, and yellows in autumn. A drive along the ridge is often the first stop for fall color enthusiasts on their annual drive along the North Shore.

Leaf watchers say there are two seasons for watching the trees burst. The inland trees start changing about September 10, and peak color occurs between September 20 and October 10. The second season—when ash, birch and poplar turn yellow against flaming sumac along Highway 61—runs from about October 5 until the 20th. Since Heartbreak Ridge is inland, get out there before mid-October.

Take the Temperance River Road (Forest Road 343) to Forest Road 166. Go east on FR 166 until you reach the Sawbill Trail (County Road 2). South on the Sawbill takes you back to Highway 61.

Onion River's Cauldron

North Shore • Inland at Milepost 86 on Highway 61

You'll find the Onion River by stopping at the Roy Berglund State Scenic Wayside just north of Milepost 86. More of a creek than a river, the Onion trickles into Lake Superior, but about a quarter mile or so upstream you'll find a gently cascading waterfall. At the base of the waterfall is a pool local residents have dubbed "The Cauldron."

The Onion River's cauldron hardly roils with the force of water fed to it from above, making it an ideal swimming hole. There are plenty of flat rock surfaces for kicking back to dry off after a dip or to spread out a picnic lunch.

To get to The Cauldron, take the rough trail located about 15 feet to the right of the Ray Berglund sign-post (between the parking lot's 6th and 7th post). The trail leads you up the east edge of the Onion and at times runs close to the edge of a drop leading down to the river, so keep the kids in hand. Look for a path leading down after a quarter mile or so of hiking (if you reach the area where trees have been cleared for power lines, you've gone about 30 yards too far). The trail continues beyond the falls for those who want a longer hike.

Ray Berglund, by the way, was a St. Paul man who worked as a lumberman and loved the natural beauty of the North Shore. He lived from 1895 to 1948.

Eagle Mountain: Lowest to Highest

North Shore • Inland at Mileposts 92/109 on Highway 61

Well, it's a bit off the shore, but if you want to go from Minnesota's lowest point to its highest, start at the lakeshore at Lutsen or Grand Marais and head on up to Eagle Mountain, 2,301 feet of erosion-resistant granite that withstood the force of glaciers. A drive of about 15 miles takes you to the head of a 3.5-mile root-covered and rocky hiking trail. The elevation rises gradually until the last half mile, which is considerably steeper and rougher.

Once at the top—a flat ridge—you'll find several excellent vistas of the Boundary Waters Canoe Area Wilderness and the Superior National Forest. Look to the west side of the ridge for a brass survey disk that marks the peak. Tread lightly: this is an environmentally sensitive area full of fragile plant life, so please stay on the main trail.

Eagle Mountain is part of the BWCAW, so you'll need a permit for a day trip. You can issue yourself a permit right at the trailhead—simply follow directions at the permit box. If you plan to stay overnight between May and September, you need an overnight permit. You can obtain one from a Forest Service office or outfitter.

From Lutsen, take the Caribou Trail (County Road 4) to Forest Road 170. From Grand Marais, start on the Gunflint Trail (County Road 12) and connect to County Road 8, then 27 and finally FR 170.

The Stone Beach at Durfee Creek

North Shore • Lakeside at Milepost 115 on Highway 61

It's not an official beach, but the stretch of lakeshore along Highway 61 a mile or so north of Grand Marais is a stone-skipper's dream. The rocks that cover the beach have been worn smooth and flat by the waves of Lake Superior, and just about any stone found there makes a great skipper.

The site is also home to great scenic beauty for those who just want to sit on some of the large outcroppings (somewhat similar to those found at Stoney Point) and soak in the view. Five-mile Rock (so-named because it rests about five miles from the center of Grand Marais) lies off to the southwest, and the lake opens up before you. Signs of small fires indicate that the spot is used for nighttime outings as well.

There's a small wayside near a blue mailbox just before the highway crosses Durfee Creek. You can park there and easily walk to the lakeshore, where the rock beach stretches hundreds of yards in both directions. A few homes can be found farther along the shore, so be careful not to encroach on private property.

Twin Falls

South Shore • Two blocks west of Port Wing on Highway 13

Slow down just before you reach Port Wing as you drive east along the South Shore on Highway 13 and you'll see a sign for Twin Falls Park—drive too fast and you'll miss it (when coming out of town from the east, the park is about two blocks west of Port Wing). Stop, back up if you missed it, and pull into the park. You'll find a circular dirt road to park along, a picnic area, and a trail leading a couple hundred yards up to a scenic overlook of the falls.

The falls are on a spring-fed creek that once must have been as big as a river, if the surrounding landscape is any testament. Spaced just a few feet apart, the falls cascade one atop the other and empty into an expansive cauldron. Part of the beauty of Twin Falls is that the erosion created by the running water has formed a cavern made of brown Lake Superior sandstone—a chance to see brownstone in its natural state and not as part of some historic building.

From the overlook you'll also see a flight of stairs on the western side of the creek leading down to an area below the falls and under the cavern. Tempting as it may be, please don't venture over to the western side of the creek—the land on that side is private property, and you'll be trespassing.

Twin Falls in late summer, as it trickles down brownstone steps.

Meyers Beach & Siskiwit Falls

South Shore • Beach: East of Cornucopia | Falls: Siskiwit Falls Road between Highway 13 and County 2

Looking for a spot to wear the kids out before expecting them to sit down and behave in a South Shore restaurant? Look no further than Meyers Beach, just outside of Cornucopia. The pristine, primitive beach, part of the Apostle Islands National Lakeshore, stretches for about a mile. Although a popular access site for kayakers, the beach is usually quiet and uncrowded. A nearby hiking trail leads to the Squaw Bay sea caves (see page 49).

The beach is located east of Cornucopia—take Highway 13 to Meyers Beach Road and head toward the lake. Parking is available, but there are no bathroom facilities, and camping is not allowed.

The Siskiwit Falls aren't much as far as dramatic descents are concerned. More of a gently flowing cascade—at least in late summer—the falls remind one of water running down a stairway rather than plunging down an elevator shaft. But they are quite lovely and provide a nice spot to rest and enjoy the outdoors accompanied by the sound of flowing water.

To find the falls, drive along Siskiwit Falls Road between Highway 13 and County Road C, about a mile east of Cornucopia, and look for the small bridge. Follow the footpath upstream 100 yards or so.

The gentle cascade of Siskiwit Falls just east of Cornucopia.

Squaw Bay Caves

South Shore • One mile east of Cornucopia's Meyers Beach

The Squaw Bay caves are a nearly mile-long string of structures carved into sandstone bedrock by wind, water, and ice. Part of the Apostle Islands National Lakeshore, the Squaw Bay caves can be found four miles east of Cornucopia (take Meyers Beach Road north off Highway 13; the caves are about one mile east of the beach). Squaw Bay contains the largest sea caves on the Apostle Islands National Lakeshore, some up to 80 feet deep. The caves are best viewed from the lake, so if you don't kayak or canoe, you'll only find partial views from the hiking path. You can also look down onto some of the caves from a narrow footbridge that spans a deep crevasse.

If you visit during the winter, the ice will provide access to a much better view. Ice forms around the cave's sandstone bedrock of brown, red, orange, and yellow layers, creating unmatched winter beauty. You can get to the caves by taking the mainland trail on boots, snowshoes, or cross-country skis, but it's quicker to simply walk along the lakeshore. Be careful! Make sure the ice is thick—call the Apostle Islands Ice Line at (715) 778-7007. Conditions are best in January and February.

Many of the Apostle Islands are home to sea caves, but it's quite dangerous to trek to them during the winter and, naturally, you need a boat in the summer.

The Squaw Bay caves in winter: multicolored sandstone adorned in ice.

Sioux River: Big Rocks & a Big Beach

South Shore • Big Rock: Outside Washburn off County C | Beach: Between Bayfield & Washburn on Hwy. 13

The 13.3-mile Sioux River between Bayfield and Washburn offers outdoor enthusiasts a variety of sights. Upstream it runs over rocky terrain but as it nears the lake, the surroundings turn to wetlands.

If you enjoy rough terrain, you'll love Big Rock Park. The park has picnic and overnight campgrounds as well as

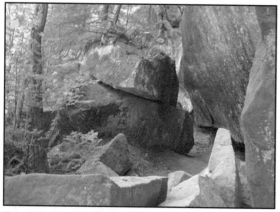

access to a rugged trail that runs along the Sioux. Many large rocks make the hike a challenge, but they also provide stunning natural beauty. This stretch of the Sioux is a popular fly-fishing spot, where brook, brown, and rainbow trout and coho salmon are often found in a deep hole below a layer of bedrock known as Big Rock Hole. To get to Big Rock Park from Washburn, take 10th Avenue out of town to County Road C, which connects to Big Rock Road, about two-and-a-half miles northwest of Washburn.

If you'd rather cool your heels than work your dogs, then the end of the Sioux is more for you. The mouth of the river is part of the Sioux River Coastal Wetlands, and alongside it you will find an expansive stretch of beach with views of Bayfield down the shore and the Apostle Islands across the water. The beach can be accessed from Friendly Valley Road off Highway 13.

Some of the big rocks at Big Rock Park on the Sioux River.

Stunning Views (often from unlikely places)

Duluth and the North Shore are home to some of the most scenic views found anywhere along the shores of Lake Superior. We've picked out twelve spots, many of which fall outside your typical idea of a scenic overlook.

Bardon's Peak

Bardon's (sometimes spelled "Barton's") Peak Forest Park is 2,775 acres of woodland west of Spirit Mountain. Skyline Parkway runs through the park as a dirt road and curves around Bardon's Peak. A stone wall keeps entranced motorists from plummeting over the side. The road is wide enough to pull off and either sit on the wall or scurry up the peak for a simply amazing look at the St. Louis River valley, Duluth, Superior, and the big lake. Besides the natural beauty, viewers can also see the entire neighborhoods of Morgan Park and Gary-New Duluth, the Oliver Bridge, and the abandoned U.S. Steel plant (as well as the scarred earth it has left behind). From Duluth, take Exit 249 off Highway 35, turn left onto Boundary Avenue and follow it to Skyline Parkway.

Thompson Hill Information Center

Folks entering Duluth from Highway 35 are always impressed with the view as they come over the ridge by Spirit Mountain—especially at night when the lights of Duluth and Superior seem to merge into one great city. That ridge is known as Thompson Hill, and it is home to one of the most scenic wayside rests anywhere. Its panoramic view can be enjoyed by the naked eye or through one of the center's view-finders. Large photos in the center itself point out islands, points, lakes, and other landmarks in the St. Louis River valley. A stainless steel sculpture by David Von Scheggel titled "The Gate," symbolizing Duluth as the gateway to the North Shore and the St. Lawrence Seaway, graces the center's grounds. From Duluth, take Exit 249 off Highway 35, turn right onto Skyline, and follow the signs.

Stunning Views, continued

Enger Tower: Sunrise, Sunset

Some think it was once an active lighthouse; others, a tribute from a grieving husband to his dead wife. Neither story is true. Sixty-foot-high Enger Tower was built in 1939 to honor Bert Enger, a prominent area businessman and Norwegian immigrant who came to this country penniless and made a fortune in furniture and real estate (see page 22 for more about the park). When the tower was finished, Crown Prince Olav of Norway visited Duluth to dedicate it. Since then, it has provided visitors with a great look at Duluth's harbor. Many people climb the tower, which stands 500 feet above the lake, during the day, but the great scenic advantage of the tower is that it's one of the few places on the Duluth hillside from which you can see the sunset. A gazebo in the park east of tower makes a great place to watch the sun rise over Lake Superior.

The tower is located off Skyline Parkway between Enger Park Golf Course and Twin Ponds.

Central High School Parking Lot

When the Duluth School Board decided to close downtown's historic Central High School (see page 71) and build its replacement up over the hill, little did they know they'd be creating a scenic overlook. Though not as architecturally impressive as its brownstone predecessor, the new school is perched high above the city, and its lower parking lot provides a stunning view. Minnesota Point juts out almost directly below the parking lot, making it a great spot to watch ship traffic come and go.

The high school is located at 800 East Central Entrance. To get there, take Central Entrance to Pecan Street (the first lights past the junction of 6th Street, Mesaba Avenue, and Central Entrance), turn left, and follow the road to the high school. Time it right: it's hard to find a parking spot during school hours.

Stunning Views, continued

The "Coppertop Church"

It's almost a trend: abandon the old brownstone building near downtown and build something modern on top of the hill, turning your parking lot into a scenic overlook. They did it with Central High School and the good folks at First United Methodist did it in 1966, when they tore down their towering church at 215 North Third Avenue West (see page 229) and built a more modern structure where Skyline Parkway merges with Central Entrance and Mesaba Avenue. The church's roof is made of copper, which has tarnished green over the years. Most Duluthians refer to it as the "Coppertop Church."

First United Methodist is located at 230 East Skyline Parkway, just east of where Mesaba Avenue and Central Entrance intersect (it has a big green roof, so you can't miss it).

Top of Chester

Ski jumpers claim the best view in Duluth is from the top of the Chester Park ski jump ramps—but you can't get there from here, unless you're willing to strap on some boards and finish with a leap. The rest of us will have to settle for the rock outcroppings found a few hundred yards behind the jumps. In summer the rocks are hidden by fields of wildflowers, and sometimes it's hard to see the lake for the trees, but on clear days the view is fantastic. If you follow one of the paths down from the rocks to a wide, grassy trail, you'll find a park bench next to a "Peace" signpost. Across from the bench, trees have been cleared to provide hikers with a place to rest and enjoy a look-see at the lake.

Chester Park is located at 1801 East Skyline Parkway. Parking is available near Upper Chester. Follow the road to the soccer fields and park, walk across the wide bridge beyond the picnic tables, then take the trails up.

Stunning Views, continued

Chi Chi's Deck / Back of Fitger's Complex

Let's face it: a Chi Chi's is a Chi Chi's is a Chi Chi's: Americanized Mexican food and mass-produced margaritas. But the Duluth Chi Chi's in the Fitger's Brewery Complex has something going for it most chain restaurants don't: two great decks just yards from the shore of the big lake. The main deck, accessible from the restaurant's bar, juts out from the top floor of the old brewery and offers the perfect place to watch the Wednesday night sailing regatta. The lower deck, made of iron, rises from the Lakewalk and stretches over the rails of the North Shore Scenic Railroad, with stairs providing a way for folks to get from the brewery to the shore (or vice versa). You don't necessarily have to patronize the restaurant to use the lower deck.

Chi Chi's is in the Fitger's Brewery Complex, 600 East Superior Street.

Golf for the View

Most folks who bring their clubs along on a trip up to these parts are headed for Giants Ridge in Biwabik or Superior National up the shore, but golfers unwilling to shell out the big bucks for an afternoon of self-torture will find two great public courses right in Duluth. These aren't the worn-down and overcrowded courses you're likely to encounter in larger cities. In fact, in 1998 *Golf Digest* ranked Duluth #1 of 309 major cities based on access to good, affordable public and municipal golf. Lester Park and Enger Park both offer 27 holes punctuated by great looks at Lake Superior (you'll see more of the harbor at Enger, more of the lake at Lester).

So if you're out to spoil a good walk, you may as well enjoy the scenery. Hackers may want to bring an extra sleeve or two of balls if they play Lester's Lake Nine. And remember, the greens always break toward the lake (well, almost always). For directions and tee times, call (218) 525-0828 (Lester Park) or (218) 723-3451 (Enger Park).

Stunning Views, continued

Park Point Beach: A View of Duluth

The previous eight overlooks offer views of Lake Superior from Duluth's hills. This one gives you a look at Duluth from next to the lake. Cross the Lift Bridge, drive a couple blocks, and pull into the parking area adjacent to the Tot Lot (a small playground; go straight when the road curves right). Walk toward the end of the Point for as long as you like. When you've had enough, turn back and head toward Duluth, but pause and take a good look at the buildings, homes, and trees that bloom from the city's hillsides. Makes you want to call it home. (Bring the kids and the dogs, but clean up after both.) The beach also makes a wonderful place to watch the sunrise.

Split Rock Lookout Station

At about Milepost 44 on Highway 61 (just past Gooseberry Falls State Park), you'll encounter the abandoned site of a commercial enterprise. It contains the charred remains of a building and the anchor from the *S.S. Medeira*, a ship that wrecked nearby in 1908. The area also has an abandoned "lookout" station with stairs you can climb for a view of the lake and Split Rock Lighthouse up the shore. **NOTE:** *This is not a state facility, and you may be trespassing* (although no signs are posted) *so try this at your own risk!* Next door you will find an official wayside, with a picnic table and trails leading toward the lake. The view's not as good, but it's a lot safer.

Palisade Head & Shovel Point

Although we've given an entire page to Palisade Head we could hardly have a section on "views" without mentioning it. The cliff stands 320-feet above the waters of Lake Superior, and you don't even have to get out of the car to enjoy a look. Shovel Point—formerly known as "Little Palisade"—is just down the road at Tetteguche State Park. (See page 37 for more information on Palisade Head and Shovel Point.)

Stunning Views, continued

Cutface Wayside

The Cutface Wayside is located at Highway 61's Milepost 104 on your way to Grand Marais. From the wayside's vantage point you can see Good Harbor Bay, Seagull Bay, and even Five Mile Rock past Grand Marais. A marker at the site is dedicated in honor of S. Rex Green, an engineer who helped establish Highway 61 "for the public's full enjoyment of the glories of forests, streams, and lakes." After taking in the view, get back in the car and head toward Good Harbor Bay. At the mouth of Cutface Creek is a lakeshore wayside, where you can park and picnic and look for thompsonite, a semiprecious rock made of concentrically banded green, white, and pink stone. Outside of the privately owned Thompsonite Beach Museum and Gift Shop down the road (and spots in Australia and Scotland), the rock is found nowhere else in the world.

Mount Josephine Wayside & Overlooks

Mount Josephine is found just past Grand Portage and has three separate waysides on both the lake and inland side of Highway 61 between Mileposts 146 and 148.

At Milepost 146 on the inland side, the winding Poplar Creek Road leads up to the Mount Josephine Wayside, a rest stop with bathrooms, picnic facilities, and a dog-walking area. It also has a few small trails and a great view of the lake and Wauswaugoning Bay.

Up the road from the wayside on the lake side of Highway 61 is a much closer view of the lake and the Susie Islands. You can also get a close look at the exposed stone of Mount Josephine where the highway cuts a path through its side.

Another stunning view of the lake is provided by an additional lakeside overlook at Milepost 148.

Architectural Adventures

(where to find great old houses & buildings)

Architectural Adventures

If you haven't noticed that Duluth is chock full of great old buildings, you're either not from around here or you spend most of your time above Skyline Parkway. Each time Duluth experienced an economic boom, the city saw some incredible structures rise from its streets. Buildings and houses constructed for lumber barons and mining executives dot downtown and the historic East End. Morgan Park, an entire community located about ten miles from downtown near Gary-New Duluth, was built to house workers at the nearby United States Steel plant, which has since closed its doors.

Duluth's structures exemplify a variety of architectural styles, from the ornate Queen Anne and Victorian to the utilitarian Arts and Crafts school. It includes examples of the Tudor Revival movement and the work of such prominent local architects as I. Vernon Hill, who introduced the "Ornamented Cube" to Duluth and influenced the city's architecture for decades after his death. Many houses and buildings, such as Old Central High School, feature the artistic flourishes of master stone carver O. George Thrana.

We've included a sample of some of the more stunning examples that still grace the city. Unfortunately, many of Duluth's finest buildings have gone. For a glimpse at some of Duluth's wonderful old buildings that have fallen victim to fire or the wrecking ball, see pages 227–236 in the "Local Lore and Places of Yore" chapter.

Certainly all the towns featured in *True North* boast some historic buildings—Ashland and Superior in particular. But Washburn—between Ashland and Bayfield—is perhaps the jewel of all the towns along Lake Superior's South Shore. The town's collection of brownstones,* constructed with stone quarried across the bay on the Apostle Islands, make it one of the most architecturally important and beautiful towns on our map. See page 82 for a description.

*"Brownstone" is actually sandstone and forms naturally in a variety of colors: brown, red, yellow, etc.

The Duluth Preservation Alliance

The Duluth Preservation Alliance was formed in 1978 to serve as a source of encouragement and technical advice for those who would undertake a restoration project and to help preserve Duluth's architectural heritage.

The DPA has advocated for the preservation of Glensheen Mansion (the Congdon estate), Old Central High School's Clock Tower, the Sacred Heart Music Center (see page 70), St. Mark's African Methodist Episcopal Church at 530 North 5th Avenue East, and is making efforts to save Duluth's historic National Guard Armory.

The following seven pages make up the DPA's "East End Walking Tour," a guide to some stunning old houses all within a four-block area. Descriptions of the homes on the tour were researched and written by Maryanne C. Norton, coauthor of *Images of America: Duluth Minnesota* (and included here with permission from the DPA). Special thanks to residents of the East End Historic District for welcoming visitors to their neighborhood.

To learn more about the Duluth Preservation Alliance, become a member, or make a donation to help save Duluth's homes and buildings, write to them at P.O. Box 252, Duluth, Minnesota 55801, or visit the DPA website at www.duluthpreservation.org.

Duluth Preservation Alliance

The DPA's East End Walking Tour

The map below guides you to the 24 Duluth homes listed on the following six pages. Take Highway 35 North and exit at 21st Avenue East. Go up the hill a few blocks to Superior Street, turn right, and find a place to park near 24th Avenue East. Then use this book as your guide to some of the best examples of the variety of architectural styles that grace Duluth's historic neighborhoods. Text courtesy of the Duluth Preservation Alliance.

The Duluth Preservation Alliance's
East End Walking Tour

East End Walking Tour, continued

1. Alex and Katherine Hartman House • 1910 • 2400 E. Superior St.
(Frederick West Perkins, architect) Today this is the Duluth Woman's Club, but originally it was the home of Alex Hartman, president of the Duluth Edison Electric Company. The house was purchased and remodeled by the Woman's Club in 1936. The stucco and half-timbered Tudor Revival sits on a steep bluff overlooking Lake Superior.

2. Albert and Louise Ordean House • 1905 • 2307 E. Superior St.
(Emmet Palmer & William A. Hunt, architects) A prominent Duluthian at the turn of the century, Albert Ordean served as president of Merchants National Bank, a founder of First National Bank, and the director of the Great Northern Railroad. An example of Georgian Revival architecture, the formal red brick house features a centered gable, end chimneys, and an elaborate entrance.

3. Frederick and Katherine Patrick House • 1901 • 2306 E. Superior St.
(I. Vernon Hill, architect) Architect I. Vernon Hill was a gifted and innovative designer whose work influenced Duluth's architecture for years after his early death at age 36. In the Patrick house, he employed stone, half timbering, and steep gables in the Tudor Revival style. Carved eagle heads on brackets support the third story gables. Patrick headed F.A. Patrick and Company, one of the country's foremost wool manufacturers.

4. Dwight Cutler House • 1906 • 5 N. 23rd Ave. E.
(William T. Bray & Carl Nystrom, architects) The stone facade facing Superior Street includes a three-story tower with battlements, suggesting the appearance of a medieval castle. The 23rd-Avenue facade features more battlements on the stone entrance as well as half timbering typical of the Tudor style. Cutler was president of a salt, lime, cement, and building materials firm.

East End Walking Tour, continued

5. George and Marion Stone House • 1901 • 2228 E. Superior St.

(P. Cooper and Son, architect) This large Renaissance Revival-style house with a red tile roof and a half tower on the front wall was built for the Stones in 1901. George Stone was an executive with Clyde Iron Works and the F.A. Patrick Company. From 1947 to 1977 the house served as a museum and offices for the Saint Louis County Historical Society. Today it is again a single family residence.

6. I. Vernon Hill House • 1902 • 2220 E. Superior St.

(I. Vernon Hill, architect) As he did with the Patrick house, Hill decorated his own home with a carved head—this time a lion—under the corner eaves of the front porch. Built for $11,000 in 1902, the house's Tudor Revival design features half timbering, carved wood braces, and decorated steep gables, all of which create a delightful example of American picturesque architecture.

7. Warren McCord House • 1903 • 2219 E. Superior St.

(Architect unknown) This shingle-style house features a stone foundation, shingle wall cladding, and a center tower with a conical roof. It cost lumber executive Warren McCord just $8,000 to build.

8. Frank and Jennie Brewer House • 1902 • 2215 E. Superior St.

(Emmet Palmer, Lucien Hall, & William A. Hunt, architects) Duluth architects Palmer, Hall, and Hunt, who also designed the Irving School and Old Main, created a grand Georgian Revival house replete with classical ornamentation, columns, pilasters, and a porte cochere to protect visitors from unpleasant weather. It has been referred to as "the wedding cake house." Brewer was a partner in a lumber company and president of Great Northern Power Company.

East End Walking Tour, continued

9. Frank and Minnie House House • 1905 • 2210 E. Superior St.
(William T. Bray, architect) Another striking example of Tudor Revival architecture, this many gabled, half-timbered house features decorative wood carvings, stone trim, and stone projections on the chimneys. Frank House was president of the Duluth and Iron Range Railroad.

10. Charles and Belle Britts House • 1892 • 2201 E. Superior St.
(John J. Wangenstein & Ernest West Baillie, architects) This home was built in 1892 for $4,000. Its wrap-around porch and distinctive shingle work are typical of the Queen Anne style. Britts worked as a banker.

11. Marcus and Sarah Fay House • 1902 • 2105 E. Superior St.
(Edwin South Radcliffe, architect) Marcus Fay, who was involved in both copper and iron mining, once ran for mayor of Duluth. The Fay's eclectic house exhibits the massing of the Queen Anne style along with the detailing of the Colonial Revival style. An impressive iron fence surrounds the property.

12. Alfred and Jane McCordic House • 1891 • 2104 E. Superior St.
(Arthur Raeder, Henry Foccin, & Benjamin Crocker, architects) Duluth attorney Alfred McCordic and his family lived here very briefly. The house was originally built in the shingle style and was faced with wood shingles; stucco was added in the 1920s. Later owners, the Andreas Miller family, provided funds for what eventually became Miller-Dwan hospital.

East End Walking Tour, continued

13. George and Charlotte Crosby House • 1902 • 2029 E. Superior St.

(I. Vernon Hill, architect) The Crosby house is considered Hill's masterpiece, the one with which he introduced a new style of architecture to Duluth. Sometimes referred to as "Ornamented Cube," the style embellishes a square or rectangular box with flared dormers, gables, and classical detailing. The Crosby house's rectangle is of sandstone block with stone carvings by master stone carver O. George Thrana. The Cuyuna Iron Range was developed by Crosby, and he founded the town that bears his name.

14. Thomas and Martha Davis House • 1909 • 2104 E. 1st St.

(William T. Bray & Carl E. Nystrom, architects) This three-story brick Tudor Revival house features prominent chimneys, a Flemish gable, carved stone ornamentation on the entrance, and a tower with battlements. It cost Davis, a Duluth attorney, $21,000.

15. Zar and Frances Scott House • 1907 • 2125 E. 1st St.

(William A. Hunt, architect) This Tudor Revival house features half timbering, steep gable roofs, and finials on the gable and dormer peaks. Scott was a partner in the Scott-Graff Lumber Company of Duluth and a leader in the reforestation movement in Minnesota.

16. Alexander McDougall House • 1910 • 2201 E. 1st St.

(William T. Bray & Carl E. Nystrom, architects) Captain Alexander McDougall, master shipbuilder and inventor of the whaleback steamer, built this house when he was a widower in his sixties. Architects Bray and Nystrom were obviously influenced by I. Vernon Hill's Ornamented Cube designs. This yellow brick box has the same flared dormer gable that Hill employed on the Crosby house, along with classical columns and ornamentation.

East End Walking Tour, continued

17. William Cole House • 1908 • 2204 E. 1st St.
(Frederick German & A. Werner Lignell, architects) Another of the many East End Tudors, the Cole house was built for $16,000 in 1908, complete with matching carriage house. Cole was president of Northern Cold Storage and Warehouse Company.

18. Clinton and Katherine Markell House • 1908 • 2215 E. 1st St.
(Architect unknown) An early pioneer and Duluth's second mayor, Markell was instrumental in the development of grain shipping. The prominent feature of this shingle-style home is the curved entrance with decorative brackets.

19. Edwin and Lucretia Bradley House • 1904 • 2229 E. 1st St.
(William T. Bray, architect) This massive Georgian-style house has fluted columns and pillasters, Greek key designs over the windows, a classically decorated portico, and a gambrel roof. Bradley's wealth came from his lumber interests.

20. Joseph Bell and Louise Cotton House • 1906 • 2309 E. 1st St.
(Fred Kees & Serenus Colburn, architects) The restrained elegance of the Renaissance Revival style shows in the yellow brick Cotton house's classical brackets, dentils, and balustrades. A corporate-law attorney, Cotton represented John D. Rockefeller against the Merritt family in the latter's unsuccessful attempt to maintain ownership of mining lands in northern St. Louis County.

East End Walking Tour, continued

21. William and Fannie Olcott House • 1904 • 2316 E. 1st St.
(William T. Bray, architect) William Bray designed this impressive Georgian-style home and its matching carriage house for William Olcott, who was president of the Oliver Mining Company and later the Duluth Missabe and Northern Railroad. Architectural historian Roger Kennedy described the Olcott house, which reportedly cost $14,000 in 1904, as "a house carrying what surely must be the most overwhelming gambrel roof in the region."

22. George and Eleanor Swift House • 1894 • 2320 E. 1st St.
(Irving A. Spear, architect) This large Victorian house features dentils under the windows, square columns on the porch, and an interesting combination of colors. George Swift, an executive with the Oliver Mining Company, paid $6,000 in construction costs.

23. John and Caroline Richards House • 1894 • 2321 E. 1st St.
(Hugh Steele, architect) Hugh Steele added interest to this Queen Anne house through the use of a palladian window in the enormous front dormer, a decorative chimney, and an open front porch. Richards was a Duluth attorney.

24. Hugh Steele House • 1893 • 2327 E. 1st St.
(Hugh Steele, architect) Just as he did with the Richards' house, building contractor Hugh Steele built his own home in the popular Queen Anne style. The distinctive corner turret is covered with patterned shingles of many shapes and is crowned with a witch's hat roof.

These Old Houses

Oliver G. Traphagen House ("The Redstone") • 1892 • 1511 E. Superior St.
(Oliver Traphagen, architect) Architects tend to build the best for themselves, as was the case when Oliver Traphagen built his family a home. The house is quite impressive from the front, with its Flemish gable and ornate carvings in red sandstone, but take a peek around back and you'll see that most of the structure is simple red brick. Traphagen and his family abandoned the home in 1896 for the sun and surf of Hawaii, and Chester and Clara Congdon lived in it before building Glensheen. The building has since been used as a single-family home, was once divided into apartments, and is now the home of H.T. Klatsky advertising.

The Sellwood/Leithead House • 1902 • 16 S. 18th Ave. E.
(William A. Hunt, architect) In 1865 miner Joseph Sellwood set out from his home in Cornwall, England, for the copper mines in northern Michigan. After finding great success in various mining partnerships, he moved to Duluth and built three homes at the corner of 18th Avenue East and Superior Street, one for himself and two as wedding presents for his daughters. His daughter Ophelia and her husband Leslie Leithead—president of Leithead Drug Company—received this little beauty on the southeast corner. The house is a fine example of Romanesque Revival architecture, featuring towers and castle-like walls made of brownstone, that "Captain" Sellwood paid just $15,000 to build. The house at the southwest corner was Sellwood's wedding gift to another daughter, who married Larue Morshan.

These Old Houses, continued

Munger Terrace • 1871 • 405 Mesaba Ave.

(Traphagen & Fitzpatrick, architects) Almost immediately after Roger Munger's Chateauesque-styled townhouse rose out of the steep Hillside on Mesaba Avenue it became *the* place for wealthy Duluthians to call home. The original structure contained eight units of 16 rooms each, but tastes changed and as Duluth's affluent moved to the east end of town, the townhouse was converted into 32 much smaller apartments. Renovated in 1978, the building's towers and turrets still turn the heads of drivers heading up or down the hill on Mesaba Avenue.

Arthur P. Cook House • 1900 • 501 W. Skyline Pkwy.

(I. Vernon Hill, architect) Most Duluthians know the Cook home as the "House of Rock" both for the rocky lot it sits on and the incorporation of the same stone by architect I. Vernon Hill, who was just 31 years old when he designed it. With arguably one of the best views of the Duluth-Superior harbor, the house was built of stone and timber for just $5,000. It became the most photographed house in Duluth and in 1931 was featured in an advertisement for the Duluth Builders' Exchange touting the future of Duluth as a "metropolis serving the great Northwest Empire and its Atlantic Gateway." Those cruising Skyline Parkway (Boulevard Drive at the time the house was built) will be remiss if they don't pull over for a long look at this much-coveted home.

Opulent Old Churches

First Unitarian Church • 1910 • 1802 E. 1st St.

(Anthony Puck, architect) Radio humorist and Minnesotan Garrison Keillor has made a living peppering his stories with good-natured fun at the Unitarians' expense. Perhaps their emphasis on democracy and freedom is too much for Minnesotans steeped in Lutheran doctrine, but Duluth has welcomed them since 1877. Their incredible Tudor Revival church was built in 1910 and held Unitarian services until 2001, when it was sold to Quakers.

St. Paul's Episcopal Church • 1913 • 1710 E. Superior St.

(Bertram Goodhue, architect) In 1913 the congregation at the first church built in Duluth—an 1869 Episcopalian structure located on the northwest corner of Lake Avenue and 2nd Street—chipped in to build a new one. Bertram Goodhue designed the church in the English Gothic style, very like an English country parish church. The church was built at a cost of $72,000. In 1929 a simple timbered parish hall was added for $105,000. In the 1990s, the roof's blue-gray slate was repaired, complete with copper flashing. Get in close for a look at the carvings. The original church was often called "Jay Cooke's Church" because the financier made a major contribution to its building finances. A statue of Cooke and his dog stands across from the Kitchi Gammi Club (see page 78).

Opulent Old Churches, continued

Sacred Heart Cathedral • 1898 • 201 W. 4th St.

(Architect unknown.) Once the home of the archdiocese of Duluth, Sacred Heart Cathedral served Catholics in Duluth for 87 years. Inside the church you'll find an Italian marble alter, beautiful wooden pews, and the original pipe organ. Although it was replaced as the seat of the archdiocese in 1957 when the Cathedral of Our Lady of the Rosary opened its doors, masses were held here until Sacred Heart merged with St. Mary Star of the Sea in 1985.

The church is now the home of the Sacred Heart Music Center, which presents a wide variety of concerts (see page 94).

First Presbyterian Church • 1891 • 300 E. 2nd St.

(Traphagen & Fitzpatrick, architects) The area in and around downtown Duluth once included large churches representing every denomination that had a parish inside the city. First Presbyterian is the last standing representative of that era. The Romanesque building, constructed of varied shades of brown Lake Superior sandstone blocks and adorned by carvings and stained-glass windows, seems to erupt from the steep hillside of 3rd Avenue East. Its corner bell tower reaches 125 feet above 2nd Street, and inside there's room enough for 1,000 parishioners. At the time it was built, the church was at the heart of Duluth's most affluent neighborhood. When parishioners moved east, attendance declined.

Old School Schools

Old Central High School • 1891–1892 • Lake Ave. & 2nd St.

(Emmet S. Palmer & Lucien P. Hall, architects) Most everyone who has ever been to Duluth has seen Old Central—its 230-foot clock tower rises above downtown and simply cannot be ignored. The Romanesque building is made of locally quarried brownstone and is modeled after the Allegheny Courthouse in Pittsburgh, Pennsylvania. In his description of Old Central's stone gargoyles, architectural historian James Allen Scott wrote that "about the cavernous entrance in the tower angelic cherubs lovingly smile while overhead grotesque animal figures leer their prurient intents." The building ceased operating as a school in 1971 and is now home to the Duluth School District's administrative offices.

Denfeld High School • 1925–1926 • 4405 W. 4th St.

(Abraham Holstead & William J. Sullivan, architects) Built in a style dubbed Collegiate English Gothic, Denfeld High School reflects Renaissance ideals. The building is shaped like an **H** with a rising clock tower that stands for "aspiring idealism." The building's eight buttresses were intended to represent "the eight types of human beings who supported the human kingdom: masters, rulers, philanthropists, philosophers, magicians, scientists, devotees, and artists." Stone carvings of Renaissance symbolism adorn the school. The building is still in use as a high school today; it takes its name from Robert E. Denfeld, Duluth's superintendent of schools for over 30 years beginning in 1885.

Old School Schools, continued

Jefferson School • 1890 • 916 E. 3rd St.
(McMillan & Radcliffe, architects) When Jefferson School opened its
doors in 1893 it was called "undoubtedly one of the finest ward school
structures in the country." The Neo-Classical Colonial structure cost
$84,000 and boasted toilets (or "water closets" at the time) with "auto-
matic flush." After closing in the mid 1980s, the school was converted
into the Jefferson Square Apartments and houses the Jefferson Children's Center.

Endion School • 1890 • 1801 E. 1st St.
(Adolph Rudolph, architect) Built in the Romanesque Revival style
of red pressure brick, the Endion School hosted students from
Duluth's Endion neighborhood for 87 years until closing its doors
in 1977. A belfry once sat atop the building, but in 1970 it was
victimized by vandals and had to be taken down. Today the building houses the Endion School Apartments.

The name "Endion" comes from a town site registered in 1856 and
is Ojibwe for *My, Your*, or *His Home*. When the town was absorbed
by a growing Duluth, it became a neighborhood. Endion Station,
now found along the Lakewalk, once stood at 15th Avenue East &
South Street, but was relocated when Interstate 35 was extended
through Duluth to 26th Avenue East.

Boomtown Buildings

Civic Center • 1909, 1923, 1928 • 5th Ave. W. & 1st St.

(Daniel H. Burnham & Company, *et. al.*, architects) Your one-stop shopping spot for some impressive Classical/Renaissance architecture, the Civic Center in Duluth includes the St. Louis County Courthouse, Duluth City Hall, and the U.S. Federal Building as well a county jail, the "Fortitude Defending the Flag" monument, and a fountain. The courthouse was designed by D.H. Burnham and went up in 1909; other architects designed City Hall and the Federal Building, but did so in a manner in keeping with Burnham's original idea. The whole complex was part of the "City Beautiful" movement of the early 20th century.

The fountain outside the St. Louis County Courthouse, the centerpiece of Duluth's Civic Center.

Duluth Union Depot • 1892 • 5th Ave. W. & Michigan St.

(Robert Swain Peabody & John Goddard Stearns, architects) Designed by Boston architects Peabody and Stearns to resemble a French Norman chateau on a grand scale, Duluth's Union Depot—including a track, roundhouse, and a shed system—was built for a cost of $615,000. At one point, it serviced over 60 trains a day from the St. Paul & Duluth Railways, Northern Pacific, and others. It closed as a railroad depot in 1969 and is now home to the St. Louis County Heritage and Arts Center, housing museums and performance stages (see pages 88 and 89). In 2001 its bricks were cleaned and the roof was replaced. (The photo at left was taken c. 1970.)

Boomtown Buildings, continued

Alworth Building • 1910 • 306 W. Superior St.

(Daniel H. Burnham, architect) Sixteen stories of concrete and steel covered in buff-colored brick and terra cotta make the Alworth building the tallest in Duluth. You have to have a good eye to see the structure's ornamental features, most of which appear at the top few floors. The building is crowned with an ornate cornice and oval window openings on the top floor and features lion's heads carved in stone. The cost to construct what the *Duluth News-Tribune* once called "a cosmopolitan office building, one that dwarfs the Tower of Babel" and "an epoch in the architectural history of Duluth"? A mere $500,000. It took workers nine months to build Duluth's "skyscraper," as much a feat today as it was in 1910 (and most of the work was done during winter months).

Board of Trade Building • 1895 • 301 W. 1st St.

(Traphagen & Fitzpatrick, architects) Fire has shaped the history of this great old building. It was built after the original Board of Trade building burned in 1894, and its cornice was removed after another fire in 1948. Built of steel, stone, brick, and marble, the ornate Romanesque structure with a two-story entrance and elaborate O. George Thrana stone carvings cost $350,000. Today the building is used as office space for attorneys and architects. The Minnesota Ballet also makes its home here and recently renovated the trading floor for use as rehearsal space. Their efforts won them an award from the Duluth Preservation Alliance. If you ask nicely and don't interrupt rehearsal, they'll let you go up to the balcony and have a look around.

Left: The Board of Trade building's ornate two-story entrance.

Boomtown Buildings, continued

Wirth Building • 1886 • 13 W. Superior St.

(George Wirth, architect) When St. Paul architect George Wirth was asked by his brother Max W. Wirth to design a combination drug store and family residence, he chose to work in the Romanesque Revival style, leaving downtown Duluth with an architectural beauty that remains the jewel of West Superior Street. The facade is made of a combination of brown- and buff-colored sandstone and features ornate carvings, arched window casings, and a projecting bay on the second floor to help flood the residence with natural light. Today the renovated building is home to the building's current owner, an antique shop, and other businesses in the upper offices.

Masonic Temple • 1904 • 4 W. 2nd St.

(C. H. Smith, architect) Mystery surrounds the Masons. George Washington was part of the order, and some say they are a secret force behind global politics. Whatever the truth, they've left quite a few interesting buildings in their wake. Home to the "Palestine Lodge #79," first established in 1869, the Masonic Temple at 2nd Street and 4th Avenue West is one of many buildings the Masons have constructed in Duluth (their first permanent home was the ornate Temple Opera Building, see page 234). Its cornerstone was laid August 10, 1904, by Masonic Grand Master of Minnesota William A. McGonagle. Joshua B. Culver, Duluth's first mayor, was the first Master of Palestine Lodge...coincidence?

Left: Columns support the Masonic Temple's Second Street entrance.

Boomtown Buildings, continued

Old Jail (& City Hall) • 1889 & 1891 • 126 & 132 E. Superior St.

(Oliver G. Traphagen, architect) After Duluth pulled itself up by the bootstraps following a recession in the 1870s, the town was rechartered in 1887. A seat of government was required, and by 1889 City Hall sat at the corner of 2nd Avenue East and Superior Street. It filled up quickly, requiring a separate jail and police headquarters, which opened next door in 1891 complete with carvings and a Flemish gable. Replaced by new buildings in 1929, the old City Hall has since had its lower facade covered by short-sighted property owners. The jail, however, was restored in 1968 and is now home to Architectural Resources, Inc.

Hotel Duluth (Greysolon Plaza) • 1925 • 227 E. Superior St.

(Martin Tullgren & Sons, architects) The compass embedded in the sidewalk outside the Hotel Duluth inspired this book's title and logo, so we're a bit partial to it. The hotel, now named Greysolon Plaza, was built in 1924 for a cost of $2.4 million. Made of reinforced steel and concrete, the hotel boasts many wonderful architectural features, such as a Classic-Revival facade, a lobby and mezzanine designed in the Italian-Renaissance style (pictured), and what its builders called a "typical Spanish dining room." Today its rooms are dedicated to senior housing while its ballroom plays host to wedding receptions and other large gatherings. It is also home to the Chinese Garden restaurant and Romano Grocery. President John F. Kennedy stayed in the hotel in the summer of 1963. See page 217 for a story of the hotel's early years.

Boomtown Buildings, continued

Engine House #1 • 1889 • 101 E. 3rd St.

(Oliver G. Traphagen, architect) Just above and across the street from Old Central High School (or directly true north) sits Engine House #1, the ironically named third firehouse in Duluth. The first, a wooden building near Minnesota Point, burned to the ground. The second, run by volunteers, remains at 22 East 2nd Street, but most of its decorative features are gone. Built in 1889, the stone and brick Engine House #1 was once crowned with an impressive bell tower; the tower was removed in 1910 and the firehouse closed in 1918. It is now used as a maintenance garage by the city school district.

Carnegie Library • 1902 • 101 W. 2nd St.

(Adolph F. Rudolph, architect) When Duluth began to outgrow its first library (housed inside the Temple Opera Building, see page 234), it used a $25,000 donation from Andrew Carnegie to help build a brick sandstone structure in a Neo-Classical design that ultimately cost $65,000. The building includes a central dome and two Tiffany windows depicting the area's history. Converted to office space in the 1980s, visitors can stop in and check out the public space (but please don't interrupt the work going on behind closed doors). The current Duluth branch of the St. Louis County library is that ore-boat like structure across from the Depot.

Boomtown Buildings, continued

Duluth National Guard Armory • 1915 • 1305 London Rd.
(Kelly & Williams, architects) Besides acting as headquarters
for Duluth's Minnesota National Guard, the Duluth Armory also
hosted hundreds of cultural events. A young Bob Dylan sat
among the Armory's audience when Buddy Holly, Richie
Valens, and the Big Bopper played here just days before taking the fateful flight that claimed their lives and inspired Don
McClean's "American Pie" ("The day the music died..."). The
Guard moved to new headquarters in 1977. A movement to
restore the Armory continues to gain support.

Kitchi Gammi Club • 1912 • 831 E. Superior St.
(Bertram Goodhue, architect) The Kitchi Gammi Club was
until quite recently a men-only club (you still have to be a
member, guest, or employee to enter). Female guests of
members, including wives and daughters, used the side
entrance as late as the mid-1980s (the club was also
once racially exclusive, as was Duluth's Northland
Country Club). At least its members had good architectural taste. The "Kitch" features elements of Gothicism
mixed with Georgian pilasters and Tudor details. Get up
close for a look at the "politically incorrect" exterior stone
carvings of American Indians holding lanterns.

Morgan Park

Folks unfamiliar with the history of Morgan Park are often taken aback the first time they encounter its concrete houses. At the turn of the 20th century, U.S. Steel decided to build a steel mill in the vicinity of Duluth to save on transportation costs (the ore came from Minnesota's Mesabi Iron Range). After Minnesota threatened to tax iron ore that crossed the state line—unless the plant was located in the state—a site near Gary-New Duluth was chosen. U.S.S. built Morgan Park (named for U.S. Steel founder J.P. Morgan; it was originally to be named "Model City") to provide nearby housing for its employees. Construction began in 1913 and by 1915 the plant was producing steel. At the time, Morgan Park had the most modern school, hospital, and community facilities in the nation. The steel plant shut down in the 1970s, but Morgan Park remains a thriving community.

All the company's buildings were made chiefly of concrete block produced at the company's own cement plant because the material needed little maintenance. The somewhat harsh look of concrete was softened by gables, eaves, and rooflines that concealed the appearance of monotonous regularity.

The heart of the community was the Goodfellowship Club, a workers' association dedicated to serving sick or needy fellow employees. The club was housed in a large, multi-use building (pictured) that included a gymnasium with a running track, an auditorium, an indoor swimming pool, and a bowling alley. It was torn down in 1981 when a more fuel-efficient building was built to replace it.

Ruins of Duluth, Part One: "Old Main"

"Old Main" (DSTC Normal School) • 1898 • 2205 E. 5th St.

(Palmer, Hall, & Hunt, architects) In 1895 the State of Minnesota created the Normal School at Duluth. It was damaged by fire while under construction and opened in 1902. In 1905 it became the Duluth State Normal School. A west wing was added in 1909, an east wing in 1915. Its name was changed to the Duluth State Teachers' College in 1921, and finally, in 1947, to the University of Minnesota, Duluth Branch ("Branch" was officially dropped in 1959). In 1948 ground was broken for the first building of the new (and current) campus. The

old campus continued to serve UMD students for many years. Its central building, affectionately dubbed "Old Main," was used as a theater until the Marshall Performing Arts Center opened on the new campus in 1974.

Old Main was consumed by fire in February, 1993. The building was once an architectural hybrid of Romanesque and Renaissance features, but today only its arches stand preserved as a monument—the site has become a Duluth city park. Most of the buildings that surrounded Old Main are still in use by the university as research facilities. Torrence Hall, a former university dormitory, has been converted into an apartment building.

Ruins of Duluth, Part Two: Minnesota Point Lighthouse

Lake Superior's first lighthouse once stood 50 feet tall and served mariners for 20 years, from 1858 to 1878. R.H. Barrett, its first and only keeper, and his family lived in a simple cottage next to the tower of red Ohio brick wrapped in limestone. Barrett kept the light burning and, when the fog became thick, actually used his own lungs to blow a warning through a logging camp dinner horn. Local residents called the horn "Barrett's Cow."

The lighthouse was abandoned in 1878. The keeper's cottage was destroyed, and the tower now stands barely 30 feet high and has to be protected by a fence, but its French lenses are still used in the west pier-head light of the Superior Entry. (See page 26 for directions to the lighthouse.)

Nearby, you'll also find the empty hull of a concrete building. It is the remains of the U.S. Lighthouse Station Depot, which was used to store buoys and acetylene used in the batteries that powered the lighthouse at Canal Park. The vessels *Amaronth* and *Marigold* loaded and unloaded acetylene at the building from 1905 until World War II. The Corps of Engineers did not want to store the potentially dangerous gas too close to Canal Park and the Aerial Lift Bridge.

Washburn's Brownstones

The town of Washburn, Wisconsin, is the seat of Bayfield County and home to some of the finest examples of buildings encased in Lake Superior brownstone you'll find along the shore of the big lake. The town is so proud of its architectural heritage that it honors the buildings each year on the last weekend of July at its Brownstone Days festival.

Much of the red Lake Superior brownstone used in Washburn's historic 19th-century buildings was quarried locally, some of it right across the bay on the Apostle Islands. Prominent structures include the current home of Chequamegon Book & Coffee (left, see page 180), the Iron Works (center) whose stone facade is also adorned with a painting, the Washburn Cultural and Art Museum (right), and the county courthouse and library.

A few of Washburn's brownstones: Chequamegon Book & Coffee, the Iron Works, and the Washburn Cultural & Art Museum (former home of the town's bank).

Arts & Culture

(museums, galleries, theatre,
ballet, symphony, etc.)

Arts & Culture

While the Twin Ports certainly don't rate as a major metropolitan area, they hold their own when it comes to the arts. It seems that souls hearty enough to inhabit what some folks might deem a hostile environment tend to be a bit more creative and expressive (or perhaps crazy?) than those who live in climates that don't require furnaces or basements or window screens. The population may be relatively small and we may never get a traveling Monet or Van Gogh exhibit to stop by, but we still have our own orchestra and a first-rate ballet company, as well as a variety of smaller theatre and comedy groups, musical groups, art museums, galleries, and artist cooperatives.

The Twin Ports, along with the North and South Shore communities, also give no short shrift to history and regional culture, evidenced by the wide variety of museums throughout the area. There are a number of active historical societies eager to share what they know about the people who first settled the region and the industries that sustained them (and made some of them ridiculously wealthy).

The region is also home to writers working in a wide variety of styles. It supports a thriving community of essayists, fiction writers, poets, and playwrights, including Anthony Bukoski, Nancy Fitzgerald, Louis Jenkins, Milan Kovacovic, Joseph Maiolo, Patrick McKinnon, Margi Preus, Barton Sutter, and Connie Wanek, among others. The Twin Ports are also home to Holy Cow! Press, the Lake Superior Writers, Poetry Harbor, and *North Coast Review*. While you're in the area, make sure to check local newspapers for special events and readings involving our homegrown wordsmiths.

While this chapter highlights permanent homes of the arts, keep in mind that art can be found (and cultural events take place) just about any time and anywhere. Live music is available somewhere every night of the week (check the "Nightlife" chapter for likely spots), readings take place at local book stores, and many of the listings in the "Annual Events" chapter center around the region's rich and varied ethnic heritage.

Art Galleries

Lizzard's Art Gallery & Framing

Downtown, Duluth • 38 E. Superior St. • (218) 722-5815 • M–Sat. 10 A.M. - 5 P.M.

There are quite a few galleries in Duluth, but Lizzard's stands out among them by offering creations inspired by more than commerce or the desire to match someone's sofa. Lizzard's features works from local, regional, and national artists as well as a full-service frame shop. The gallery's high tin ceilings, glossy wood floors, and ample windows create a welcoming browsing environment in its two large rooms filled with paintings, sculpture, pottery, photography, jewelry, glassware, and textile works. While some items are priced (justifiably so) for the rich and famous, Lizzard's also features a variety of posters and pre-matted photographs and prints that are a bit more affordable, plus a selection of unique greeting cards.

Dirtygirlz Cooperative

Downtown, Duluth • 114 N. 1st Ave. W. • (218) 733-9595 • F & Sat. 10 A.M. - 6 P.M. / Sunday hours vary (call first)

When ceramics students at Lake Superior College, a Duluth technical college, found that they were losing badly needed work space, Mary Pechacek and some other "dirty girls" (so called because they tended to leave clay footprints around) decided to take matters into their own hands. They searched for and found space, not only to work in, but also to display and sell their creations. Now at their second location, the cooperative is open to both men and women artists and is not restricted to those who play with clay. Members have access to the cooperative's workspace—which includes two kilns, tables for potters, and lots of open space for easels and other equipment—24 hours a day, seven days a week. In exchange, members keep the studio space clean and help staff the gallery. The gallery's hours can fluctuate throughout the year, so it's not a bad idea to call before you visit.

Art Galleries, continued

Washington Galleries

Central Hillside, Duluth • 315 Lake Ave. N. • (No Phone Number) • Sat.–Sun. 1 P.M. - 5 P.M. / Special Events

The story of Washington Galleries begins in 1911 when the building it occupies was erected just up the street from Duluth's historic Central High School. The structure served as Washington Junior High School until 1992 when it was purchased by Artspace, a Minneapolis-based non-profit developer taking on its first project outside the Twin Cities area. Since that time, Artspace has completed similar projects in major cities around the country. Renovations converted the classic old school's six stories and 44,000 square feet into 39 apartments as well as gallery space, two dance studios, three musical rehearsal rooms, and other meeting rooms. Washington Studios, as the building is now known, functions as a cooperative, providing living and working space for its artist members. Artists have the opportunity to show their works in the on-site gallery. While the gallery has somewhat limited hours, be sure to check local newspapers for special events and openings that afford more opportunities to see the fruits of this creative environment.

Alternative Outlets for Local Art

Not all art is found in galleries or museums. The establishments listed below also display and sell original art by local artists.

Beaner's Central • 324 N. Central Ave. • (218) 624-5957 • opens M–F 6:30 A.M., Sat. 8 A.M., Sun. 10 A.M. / closes 9 - 11 P.M.

Coco's to Geaux • 324 W. Superior St. • (218) 740-3039 • M–F 7 A.M. - 5 P.M. (lunch 11 A.M. - 1:30 P.M.)

Lakeview Coffee Emporium • 600 E. Superior St. • (218) 720-4464 • M–Sat. 7 A.M. - 8 P.M. / Sun. 8 A.M. - 6 P.M.

Round About Records • 205 E. Superior St. • (218) 733-0132 • M–F 11 A.M. - 8 P.M. / Sat. 10 A.M. - 9 P.M. / Sun. 12 P.M. - 5 P.M.

Museums

Tweed Museum of Art

UMD Campus, Duluth • 10 University Dr. • (218) 726-8222 • T 9 A.M. - 8 P.M. / W–F 9 A.M. - 4:30 P.M. / Sat.–Sun. 1 P.M. - 5 P.M.

The Tweed Museum of Art on the University of Minnesota Duluth campus houses nine galleries and displays works in all media. The museum strives to represent the history of art as well as contemporary trends, and to present artwork from various world cultures. To that end, each year the Tweed organizes eight to ten major exhibitions and presents rotating exhibits from its permanent collection. The permanent collection includes works from the 14th century to the present, with strong representations of 16th- to 19th-century European painting, 19th- and 20th-century American painting, and modern and contemporary art. The Tweed's museum store is a great place to find quality gifts like posters, art books, and unique jewelry. Closed university holidays.

Graffiti Graveyard

Between Downtown and Bayfront Park • Always Open

Graffiti Graveyard is the unofficial name of an area underneath Interstate 35 between Bayfront Park and the Depot (park near Bayfront and walk across Railroad Street and a set of tracks, then follow the wall that passes below the highway until you find the entrance—watch out for the water). Wide as four lanes of highway and nearly a half mile long, the Graveyard has become a haven for graffiti artists. Every wall and pillar has been hit with paint, some of it amateur scribblings, some of it well-executed works of art. From original creations to your favorite Warner Brothers cartoon characters, you'll find miles of self-expression and slogans along with the typical declarations of who was here and who loves whom. Another local site for graffiti artists is found under the Eighth Street bridge that crosses over Chester Creek. As you walk under the bridge, look up: directly under the mid-point of the arch you'll see the words "Beat This! 10-2-91".

Museums, continued

The Depot

Downtown, Duluth • 506 W. Michigan St. • (218) 733-7500 • Summer: Daily 9:30 A.M. - 6 P.M. / Winter: M–Sat. 10 A.M. - 5 P.M. / Sun. 1 P.M. - 6 P.M.

Technically, the Depot is actually the St. Louis County Heritage and Arts Center, but local residents call it the Depot for obvious reasons: it's a whole lot easier to say, and the building once functioned as a railroad depot. Built in 1892, the building was a Union Railroad depot that by 1910 served seven lines with as many as 5,000 passengers per day passing through its doors until it closed as a railroad depot in 1969 (see page 73). In 1971 the building earned a spot on the national register of historic places, and in 1973 it began operating as a cultural center. Today the Depot is home to four museums and provides office, theater, and studio space for five performing arts organizations including the Duluth Art Institute, Duluth Children's Museum, Minnesota Ballet, and Duluth Playhouse.

Given the range of organizations it hosts, the Depot is a sort of cultural one-stop shop, offering something to interest just about anyone. The main entrance, located at street level, leads to The Great Hall, an impressive open area where travelers once bought tickets, waited for trains, and perhaps grabbed a quick meal and a shoe shine. Make sure to pause here and check out the vaulted ceiling on your way through to the St. Louis County Historical Society's (SLCHS) exhibits. Up one floor you'll find the Lake Superior Ojibwe Gallery, also operated by the SLCHS, and the Duluth Art Institute. Down one floor from the Great Hall, you'll find the Duluth Children's Museum, which continues down yet another level. The best way to get to there is through the Children's Tree, a spiral staircase that wends its way through a life-sized diorama of a tree's interior. The lower level, called the Track Level since this was the actual train arrival and departure area, holds what is indisputably the Depot's finest exhibit: the Lake Superior Railroad Museum. Plan to spend a lot of time here and expect to feel about ten years old by the time you leave. If you're not convinced yet, read more about the Railroad Museum on page 89.

Museums, continued

Lake Superior Railroad Museum
Downtown, Duluth • 506 W. Michigan St. • (218) 733-7590 • (Same operating hours as the Depot, previous page)

Located on and around the original tracks that used to service trains coming in and out of the Duluth Union Depot, the Lake Superior Railroad Museum is more than a museum, it's a trip back in time. As you descend the wide, crowd-accommodating staircase from the Depot's Great Hall you begin to detect the aroma of old trains: oil and grease and soot and who knows what else, all comingling to form the smell of history. Along six tracks, the museum displays carefully restored train cars of all types, including plows, steam locomotives, and passenger and dining cars. Some can be viewed from platforms, others you can actually walk through to get a closer look. To further enhance your time travel, the trains are surrounded by Depot Square—a meticulous recreation of turn-of-the-century shops and offices that could be a museum unto itself. Each building is outfitted with period-appropriate signage, window-dressing, furniture, wares, etc. The Railroad Museum is simply not to be missed. (And if you have the time, you can take the North Shore Scenic Railroad to Two Harbors and back.)

Old Fire House & Police Museum
East End, Superior • 402 23rd Ave. E. • (715) 398-7558 • Open seasonally (call ahead)

The last of Superior's turn-of-the-century fire houses, the museum was originally the East End Fire Hall, built to replace an old wooden firehouse that stood on the same spot until, ironically, it burned down in 1896. In 1982 the old fire hall became a museum dedicated to firefighters and police officers, and in 1996 it became the home of the Wisconsin State Fire and Police Hall of Fame, honoring the heroic deeds of firefighters and police officers throughout the state's history. Visitors will find vintage firefighting and police memorabilia, including several old firefighting rigs. The museum is open seasonally for self-guided tours at the cost of a small donation.

Museums, continued

Karpeles Manuscript Library Museum

Duluth • 902 E. 1st St. • (218) 728-0630 • Daily 12 P.M. - 4 P.M. / Closed Holidays & Mondays from Labor Day to Memorial Day

This Duluth museum is one of seven Karpeles sites located throughout the U.S. Together, the libraries house the world's largest private holding (over one million items) of important original manuscripts and documents from the fields of literature, science, religion, history, art, and even popular culture. Every three months a new exhibit is featured, along with the museum's ongoing displays. During 2001 some of the featured exhibits traveling among the Karpeles libraries included design and concept sketches for *Star Trek: The Next Generation*, early baseball documents, original nursery rhyme illustrations, and a collection of Eva Peron material, including letters and drafts of addresses. Admission is free.

Museums You May Already Know

Fairlawn Mansion (Pattison estate) • 906 E. 2nd St. • (715) 394-5712 • Tours: M–Sat. 9 A.M. - 5 P.M. / Sun. 12 P.M. - 5 P.M.
Tours of a 42-room Queen Anne-style house built by Superior's three-time mayor Martin Pattison in 1891.

Glensheen Mansion (Congdon estate) • 3300 London Rd. • (218) 726-8910 • Tours: M–F 9:30 A.M. - 4 P.M., May–October
Tours of the house Chester and Clara Congdon finished in 1908, modeled after an early 17th-century English country estate.

Great Lakes Aquarium • 353 Harbor Dr. • (218) 740-3474 • M–Sun. 10 A.M. - 6 P.M. • Fresh water fish and marine life.

Lake Superior Maritime Museum • Canal Park • (218) 727-2497 • Summer: Daily 10 A.M. - 9 P.M. / Winter: F–Sun. 10 A.M. - 4:30 P.M.
History of shipping and shipwrecks on the Great Lakes.

***S.S. Meteor* Museum • 300 Marina Dr. • (715) 392-5742 •** Tours of the *S.S. Meteor* whaleback and *Col. D.D. Gaillard* dredger.

William A. Irvin • 350 Harbor Dr. • (218) 722-7876 • Tours: Sun.–W 9 A.M. - 6 P.M. / Th.–Sat. 9 A.M. - 8 P.M. • Ore boat tour.

Theatre

Manion Theatre & University Experimental Theatre (UWS)
UWS Campus, Superior • Belknap St. & Catlin • (715) 394-8380 • Call for performance schedule

The University of Wisconsin-Superior's 237-seat Manion Theatre offers a wide range of theatre—from musical to drama to opera—produced by the school's theatre department and occasionally involving guest directors and performers. The University Experimental Theatre is home to department productions as well as shows produced entirely by students. Tickets range from $6 to $12 and just $1 for UWS students.

Mitchell Auditorium & the Little Theatre (CSS)
St. Scholastica Campus, Duluth • 1200 Kenwood Ave. • (218) 723-5900 • Call for performance schedule

Theatre students at College of St. Scholastica have two venues on campus in which to showcase their talents: Mitchell Auditorium, seating 500 (also home to musical performances, lectures, and concerts) and the Little Theatre, a 150-seat "black box." The Theatre Department stages three professionally directed productions each year. Tickets $8, seniors and students $5, and just $3 for CSS students.

Marshall Performing Arts Center & Dudley Experimental Theatre (UMD)
UMD Campus, Duluth • 10 University Dr. • (218) 726-8561 • Call for performance schedule

MPAC is the home of the University of Minnesota Duluth's award-winning theatre department, which has sent several plays to the Kennedy Center as part of the American College Theatre Festival since 1987. Each year the UMD Theatre Department stages several productions, including a musical, a modern drama, and a classic Greek or Elizabethan play, as well as plays written and produced by students. The main theater seats 700 people; Dudley Experimental Theatre holds about 100. Tickets $12, students and seniors $9, and $6 for UMD students.

Theatre, continued

Renegade Comedy Theatre

Downtown, Duluth • 404 W. Superior St. • 800-722-6627 or (218) 722-6775 • Call for show times

Since 1991 Renegade Comedy Theatre has been producing and performing original material as well as the works of other writers. Each year, the troupe puts together several shows, including Halloween- and Holiday-themed sketch programs. Renegade also produces works for kids through the Renegade Children's Theatre. But even if there's not a show running, you can always catch the Renegade folks in action at the Comedy Olympics every Friday and Saturday night at 9:30 P.M. The Comedy Olympics is a show structured like television's *Whose Line is it Anyway* in which two teams of two troupe members compete to come up with the best improvisational response to audience suggestions while a referee officiates. To find out if a regular show is running, check local newspapers or call the Renegade box office.

Colder by the Lake

Duluth • No permanent address • www.colderbythelake.com • Check website for show times and locations

Colder by the Lake is the area's oldest surviving comedy theatre troupe, entertaining Duluth audiences since 1983. Throughout the '80s, Colder performed several sketch-based revues each year, but of late they have focused on producing one or two full-scale shows per year based on original material or well-known works such as Shakespeare's *A Midsummer Night's Dream*. They last entertained local audiences in January 2002 with a revival of their highly acclaimed and downright hilarious 2001 production *Les Uncomfortables*, an original comic opera about Duluth's founder, Daniel Greysolon Sieur du Lhut, written by Colder founder Margi Preus and long-time Colder writer/performer Jean Sramek. It's difficult to predict when the Colder crew will stage another show, so check their website or the entertainment calendars in local newspapers when you're in the area.

Theatre, continued

Duluth Playhouse
Downtown, Duluth • 506 W. Michigan St. • (218) 733-7555 • Box Office: M–F 9 A.M. - 5 P.M. / Sat. 12 P.M. - 6 P.M.

The Duluth Playhouse, staging musical and nonmusical productions since 1914, bills itself as "excitement for the whole family" and reflects this motto in its choice of material. The 2001-2002 season featured titles such as *Annie*, *The Miracle Worker*, and *The Adventures of Tom Sawyer*—all suitable for theater-goers of all ages. But for those who might find these choices a bit too advanced, the Playhouse also has a children's theatre that puts on shows performed by children for children, based on material that most kids will find familiar and entertaining. Performances take place Wednesday through Saturday with matinees on Saturday and Sunday. Individual tickets for the 2001–2002 season ranged from $12 to $14 for adults, $10 to $12 for seniors and students, and $6 to $11 for kids, depending on age.

Minnesota Ballet
Downtown, Duluth • Box Office: 301 W. 1st St. • (218) 529-3742 • M–F 9 A.M. - 4 P.M.

The Minnesota Ballet is a professional company of 12 dancers that makes its home in Duluth's historic Board of Trade building (see page 74). The company tours internationally and throughout the U.S. and performs each season in Duluth and the Twin Cities. The Ballet performs a variety of works from both classical and modern ballet, as well as theatrical ballroom and jazz styles. It also conducts residency, outreach, and education programs to teach the art and history of ballet to area students and residents through lectures and demonstrations, and offers classes to all age groups and to people with physical challenges. Individual tickets for the 2001–2002 season ranged from $15 to $27 for adults, $12 to $20 for students age 13 to college (with identification) and $10 to $18 for children 12 and under.

Music*

Duluth–Superior Symphony Orchestra

Duluth • Box Office: (218) 733-7579 • M–F 8:30 A.M. - 5 P.M. • Performances: DECC Auditorium, 350 Harbor Dr.

The Duluth–Superior Symphony Orchestra got its start in 1931, though it was then called the Duluth Civic Orchestra, performing in the historic Duluth Armory building (see page 78). In 2001 the DSSO celebrated its 70th year and the addition of its new conductor, Markand Thakar. The orchestra performs 20th-century American and contemporary works along with classical works of the Western European symphonic tradition. Each season features ten regular performances (some with classical programs, some pops) as well as a performance of Handel's Messiah. Individual tickets for the 2001–2002 season ranged from $16.50 to $38 for adults, half price for students ages 6 to 17, with seniors over 65 receiving a $2 discount.

Sacred Heart Music Center

Central Hillside, Duluth • 201 W. 4th St. • (218) 723-1895 • Open for performances and tours (call for schedules)

The former Sacred Heart Cathedral (see page 70) was completed in 1896 and is now managed by a non-profit organization. The group is dedicated to the preservation and renovation of the 100-year-old landmark and to providing a venue for the performing arts in Duluth by regional, national, and international artists. From the early music of the Twin Cities' renowned Rose Ensemble to the modern, ethereal sound of Duluth's own Low, the Music Center's architectural features and superb acoustics provide a unique setting for a wide variety of aural entertainment. The former cathedral has also retained its historic 1898 Felgemaker pipe organ. The center often provides visitors opportunities to hear (and even play) the organ. Self-guided and group tours are available; contact the Music Center for schedule and details.

*For additional live music venues, see pages 108–110.

North Shore Galleries & Museums

3M/Dwan Museum
Two Harbors • 201 Waterfront Dr. • (218) 834-4898 • May–October: Daily 9:30 P.M. - 5 P.M.

Displays and interactive programs on the history of 3M in the building where it all started in 1902.

Lake County Historical Museum
Two Harbors • 520 South Ave. • (218) 834-4898 • M–Sat. 9 A.M. - 5 P.M. / Sun. 10 A.M. - 3 P.M.

Exhibits on the pioneering history of Lake County, North Shore dogsled mail delivery, logging, and more.

North Shore Commercial Fishing Museum
Tofte • Highway 61 & County Rd. 2 • (218) 663-7804 • Summer: Daily 9 A.M. - 7 P.M. / Winter: Daily 9 A.M. - 5 P.M.

Displays on commercial fishing, Lake Superior, and the people who settled the area.

Johnson Heritage Post Art Gallery
Grand Marais • 115 W. Wisconsin • (218) 387-2314 • Summer: M–Sat. 10 A.M. - 5 P.M. / Sun. 12 P.M. - 4 P.M. / Winter: T–Sun. 12 P.M. - 4 P.M.

Revolving exhibits, plus a permanent collection of paintings by Anna Johnson, a regional pioneer.

Grand Portage National Monument
Grand Portage • 211 Mile Creek Rd. • (218) 378-2788 • May–October: Daily 9 A.M. - 4:30 P.M.

Exhibits on the fur trade and area history, craft and cooking demonstrations, American Indian artifacts, and more.

South Shore Galleries & Museums

Bayfield Maritime Museum
Bayfield • 131 S. 1st St. • (715) 779-9919 • July–Aug.: Daily 10 A.M. - 7 P.M. / June, Sept., Oct.: Daily 10 A.M. - 5 P.M.

Displays on commercial fishing, lighthouses, sailor crafts, shipwrecks, and more.

Native Spirit Gifts and Gallery
Bayfield • 14612 Highway 13 • (715) 779-9550 • May–Oct.: M–Sat. 10 A.M. - 5 P.M. / Sun. 12 P.M. - 5 P.M. / Wknds. until Christmas

Cultural displays, American Indian art from the Great Lakes region, craft demonstrations, and birch bark canoes.

Apostle Islands National Lakeshore Museum
Bayfield • 415 Washington Ave. • (715) 779-3397 • Mem. Day–Labor Day: Daily 1 P.M. - 4 P.M. / After Labor Day: wknds. only

Exhibits on logging, lumbering, agriculture, and more, plus an extensive collection of historic photographs.

Washburn Historical Museum and Cultural Center
Washburn • 1 E. Bayfield St. • (715) 373-5591 • April–December: Daily 10 A.M. - 4 P.M.

Local and regional history exhibits, dioramas, and fine art.

Northern Great Lakes Visitor Center
Ashland • 29270 Highway G • (715) 685-9983 • Summer: Daily 9 A.M. - 7 P.M. / Winter: Daily 9 A.M. - 5 P.M.

Observation tower, interpretive and historic exhibits, boardwalk trail, visitor information, and trip planning.

Nightlife
(libations, live music, dancing, etc.)

Nightlife

You can find just about anything to do in the Twin Ports on a weekend night (and most weeknights). Both Duluth and Superior have plenty of watering holes, but Superior in particular offers many places to drink. They say "Soup Town" has more bar stools than church pews, and they might be right: Twenty-six bars operate along one 10-block strip of Tower Avenue, and nine more can be found a block or less from the Tower Avenue strip.

With that many bars on one Superior street, we couldn't do a fair job describing each and every bar in Superior and Duluth without developing a serious drinking problem, so we've hand-selected a number of places because of their authentic atmosphere or specialty (e.g., gay-lesbian-bisexual-transgender establishments, microbreweries, etc.). We also profiled some neighborhood taverns in case you find yourself on an unfamiliar side of town and want to stop for a cold one in a comfortable setting. We tried to avoid places you could find anywhere—in other words, no chains, sports bars, or typical college bars.

For those who like to do more than just drink, we've listed Twin Ports dance clubs, bowling alleys, pool halls, and live music venues. The Twin Ports enjoys an eclectic music scene and has recently seen some of its local musicians achieve regional, national and even international acclaim. Check the local arts & entertainment papers to find out where you can see college chart-toppers Low, the Lake Superior surf guitar of the Black Labels, the Black-Eyed Snakes' power blues, the sleepy pop of Fair Weather Friend, folkster Jamie Ness, "rawk and/or rollers" Giljunko, Max Dakota's reggae-fusion, the eclectic glam of Gild, Father Hennepin's Hillsidebilly alt-country, the ska-meets-Phish sound of No Room to Pogo, comic super-hero rockers First Ladies, and many more.

Check out the end of this section for some great places to drink along the shores. By the way, Minnesota bars are open until 1 A.M. and Wisconsin bars serve until 2 A.M. weeknights and 2:30 A.M. weekends. And if you're out at a Superior nightspot and think you've spotted Rod Stewart slumming it, you're wrong—but you're not the only person to make that mistake. That's just Rod's local doppelganger.

Authentic Atmosphere

The Anchor Bar
North End, Superior • 413 Tower Ave. • (715) 394-9747 • Sun.–Th. 'til 2 A.M. / F & Sat. 'til 2:30 A.M. • Full bar

If you're looking for a place with character, the Anchor has it in spades. No fake antiques or sports memorabilia here, just real things from real ships in a real harbor town: diving suits, flags, life rings, etc. If you're lucky, the barber chairs will be unoccupied when you get there. Besides that, beer is inexpensive and the Anchor boasts one of the best selections of imports and microbrews in the Twin Ports—and the best burgers and fries, hands down.

Molly's
North End, Superior • 411 Tower Ave. • phone number unavailable • Sun.–Th. 'til 2 A.M. / F & Sat. 'til 2:30 A.M. • Full bar

From its pressed tin ceiling to the Tiffany-esque stained glass lamps behind the bar, Molly's has about the best décor you're likely to find in a dive. Molly's son Oscar has decorated the bar with great old memorabilia, including antique signage such as an advertisement for land at Tower and Belknap—now the heart of downtown—at just $1 an acre. Leinies cost a buck, and Molly's has the best classic R & B jukebox in the midwest. Molly's was once considered a GLBT bar, but these days you'll find all kinds of folks enjoying themselves under its roof.

Choo Choo Bar
Itasca, Superior • 5002 E. 3rd St. • (715) 398-3788 • Sun.–Th. 'til 2 A.M. / F & Sat. 'til 2:30 A.M. • Full bar

Structure sets the Choo Choo apart from any other bar in the Twin Ports. Made from old railroad cars (it sits along the tracks in Superior's Itasca neighborhood), the Choo Choo's ceilings are low and curved, and the bar itself is quite narrow, creating a cozy atmosphere. Not much of a choice in beer, just a few domestic taps, cans, and bottles. You can play pool or darts, and the jukebox selection runs from Johnny Cash to the Backstreet Boys.

Authentic Atmosphere, continued

Kom-On-Inn

Spirit Valley (West Duluth), Duluth • 332 N. 57th Ave. W. • (218) 624-3385 • Open 'til 1 A.M. • Full bar

For a glimpse of what West Duluth once looked like, all you need do is come inside the Kom-On-Inn. The highlight of this long, narrow drinking hole is the line of wooden booths, each sporting an original oil painting by Art Fleming depicting the mills and factories that flourished in this once-industrial end of town. The Kom-on-Inn has been open since Prohibition ended, and it hasn't raised its prices much since. A must stop in West Duluth.

NorShor Theatre

Downtown, Duluth • 211 E. Superior St. • (218) 727-7585 • Open 'til 1 A.M. • Full bar

Duluth's historic Orpheum Theatre (see page 234) was renovated in the late 1930s, transforming the vaudeville house into an art-deco movie theater. It is now a bar/nightclub that shows independent and foreign films and acts as the epicenter of Duluth's ever-growing live music scene. Three-dimensional art deco reliefs decorate the stairway walls and those adjacent to the main stage. The mezzanine lounge features a classic wooden bar where you can choose from a good selection of imports and microbrews—or ask Rick to twist you up a martini.

Sir Benedict's Tavern

Downtown, Duluth • 805 E. Superior St. • (218) 728-1192 • Open 'til 11 P.M. • Beer & wine only

Sir Ben's strives to be an authentic British pub, and while it's not exactly what you'd find in the U.K., it does have a warm, comfy feel and an incredible selection of imported beers from around the globe. The pub hosts live music on weekends and a bluegrass jam every Wednesday night. In the summer, Sir Ben's patio makes a great spot to enjoy a beer and gaze at the big lake. If you're hungry, Sir Ben's also serves soups and sandwiches.

Under the Rainbow (GLBT Establishments)

Bev's Jook Joint
Downtown, Superior • 820 Tower Ave. • (715) 392-5373 • Sun.–Th. 'til 2 A.M. / F & Sat. 'til 2:30 A.M. • Full bar

Bev's is about the friendliest place in downtown Superior. People of all orientations gather to listen—and some-time join in on—live music performances from local and national acts (primarily blues). A variety of instruments adorn the walls, and all may be taken down and played if you care to jam with the band (and if the band's into it). In the summer, step out back for some fresh air when the band takes a break. Good beer selection.

J.T.'s
North End, Superior • 1506 N. 3rd St. • (715) 394-2580 • Sun.–Th. 'til 2 A.M. / F & Sat. 'til 2:30 A.M. • Full bar

One of three remaining bars along Superior's once notorious 3rd Street (filled with speakeasies and brothels during Prohibition), J.T.'s erupts on weekend nights as the dance floor fills with folks of all ilks who just want to shake their groove thang. If you're not into dancing, J.T.'s has a couple of pool tables to keep you busy, and they open the grill in the afternoon. Good selection of beer and wine, and the bar occasionally hosts drag shows.

The Main Club
Downtown, Superior • 1217 Tower Ave. • (715) 392-1756 • Sun.–Th. 'til 2 A.M. / F & Sat. 'til 2:30 A.M. • Full bar

If you've come back for a visit, don't look for the Main in its old location in the North End—that burned to the ground. Now located next to the Androy Hotel on Tower, the Main has long served the Twin Ports' GLBT com-munity and plays host to an annual ball and Gay Pride celebration. The Main has a small dance floor with music spun by a D.J. and its bar offers a fine selection of beers.

Brewpubs

Fitger's Brewhouse

Downtown, Duluth • 600 E. Superior St. • (218) 726-1392 • M–Sun. 11 A.M. - 1 A.M. • Beer & wine only • Smoke free

Even though the Brewhouse is located inside the somewhat tourist-oriented Fitger's Brewery Complex, we had to include it for one simple reason: hands down, the best beer you'll find in Duluth or up the North Shore (maybe even Minnesota). From the Witch Tree ESB to the Bigboat Oatmeal Stout, master brewer Dave Hoops and his crew cook up an excellent assortment, including seasonal beers. (In honor of the annual Home Grown Music Fest, the Brewhouse offers "Home Grown Hempin' Ale.") You can enjoy live music from local and national singer/songwriter acts most weekends, and Thursday night is home to Starfire Lounge: inexpensive pitchers and an eclectic mix of music. The Brewhouse also makes great food, from gourmet sandwiches to vegetarian entrées.

Twin Ports Brewing Company

Downtown, Superior • 1623 Broadway St. • (715) 394-2500 • Sun.–Th. 'til 2 A.M. / F & Sat. 'til 2:30 A.M. • Beer only

The Twin Ports Brewing Company features the handcrafted brews of Rick Sauer and the only hand-poured beer north of the Twin Cities, thanks to its Victorian beer machine. (It pulls the beer out of the cask the old way, without the aid of carbon dioxide.) Sauer puts up a regular line of brews such as the Derailed Ale, Burntwood Black, and Twin Ports ESB as well as seasonal brews like the Apple Harvest Ale, which isn't overly fruity despite its name. Located inside the old Russell Creamery, Twin Ports's glazed-tile walls are adorned with old signs from Superior's brewing history, especially those advertising the Northern Brewing Company. Limited food available, including a smoked salmon platter. Wednesdays after 9 P.M., pitchers are just $7, and weekdays from 4 to 6 P.M., pints are only $2.50. If you're bored with pool or darts, ask for a cribbage board, chess set, or Yahtzee game.

Neighborhood Saloons

The Reef

Endion, Duluth • 2002 London Rd. • (218) 724-9845 • Open 'til 1 A.M. • Full bar

Besides Black Woods restaurant, The Reef is the only place you can get a drink east of downtown. Its clientele ranges from neighborhood regulars to UMD and St. Scholastica students. The Reef has lots of games to play (pool, darts, foosball, video games) and plenty of TVs to stare at, including a couple big screens (and they're not always tuned to sports). A limited number of imports and microbrews. Live music on weekends.

The North Pole

Irving (West Duluth), Duluth • 5606 Raleigh St. • (218) 624-9623 • Open 'til 1 A.M. • Full bar

The North Pole is a classic neighborhood saloon. Its west wall is dominated by a superb wooden bar with wooden coolers and a modestly ornate back covered with years of memorabilia, Swisher Sweet cigars, Hav-A-Hank handkerchiefs, and Ronson lighter flints. Tap beer (domestic only) sells for $1.25, but 20-ouncers go for $1.50 during NFL games. The only jukebox anywhere that still has Boyce & Hart's "I Wonder what She's Doing Tonight."

Buena Vista Lounge

Central Hillside, Duluth • 1144 Mesaba Ave. • (218) 722-1371 • Open 'til 1 A.M. • Full bar

Located where the 'Heights meets the Hillside, the Buena Vista Lounge is the last non-chain drinking establishment in Duluth until you near the outskirts of Hermantown out past the Miller Hill Mall shopping corridor. The Buena's simple décor is dominated by a large, rectangular bar—nothing fancy here, just a good, comfy spot for a drink. Domestics and a couple microbrews on tap; many TVs, dartboards, and video games to entertain you.

Neighborhood Saloons, continued

Alpine Bar & Lounge

Gary-New Duluth, Duluth • 1308 Commonwealth Ave. • (218) 626-9979 • Open 'til 1 A.M. • Full bar

Although the bar is topped in Formica, the rest of the Alpine has an authentic touch, from the mosaic tile floor to the bar's brass rail—they even sell pork rinds, pickled eggs, and pickled turkey gizzards. And although a sign proclaims "Alpine Proudly Serves Pabst Blue Ribbon on Tap," it actually sells no tap beer. Plenty of domestic bottles and cans, though, and everything from Buddy Holly to Duran Duran on the jukebox. Karaoke on weekends.

Congress Bar

Gary-New Duluth, Duluth • 1334 Commonwealth Ave. • (218) 626-9967 • Open 'til 1 A.M. • Full bar

The centerpiece of the Congress is its classic wooden bar and bar back, complete with a mirror held in place by tufted leather (which, sadly, has been covered over). In the summers, an outdoor beer garden opens out back. You'll find Old Style, Killian's, and MGD on tap plus domestic and a few Mexican imports in the cooler. Register to win the "Customer of the Week" drawing for free drinks every night for a week.

The Wabegon Inn (and Last Chance Café)

Fond du Lac, Duluth • 14030 W. Highway 23 (keep driving past Fond du Lac) • (218) 636-1700 • Open 'til 1 A.M. • Full bar

If you've spent the day in Jay Cooke or are heading down to the 'Cities on Scenic Highway 23, the Wabegon makes a great spot to wet your whistle. Small and simple, the Wabegon has darts, a pool table, and a juke box (mostly new country). You'll find Bud and Miller on tap for just $1.50. You'll also find an anomaly in this place so close to where Packerland intersects with Vikingland: a Tampa Bay Buccaneers mirror. The Wabegon also sells off-sale liquor and houses the Last Chance Café (burgers, steaks, barbecued ribs, spaghetti).

Neighborhood Saloons, continued

El Dorado
Oliver, WI • 2110 E. Union St. • (715) 392-3717 • Sun.–Th. 'til 2 A.M. / F & Sat. 'til 2:30 A.M. • Full bar

Before the El Dorado changed hands in 1999, it looked like a hybrid saloon/thrift store—you could get a beer and a ceramic trout-shaped flower pot. Today the knick knacks are gone, but the El Dorado still makes a great place to have a beer, shoot a game of pool, or play one of their many video-gambling machines. Named by its original owner who had made his fortune in a silver mine, the El Dorado is decorated with authentic wagon wheels and oxen harnesses. You can enjoy a can of domestic beer for $1.50. Some food and off-sale available.

Charlie Brown's
Billings Park, Superior • 1828 Iowa Ave. • (715) 394-5295 • Sun.–Th. 'til 2 A.M. / F & Sat. 'til 2:30 A.M. • Full bar

Next door to the antique shop, across the street from the bakery, and a few doors away from the café, Charlie Brown's helps make up "downtown" Billings Park. This tiny corner bar is decorated with an array of beer steins and—because of its name—Peanuts memorabilia. Where else can you get drunk while staring at Snoopy and Woodstock without feeling like some kind of creep? Pool table in back, and domestic taps are just $1.

The Office
East End, Superior • 2129 E. 5th St. • (715) 398-7536 • Sun.–Th. 'til 2 A.M. / F & Sat. 'til 2:30 A.M. • Full bar

Another great neighborhood saloon with an old wooden bar and coolers, The Office is located in the heart of Superior's East End business district. The walls are covered with photos of patrons from days gone by, and you'll find everything from Patsy Cline to the Beatles on the jukebox. It will cost you $1.25 for a domestic tap, and don't bother asking if they have imports or microbrews. Limited off-sale liquor and beer available.

Bowling Alleys*

Incline Station Bowling Center
Downtown, Duluth • 601 W. Superior St. • (218) 722-0671 • Every day 9 A.M. - 12 A.M.

Features Atomic Bowling (disco and black lights, music) and bumper bowling. Attached bar & grill.

Landmark Lanes
Downtown, Superior • 1914 Broadway St. • (715) 394-4422 • Every day 11 A.M. - 12 A.M.

Bumper bowling and birthday party reservations available.

Stadium Lanes
Lincoln Park, Duluth • Grand Ave. at 34th Ave. W. • (218) 628-1071 • Sun.–Th. 12 P.M. - 12 A.M. / F & Sat. 'til 1:30 A.M.

Bumper bowling available. Leagues from 5 P.M. to 9 P.M. Monday–Thursday. Attached bar (Mary's Place).

Tanski's Ridgeview Lanes
Woodland, Duluth • 3930 E. Calvary • (218) 728-3614 • M–F 3 P.M. - 12 A.M. / Sat. & Sun. 12 P.M. - 12 A.M.

A great old bowling center. Call ahead for bumper bowling. Full bar and pizza available.

Village Lanes
South End, Superior • 6419 Tower Ave. • (715) 394-4436 • M–Th. 10 A.M. - 12 A.M. / F & Sat. 'til 2:30 a.m. / Sun. 'til 12 A.M.

Bumper bowling available; full bar and grill.

*Call ahead to make sure it's not league night! Duluth bowling alleys go smoke free April 1, 2003.

Billiard Parlors

Horseshoe Billiards

Lincoln Park, Duluth • 2415 W. Superior St. • (218) 727-5144 • Sun.–Th. 10 A.M. - 2 A.M. / F & Sat. 10 A.M. - 3 A.M.

You'll find twenty pool tables at Horseshoe's: ten bar-sized (7-foot), nine 9-foot, and one snooker table (6 x 9 feet). You'll also find several dart boards as well as ten TVs—one large screen—in case you want to watch a ball game while you shoot some stick. Beer and soft drinks available. **Duluth billiard halls go smoke free April 1, 2003.**

Mr. Lucky's

Downtown, Superior • 1022 Tower Ave. • (715) 395-9789 • Sun.–Th. 'til 2 A.M. / F & Sat. 'til 2:30 A.M.

Mr. Lucky's, a self-proclaimed "modern, upscale billiards parlor," has thirteen bar-sized pool tables, four 9-foot tables, and one snooker table. Mr. Lucky's also has a full-service bar, serves pizza, and buys and sells pool cues and tables.

Bars with Above-Average Billiard Facilities

Capri Bar • Downtown, Superior • 1224 Tower Ave. • (715) 395-1908 • Sun.–Th. 'til 2 A.M. / F & Sat. 'til 2:30 A.M.

The Palace • Downtown, Superior • 1108 Tower Ave. • Sun.–Th. 'til 2 A.M. / F & Sat. 'til 2:30 A.M.

The Pioneer • Downtown, Duluth • 323 W. 1st St. • Open 'til 1 A.M.

The Reef • East End, Duluth • 2002 London Rd. • (218) 724-9845 • Open 'til 1 A.M. • (see page 103)

The Lounge • Downtown, Superior • 715 Belknap St. • (715) 392-5341 • Sun.–Th. 'til 2 A.M. / F & Sat. 'til 2:30 A.M.
(The Lounge's billiard facilities aren't all that impressive, but they do have an **L**-shaped table.)

Live Music Venues

Beaner's Central

Spirit Valley (West Duluth), Duluth • 324 N. Central Ave. • (218) 624-5957 • open 'til 11 P.M. most nights

Eclectic: singer/songwriter, reggae, rock, country, etc. (see page 127 for details).

Bedrock Bar

Lincoln Park, Duluth • 2023 W. Superior • (218) 720-4755 • Open 'til 1 A.M.

Mostly hard rock and heavy metal cover bands.

Bev's Jook Joint

Downtown, Superior • 820 Tower Ave. • (715) 392-5373 • Sun.–Th. 'til 2 A.M. / F & Sat. 'til 2:30 A.M.

Blues and much more (see page 101 for details).

Charlie's Club

Spirit Valley (West Duluth), Duluth • 5527 Grand Ave. • (218) 624-3150 • Open 'til 1 A.M.

Mostly hard rock and heavy metal cover bands.

Fitger's Brewhouse

Downtown, Duluth • 600 E. Superior St. • (218) 726-1392 • M–Sun. 11 A.M. - 1 A.M.

Singer/songwriters on weekends (see page 102 for details).

Live Music venues, continued

The Limit
Gary-New Duluth, Duluth • 1426 Commonwealth Ave. • (218) 626-3398 • Open 'til 1 A.M.

Local and regional country and top 40 pop cover bands.

Norm's Beer & Brats
Downtown, Superior • 1901 Broadway St. • (715) 394-9689 • Sun.–Th. 'til 2 A.M. / F & Sat. 'til 2:30 A.M.

Local and sometimes national rock acts (original and cover bands).

NorShor Theatre
Downtown, Duluth • 211 E. Superior St. • (218) 727-7585 • Open 'til 1 A.M.

The epicenter of the Twin Ports' live music scene, featuring local, regional, and national acts. Rock, alt-country, Hillside "rawk and/or roll," singer/songwriters, folk, reggae, ska, you name it (see pages 100 and 234).

Red Lion
Downtown, Duluth • 220 E. Superior St. • (218) 722-9440 • Open 'til 1 A.M.

During most of the week, The Red Lion is a popular watering hole for folks who live close to downtown, but on Wednesday nights the regular crowd is infused with college students and the hipster crowd as they gather to enjoy the surf-guitar-and-reefer inspired Black Labels.

Live Music venues, continued

The Reef
Endion, Duluth • 2002 London Rd. • (218) 724-9845 • Open 'til 1 A.M.

Local and regional original and cover bands on weekends (see page 103 and 107 for details).

The Saloon
Downtown, Superior • 1807 N. 11 St. • (715) 392-6400 • Sun.–Th. 'til 2 A.M. / F & Sat. 'til 2:30 A.M.

DJs—including guest DJs from Minneapolis, Madison, and Chicago—spin underground house music on weekends.

Sir Benedict's Tavern
Downtown, Duluth • 805 E. Superior St. • (218) 728-1192 • Open 'til 11 P.M.

Bluegrass jams and singer/songwriters (see page 100 for details).

Tap Room
Downtown, Duluth • 600 E. Superior St. (in the basement of the Fitger's Brewery complex) • (218) 722-0061 • Open 'til 1 A.M.

College crowd on weeknights, but live local and national acts on weekends.

Third Rock
Downtown, Superior • 1201 Tower Ave. • (715) 394-7171 • Sun.–Th. 'til 2 A.M. / F & Sat. 'til 2:30 A.M.

Hard rock; occasional national acts.

Dance Clubs

Stargate
Downtown, Superior • 619 Tower Ave. • (715) 395-2222 • Sun.–Th. 'til 2 A.M. / F & Sat. 'til 2:30 A.M.

DJ spins top 40 dance, rap, and hip hop.

Club Key West
Downtown, Superior • 705 Tower Ave. • (715) 392-3277 • Sun.–Th. 'til 2 A.M. / F & Sat. 'til 2:30 A.M.

Top 40 dance (you might remember this place as the former Cove Cabaret; the leaking bathroom has been fixed).

Hall of Fame
Downtown, Superior • 1028 Tower Ave. • (715) 394-4225 • Sun.–Th. 'til 2 A.M. / F & Sat. 'til 2:30 A.M.

DJs play top 40 dance, rap, and hip hop.

The Main Club
Downtown, Superior • 1217 Tower Ave. • (715) 392-1756 • Sun.–Th. 'til 2 A.M. / F & Sat. 'til 2:30 A.M. • Full bar

The dance floor is tiny, but the beats are big, and the pool table has pink felt (see page 101 for details).

J.T.'s
North End, Superior • 1506 N. 3rd St. • (715) 394-2580 • Sun.–Th. 'til 2 A.M. / F & Sat. 'til 2:30 A.M.

Gay, straight, or anywhere in between—you're welcome on the dance floor (see page 101 for details). Top 40 dance.

North Shore Nightspots

The Landing

Two Harbors, MN • 621 7th Ave. • Open 'til 1 A.M.

Housed within the historic Pearson Motors building that dates back to 1920, the Landing is a combination small-town tavern and sports bar. Inside you'll find high ceilings, pine walls, and a large wrap-around bar, behind which bartenders pour plenty of domestic beers and a limited number of imports. The Landing has two pool tables, foosball, and darts, and you can order a Shirk's pizza or Asian food from the Vietnamese Lantern, next door.

The Green Door

Beaver Bay, MN • Highway 61 • Open 'til 1 A.M.

The Green Door was once the Beaver Bay schoolhouse, and not much has changed inside—the blackboards are still in place, and some of the regulars at the Thursday afternoon cribbage matches attended grammar school there. A standard domestic beer selection and few imports; off-sale available as well. You can play pool, foosball, and darts and dance to live music on weekends. Look for the giant beer keg as you drive through town.

Gunflint Tavern

Grand Marais, MN • 111 W. Wisconsin • M–Sun. 'til 12 A.M. / F & Sat. 'til 1 A.M.

We weren't sure whether to put the Gunflint under "Eats" or "Nightlife," but since it has arguably the best beer selection on the North Shore, nightlife got the nod. You'll find selections from Ireland's Guinness to Duluth's Lake Superior Brewing Co. and just about everything in between. They also have great food for meat-eaters (Jamaican jerk tuna steak) and for veg heads (too many selections to mention). As if that weren't enough, the Gunflint is housed inside the historic Grand Marais State Bank—the vault is behind the bar.

South Shore Nightspots

Rum Line Tavern
Bayfield, WI • 31 S. 1st St. • Sun.–Th. 'til 2 A.M. / F & Sat. 'til 2:30 A.M.

Housed in an unassuming blue brick building shaped somewhat like a quonset hut and sporting a cow weather vane, the Rum Line is found just off Bayfield's beaten path of often overly quaint "shoppes." The Rum Line helps keep the Caribbean in the booze business by offering 24 varieties of rum. On tap you'll find seasonal Leinenkugel's and Summit Pale Ale, plus the usual suspects of imports in bottle. Bloodies on Sunday for $3.

Morty Muldoon's (a.k.a. Morty's Pub)
Bayfield, WI • 108 Rittenhouse Ave. • Sun.–Th. 'til 2 A.M. / F & Sat. 'til 2:30 A.M.

Recently renovated, Morty Muldoon's makes it into *True North* due to its history (the original Morty was one of the first to swim from Bayfield to Madeline Island and back). The linoleum has been removed to expose hardwood floors, which replaced the sawdust floors of 100 years ago. Morty's still features a beautiful stone fireplace, and the owners may bring back the Saturday night potluck dinners of days gone by. Behind the bar you'll find Leinie's and Summit on tap plus bottled imports and microbrews. Live music on weekends.

Patsy's Bar
Washburn, WI • 328 W. Bayfield • M 4 P.M. - 2 A.M. / T–Th. 9:30 A.M. - 2 A.M / Fri. & Sat. 'til 2:30 A.M. / Closed Sundays

On August 13, 2001, Patsy claimed she'd been behind the wood 28 years, 7 months, and 3 days, and that she'd had enough—the place was for sale. We can only hope that if someone's bought it since, they haven't removed Patsy's attitude. Patsy's is furnished with a classic wooden bar and coolers, and the men's room is decorated with a painting of naked ladies on bar stools. Patsy's is the unofficial office of Warren Nelson and the gang from Big Top Chautauqua, so you might stumble across a free show. If not, Nelson's music is also on the jukebox.

South Shore Nightspots, continued

Club 13

Between Washburn & Ashland, WI · 35 Highway 13 · Sun–Th. 11 A.M. - 2 A.M. / F & Sat. 'til 2:30 A.M.

At the edge of Bayfield County (geographically the second largest county in Wisconsin and second smallest by population—there isn't a single traffic light within its borders) stands an example of Americana you rarely find in these parts: a roadhouse. Club 13 has everything you'd expect from a roadhouse short of chicken wire in front of the stage. You'll find Leinenkugel's and Miller's Lite on tap along with lots of domestic beers, and you won't have to spend much to enjoy a few. Tap beer is a buck ($1.50 for a 16-ounce glass), canned beer and rail drinks two bucks, and call drinks just $2.50. They also sell off-sale beer to get you further on up the road. Anyone (yes, *anyone*) wearing lipstick on Monday night is entitled to two-for-one drinks. Thursday night has a dart league, and each and every Friday you'll find live music by local bands—that's what makes a roadhouse a roadhouse.

Tom's Burndown Café

La Pointe, WI · (on Madeline Island) · #1 Middle Road · (715) 747-6100 · Seasonal (call before you get on the ferry)

According to owner Tom Nelson, Tom's Burndown Café is "an open-air tent bar, slapped together from a deck, a semi trailer, a scrap of circus tent, a few beer coolers, and a lot of good patch work and rope." The bar also incorporates derelict cars, decks, and stages, each of which has its own tale to tell. Tom's brings in musicians on some weekends to entertain the crowd, ranging in styles from folk to jazz to reggae. And the café plays host to The Middle Road Literary/Arts Society, Inc., and the aptly named Nelson Phoenix Gallery. And just who was Madeline Island named for? Its Ojibwe name is Moningwunakauning or "home of the golden-breasted wood-pecker." It became Madeline Island after Equaysayway, daughter of Chief White Crane, married Michel Cadotte, a Frenchman who established a trading post in 1793. She was baptized a Christian and adopted the name Madeleine, after which her father renamed the island. (No one knows how Madeline lost that extra "e".)

Places to Eat

(or grab groceries or something to go)

True North Dining

When choosing which restaurants to include in *True North*, we decided to select from locally owned and operated establishments (no chains!), particularly those that offer a taste of the region, either in their menu, their décor, or their history. (Careful readers will note the absence of any Bayfield eateries: while we found no restaurants there that met our criteria, many folks suggested we include Maggie's because of its excellent food, but space would not allow it.) Few of the restaurants would place high on a gourmet restaurant reviewer's "best of" list, but all make great examples of true north dining. Local residents might be surprised that some area eateries don't appear in this section, including the Anchor Bar, considered to have the best burgers around. We placed drinking establishments that serve food in the Nightlife chapter, so look there for the Anchor, the Brewhouse, and others. Prices are based on summer 2001 menus.

Unfortunately, many great spots that would have been at home among these pages no longer exist, but we haven't forgotten them. In Duluth, the Flame was once one of Duluth's best-known restaurants—the Great Lakes Aquarium now sits at its former location. When Natchio's on 2nd Avenue West closed its doors, it also closed the book on excellent, authentic Greek cuisine in the Twin Ports (and belly dancers). The Chinese Lantern never came back after a fire in the early '90s (despite the fact that its bar was named The Brass Phoenix). Before Canal Park was permanently disfigured by the presence of a Burger King, the Canal Park Inn served up hometown burgers and french fries that fed local teens and seagulls. In 2001 one of the last great neighborhood grocers faded into history as Taran's Market on the East Hillside closed its doors. The turn of the century was also tough on restaurants across the bay, as 2001 saw the closing of longtime local favorite The Library/Zona Rosa. Bob's Chop Suey also shut down. Bob's was the ultimate taste of true north: Asian food that few Asian folks would recognize served in a dining room decorated with neon lobsters and roast turkeys on the ceiling and divided into private rooms by pegboard walls like those in your dad's basement workshop. Bob's didn't serve alcohol, but you were free to bring your own, and they'd supply the set-ups. Alas....

The Duluth Smoking Ban

On January 1, 2001, after a great deal of debate, a Duluth City Council ordinance banning smoking in Duluth's restaurants went into effect. It prohibited smoking in any restaurant unless the establishment had a smoking area sealed off from the rest of the dining areas and with a separate ventilation system. Restaurants with bars were allowed to let customers smoke after 8 P.M. but prohibited minors from being in the establishments when smoking was allowed. The ban was met with both praise and criticism. Anti-smoking groups considered it a victory for public health. Small restaurants with a majority of smoking customers worried it would be their financial ruin. Diners, for the most part, were confused. The main complaints about the ban were that it didn't go far enough, that there were too many gray areas, and that it was unenforceable.

It soon affected area restaurants. The owner of the Duluth Grill shut down her restaurant, claiming the ban made it financially impossible to continue (the Duluth Grill has reopened as an Embers). The Pickwick and Sammy's Pizza refused to comply with the ban, drawing the attention of anti-smoking protesters. Eventually, five restaurants were given smoking ban exemptions after proving they had lost 15 percent of their business because of the ban. After the exemptions were granted, other restaurants cried foul. The City Council again debated and attempted to change the ordinance, making it hard and fast: no smoking in restaurants, period. The Duluth Hospitality Association collected 2,880 valid signatures on a petition for a referendum so that Duluth citizens could decide the ban's fate in November 2001 elections. The new ban passed. Patrons can no longer smoke in a Duluth restaurant or bar/restaurant, period. Restaurants that allow smoking face fines up to $750. And starting April 1, 2003, smoking will also be banned in billiard halls and bowling alleys. But don't count the Hospitality Association out just yet—efforts to repeal the ban continue.

Restaurants that received exemptions from the original bans may allow smoking until April 1, 2003. Those restaurants include Uncle Louis', Jim's Hamburgers, 21st Delight, the Miller Hill Mall Country Kitchen, and Perkins West.

Burger Joints

A & Dubs

Lincoln Park, Duluth • 3131 W. 3rd St. • (218) 624-0198 • Open during the summer for lunch and dinner

Besides Gordy's Hi-Hat in Cloquet, A & Dubs is the only drive-in restaurant left in the region. The menu teems with unbelievably underpriced burgers, coneys, shrimp, and steak and chicken sandwiches. Baskets with fries and slaw go for as low as $3.10 (cheeseburger), and the crinkle-cut fries are another reminder of days gone by. You won't find any vegetarian options at A & Dubs, but its deep fryer gets a work out, producing golden brown onion rings, potato wedges, cheese sticks, and chicken chunks. Besides the service, the real treat at A & Dubs is the homemade root beer, available by the mug, the quart, or the gallon. If you're taking the family to the Wade for a Dukes' game, grab dinner at A & Dubs on the way.

Ray's Place

Lakeside, Duluth • 5231 E. Superior St. • (218) 525-6493 • T–Sat. 11 A.M. - 8 P.M.

If you like burgers, and you like 'em big, you'll want to give Ray's Place a try. Ray's doesn't mess around with size, serving up third-, half-, and full-pound burgers made of beef or buffalo. Take the Big Ray, for instance: a full pound of burger topped with two slices of cheese and four—count 'em, four—slices of bacon. Besides burgers, Ray's makes hot sandwiches, hot dogs, fries, onion rings, and deep-fried cheese curds and serves ice cream, sundaes, shakes, and malts. Most burgers range in price from $2 to $5, but the Big Ray will cost you $6.25 (and perhaps a trip to the cardiologist). Sandwiches start at $2.75 (grilled cheese) and top out at $4.25 (grilled chicken). Inside Ray's you'll find it sunny and clean, but spare—not much décor—with a children's play area outside. It's basically locally owned fast food without a drive through. It's also the last restaurant in town if you're heading up the north shore (or the first if you're coming off the shore).

Burger Joints, continued*

Mr. Nick's
Downtown, Duluth • 220 W. Superior St. • (218) 722-5373 • M–Th. 7:30 A.M. - 5 P.M. / F & Sat. 7:30 A.M. - 7 P.M.

Home of the Charburger, Mr. Nick's was a staple of downtown Duluth. Then it closed, and a Burger King moved in. Then the Burger King closed, and so did the McDonald's across the street. And now, Mr. Nick's is back, serving up breakfast and lunch to the downtown crowd. Burgers range in price from $1.89 to $4.09 (add $1.39 if you want a half-pound burger) and range in style from classics like a California or a bacon cheeseburger to new tastes like Italian, Cajun, and something with Canadian bacon added that Mr. Nick's calls a Royal. The restaurant also makes a variety of sandwiches, including fish and veggie, as well as great fries and homemade onion rings. The décor is clean and simple, with enlarged black-and-white photos from Duluth's past adorning the walls. Connected to the Skywalk system; one vegetarian option.

Ray's Grill
Irving (West Duluth), Duluth • 5610 Raleigh St. • (218) 628-1865 • T–Sat. 8 A.M. - 8 P.M. / M 8 A.M. - 1 P.M.

More than a burger joint, Ray's Grill is hard to categorize. The menu reads like a diner's, but the interior looks like a neighborhood bar—and it was, up until the smoking ban. Burgers range from $2.35 to $4.50 (Big Boss Double) and you can also get sandwiches, coneys, and Polish and Italian sausage sandwiches. Daily specials include a roast beef dinner for $5.50, and twice a week you can get all-you-can-eat spaghetti and meatballs for $4.35. The menu also has a few more spendy items, including a 13-ounce steak for $17 and some pretty atypical choices for a blue-collar eatery, such as mostaccioli and sausage topped with baked mozzarella cheese. A second dining room connects Ray's to the North Pole (see page 103).

***See also the Anchor Bar (page 99), Jim's Hamburgers (page 121), and T-Bonz (page 130).**

Coneys!

Original Coney Island

Downtown, Duluth • 107 E. Superior St. • (218) 727-1077 • M–Sat. 6 A.M. - 11 P.M. / Sun. 8 A.M. - 9 P.M.

The Original Coney Island has been slinging chili sauce on top of skin-on, all-beef wieners in downtown Duluth since 1921, and they've gotten mighty good at it. Coneys are just $1.35 (99¢ on Wednesdays, $16.20 for a baker's dozen), and everything else on the menu is just as cheap (that goes for breakfasts, too, including biscuits & gravy). Besides coneys and breakfast, the Original offers bratwurst, polish sausage, coney burgers, and chili. The Original's décor is a treat. Wood floors, tall wooden booths, and a bar-like counter complete with a brass footrail and bolted-down, high-back stools take diners back in time. (The oldies station on the radio and a 1959 wall menu advertising coneys for 25¢ and malts for 40¢ help, too.) Try your hand at the Bally's Skill-Roll game; if you score over 380 points, you win a free coney.

Coney Island Deluxe

Downtown, Duluth • 112 W. 1st St. • (218) 722-2772 • M–Sat. 6 A.M. - 9 P.M. / Sun. 8 A.M. - 8 P.M.

Part coney shop, part Greek grocery, the Coney Island Deluxe serves up good cheap food at lunch counter prices that keep the downtown crowd happy. Besides coneys, burgers, and fries, Deluxe has a salad bar and also makes a mean gyros. Its Greek owners also stock feta cheese, kalamata olives, and other jarred and canned Greek delicacies for retail sale. Extremely clean and bright, Deluxe has plenty of booth, table, and counter seating. Its walls are adorned with large photos of Lake Superior ore boats and tugs, including a beauty of the *Edmund Fitzgerald*. And if the trophies are any indication, Deluxe once sponsored one heck of a bowling team.

So who makes the more authentic coney, Deluxe or Original? That's a matter of taste, but this may be telling to die-hard coney enthusiasts: Deluxe has another branch—in the Miller Hill Mall food court.

Downhome Diners

21st Delight

Lincoln Park, Duluth • 2125 W. Superior St. • (218) 727-5804 • M–Sat. 6:30 A.M. - 7 P.M. / Sun. 7 A.M. - 4 P.M.

It used to be if you took the Greyhound into Duluth, your first stop was often the Bridgeman's across the street from the depot. The decline of bus travel forced the station to move, and the Bridgeman's is no longer there—as a Bridgeman's, anyway. In 1988 it became the 21st Delight, and it's been delighting West Enders ever since. The diner serves up heapin' helpings of diner chow, from breakfast (biscuits & gravy) to dinner (meat loaf, liver & onions) and lots of burgers and sandwiches for lunch—and nothing over $8 (even the sirloin steak). The Delight still has that Bridgeman's feel: clean and bright with a large center island "bar" offering both stool and booth dining, not to mention the sea-foam green Hamilton-Beach mixer to stir up thick malts). Everything is available to go; few vegetarian options. **Smoking Ban exempted until April 2003.**

Jim's Hamburgers & Café

Central Hillside, Duluth • 502 E. 4th St. • (218) 727-9117 • M–Sat. 6 A.M. - 7 P.M. / Sun. 7 A.M. - 7 P.M.
Lincoln Park, Duluth • 2005 W. Superior St. • (218) 727-9400 • M–Sat. 6 A.M. - 7 P.M. / Sun. 7 A.M. - 7 P.M.

Jim's is a Duluth institution, and that has nothing to do with the brown-and-orange color scheme. With good ol' diner chow and no fuss made over the décor, Jim's passes the savings along to you. Breakfasts (served any time) start at $1.65, and nothing on the menu costs more than $5.50. Jim's has plenty of traditional diner options (even gravy for your fries), but the focus is hamburgers. You have your choice of quarter-, third-, or half-pound burgers, and if you take a seat at the counter, you can watch the cook fry them up. We do have one minor complaint about Jim's: even though its menu highlights burgers, you have to ask for the mustard, and they serve it to you in those little plastic packets. Few veggie options. **Smoking Ban exempted until April 2003.**

Downhome Diners, continued

Joyce's Kitchen

Spirit Valley (West Duluth), Duluth • 5517 Grand Ave. • (218) 624-9798 • M–F 6 A.M. - 7 P.M. / Sat.–Sun. 8 A.M. - 3 P.M.

Joyce's has to be the epitome of old-fashioned home cookin' in Duluth. Let's put it this way: if you order the hot meat loaf sandwich with mashed potatoes, all you'll *see* when it arrives is a heaping plate full of gravy. Breakfast, lunch, or dinner, you won't pay more than $6 for any complete meal, whether you order the baby beef liver, breaded veal, scalloped potatoes & ham, or the baked ribs with kraut. A half-pound burger with fries is just $3.75, and you can get a grilled cheese sandwich with a full bowl of chili for $4. The setting is also a classic—a sprawling lunch counter at its center completed by low stools with backs, jutting islands, and attached booths. More tables and booths surround the counter, providing additional seating. The only thing Joyce's Kitchen needs is new ceiling tiles. Very limited vegetarian options.

Sunshine Café

Spirit Valley (West Duluth), Duluth • 5719 Grand Ave. • (218) 624-7013 • M–F 6 A.M. - 5 P.M. / Sat. 6 A.M. - 3 P.M. / Closed Sundays

A tiny diner in the heart of West Duluth, the Sunshine Café serves arguably the best breakfast in town. The diner itself claims to have the best omelettes in town, and no one is making an argument over that statement. They start with up to three eggs and give diners a variety of options, including veggie, Denver, "everything," ham and cheese, and even corned beef hash. If eggs aren't your game, try the Swedish pancakes or come back at lunch time for a hot sandwich or burger ($2.25–$4.95) with homemade fries or a complete dinner—roast beef, chicken, shrimp, etc.–for less than $7. You'll find the Sunshine's décor clean but an odd mix, such as faux-brick wainscotting offset by wallpaper and a lamp near the counter that would look more at home in a 70s-era bachelor pad, but no one's complaining. The Sunshine proudly proclaims that it has been smoke free since before the ordinance. Some vegetarian choices.

Downhome Diners, continued

Ketola's Kafé

Denfeld (West Duluth), Duluth • 3901 Grand Ave. • (218) 624-2725 • M–F 7 A.M. - 2 P.M.

Open for just seven hours a day, Ketola's is a true neighborhood diner. It's not much to look at—several booths and low counter dining set off by black faux marble tile (a classic diner look) and collector's Wheaties boxes on the shelves. It's the kind of a place where the waitresses seem to know everyone in the place, and you can guess that few of the customers ever need to look at the menu. But when you do, you'll be pleased to find good ol' diner grub at good ol' diner prices. Traditional breakfasts run from $2.25 to $6.25 (three eggs, three sausages, three bacon strips, and toast) and burgers and hot sandwiches go for $2 to $3.50, including a hot beef sandwich with mashed potatoes. Old fashioned dinners, such as pork chops and apple sauce, range from $5.50 to $6.50. Try the french fries, thick and freshly cut with the skin left on—outstanding! Vegetarians, this probably isn't the place for you....

East End Café

East End, Superior • 2209 E. 5th St. • (715) 398-3461 • M–Sun. 6 A.M. - 8 P.M.

Located right next door to East End Hardware (a great neighborhood hardware store housed inside an old movie theater), the East End Café just about drips with local color. Its two large rooms are furnished with chairs and tables, and the plastic tablecloths are adorned with colorful prints in a variety of patterns. (The smoking section also has low counter dining.) Pretty much diner fare here, with hot and cold sandwiches, burgers, and basic breakfasts and dinners. For breakfast, you can order an egg, toast, and hash browns for only $1.75 or splurge and go for the three-egg ham-and-cheese omelet for $4.05. Dinners are equally inexpensive, with burger baskets going for $2.05 and an eight-ounce sirloin steak with soup and a salad or choice of potato—the most expensive item on the menu—for $7.99.

Downhome Diners, continued

Billings Park Café

Billings Park, Superior • 1802 Iowa Ave. • (715) 394-6792 • M–F 11 A.M. - 7 P.M.

If you're looking for a real neighborhood café in a real neighborhood, get yourself over to Superior's Billings Park. The Billings serves good, simple food at simple prices—only the steak will cost you more than $7. The menu features mostly burgers and hot sandwiches as well as some dinners, including a fish fry, barbecued ribs, and spaghetti. The café is home to the Big Izzy (a triple-patty cheeseburger) and the best patty melt in the Twin Ports, as far as we're concerned. The french fries are homemade, and you can even get a fried egg sandwich. Homey touches decorate the dining room, but the floral print curtains and paintings do little to off-set the browns and beiges of the tables, booths, and aged carpet. The friendly clientele and staff, however, more than make up for the earthy color scheme. Canned beer available.

The Kitchen

North End, Superior • 803 N. 5th St. • (715) 392-4500 • M–Sat. 5:30 A.M. - 2 P.M.

The Kitchen is about as stripped down as a diner can be: simple tables and chairs, linoleum tile floors, paneled walls, and a ceiling with fans and fluorescent lighting. The only adornments come from a rather impressive collection of Marilyn Monroe memorabilia and the bleached skull of a long horn steer. But as far as diners go, simple equals good, and the Kitchen echoes that equation in its food. About the fanciest item on the menu is an omelette called the Nite Owl that includes ham, cheese, onions, peppers, tomatoes, and hash browns all wrapped inside three eggs. Breakfasts range from $2.85 for eggs, toast, and hash browns to $4.50 for steak and eggs. For lunch and dinner (the Kitchen closes at 2 P.M.), you can order from a list of burgers, sandwiches, and baskets ($2 to $6) or complete dinners featuring roast beef, roast pork, pork cutlets, ham, or chicken ($5.50 to $6). Have some pie for dessert, wear plaid if you want to blend in, and expect to dine next to smokers.

Downhome Diners, continued

Louis' Café & Restaurant
Downtown, Superior • 1602 Tower Ave. • (715) 392-3058 • M–Sat. 24 hours / Sun. 12 A.M. - 9 P.M.

Although it has been operated by the same Greek family for three generations since either 1929 or 1946 (the menu gives conflicting stories), few local residents go to Louis' for its Greek cuisine. Most, in fact, go for the pancakes. Huge and tasty, there's something special about Louis' pancakes (nutmeg?), and they offer lots of toppings. Louis' menu also serves up American and Greek fare, but you get the feeling they aren't exactly using old family recipes. Still, if you've got a hankering for moussaka, dolmades, or spanikopita, they're the only game in town. The café's décor follows the Greek theme, with white plastered walls and photos of Greece. Its doors remain open almost constantly, so add it to your mental list of late-night options. Good selection of veggie options. (There's another Louis' on London Road at 15th Avenue East in Duluth: same menu, but with all the atmosphere of a Perkins.)

Uncle Louis' Café
Central Hillside, Duluth • 520 E. 4th St. • (218) 727-4518 • M–F 6 A.M. - 3:30 P.M. / Sat.–Sun. 7 A.M. - 3 P.M.

Over the past few years Uncle Louis' has become a favorite among Hillsiders and the weekend hangover crowd of hipsters and UMD students. Although it has no affiliation with Louis' in Superior (there was once a family connection), its pancakes are just as delicious—it has to be the same recipe—but less expensive. Same goes for the gyros/feta omelette and the rest of the breakfast menu. Lunch time at Louis' provides you with a variety of options, from burgers and sandwiches to dinner specials such as au gratin taters & ham, meat loaf, and roast turkey, and nothing costs more than $10. Not many veggie options, but the grilled feta, raw onion, and tomato sandwich is tasty. The sign on the door may say Uncle Louis', but make no mistake: this is Penny's kitchen, where they say the food is so good "you'll think we stole your mom!" **Smoking Ban exempted until April 2003.**

Late Night Delights*

Frank's Fast 'n' Fresh Deli

North End, Superior • Inside the Hammond Spur at Hammond & 5th St. (base of the Blatnik Bridge) • M–Sun. 24 hours

Many folks discover Frank's after a night of drinking when, out of cigarettes, they pull into the Hammond Spur for cheap smokes before hopping on the Blatnik Bridge and heading back to Duluth. And that's just about perfect, because Frank's serves up an array of late-night gastronomic delights all deep-fried the same golden-brown hue and ready to help diners head off a hangover. Frank's late-night spread includes chicken breasts & wings, jalapeno poppers, mushrooms, cheese sticks, egg rolls, a vaguely Mexican treat called a tacito, mashed-potato balls, and chunky fried taters known as jojos. During the day you can get homemade unfried fare such as meat loaf and mac & cheese. Best of all, it's so cheap you can pay for it with change and crumpled one-dollar bills.

House of Donuts

Central Hillside, Duluth • 624 E. 4th St. • (218) 727-7421 • M–Th. 6 A.M. - 3 A.M. / F 6 A.M. 'til Sunday 3 A.M.

Affectionately known as the H.O.D., for years the Hillside's House of Donuts has been keeping smiles on the faces of college drinkers long after the bars have closed or the last keg has run dry. Despite its name, the H.O.D. is best known for its hot and cold subs, featuring mammoth amounts of meat stuffed into a hoagie roll and topped with big chunks of tomato, onion, and pickles—a sandwich served with a knife and fork. At $4.25, the 12-inch sub is the most expensive item on the menu. The H.O.D. also serves tacos, nachos, potato nuggets, and a burger & fries combo for just $3.25. And let's not forget the donuts: cake or raised, plain or glazed, they've got 'em all. Try a butter bar, named, we guess, because there must be an entire stick of butter in each one. And despite what the sign says, the H.O.D. is no longer "Open 24 hours, Sundays 'til 5."

*See also Louis' Café & Restaurant (page 125) and Amigo's Mex-Express (page 142).

Soup, Sandwiches, & Coffee

At Sarah's Table
Chester Park, Duluth • 1904 E. 8th St. • (218) 723-8569 • M–Sun. 10 A.M. - 5 P.M. (hours may change)

At the time we wrote this, At Sarah's Table was located just over the Lift Bridge on Park Point and planned to move into the old Taran's Market location on the East Hillside. (Some may remember that Sarah's was once found on London Road near the Portland Malt Shop.) The old Sarah's was a combination coffee shop/bookstore that served homemade soups and sandwiches, and we expect the new one to be much the same on a larger scale. The soups at Sarah's are all made from scratch, and each day diners have their choice of a vegetarian or nonvegetarian selection. Sandwiches range from Boca™ Garden Burgers and hummus to roast chicken and a BLT many consider the finest around. Sarah's even has a few breakfast selections such as bagels and a diced potato treat with red and green peppers, onions, and garlic fried up and topped with cheddar cheese.

Beaner's Central
Spirit Valley (West Duluth), Duluth • 324 N. Central Ave. • (218) 624-5957 • opens M–F 6:30 A.M., Sat. 8 A.M., Sun. 10 A.M. / closes between 9–11 P.M.

Much more than a coffee shop, Beaner's is a concert café that serves up gourmet coffees, chai, teas, a variety of unusual sodas, and even beer and wine along with great live music. They also offer tasty soups and panini and deli sandwiches (with veggie options) as well as muffins, scones, and cheesecake. Owners Jason and Anne Wussow have created an atmosphere unique to West Duluth, first by making their establishment more than an eatery—its stage and sound system are first rate, and the décor can't be beat—and then by inviting a variety of musicians who play anything from folk to reggae, rock to country, and just about everything in between. If you plan to see a show, come early so you can grab one of the comfy chairs near the windows.

Quick Lunches

Exchange Deli & Bakery
Downtown, Duluth • 301 W. 1st St. • (218) 727-8836 • M–F 6:45 A.M. - 4 P.M.

The Exchange plays on a little Duluth history as it serves the downtown crowd tasty morning treats and quick, inexpensive lunches. Located on the ground floor of the historic Board of Trade building (if for nothing else, stop by to admire the architecture), the Exchange's walls are adorned with photos of Duluth in days gone by and the stunning watercolors of famed Duluth painter Cheng Khee Chee. Even its menu reflects the town, with sandwiches named after neighborhoods, including the "East Ender" (veggies), the "Park Point" (95% fat-free ham), the "Morgan Park" (tender roast beef), and the "Gary-New Duluth (hard salami and capicola). The sandwiches cost less than $4 and can be enjoyed with a cup of homemade soup or chili or a salad. The Exchange also has a wide variety of bars, cookies, and muffins, and other baked sweets.

Holmes East End Bakery
East End, Superior • 2123 E. 5th St. • (715) 398-5523 • M–F 6 A.M. - 2 P.M. (lunch at 11 A.M.) / Sat. 6 A.M. - 12 A.M.

Essentially, Holmes is a tiny bakery that serves lunch—and it closes by two o'clock every afternoon, so it's not a place to grab a snack in the evening. Inside, a glass counter filled with bakery treats lines the left side of the store, and a lunch counter with low stool seating lines the right, creating a corridor to a few small tables in the rear. It's clean, bright, and simple. Simple, in fact, is a great way to describe the food. No frills here, just good eatin'. The lunch menu consists almost entirely of burgers and sandwiches on a plate with chips and pickles or in a basket with fries, onion rings, and a cookie—and nothing costs more than $6. You can also enjoy homemade soup or chili, but we recommend saving room for some baked goodies. Holmes makes all sorts of bakery treats, from cookies and bars to turnovers and chocolate-iced cream puffs.

Gourmet to Go (and catering)

Savories
Endion, Duluth • 5 S. 13th Ave. E. (Plaza Shopping Center) • (218) 625-5555 • M–Sat. 10 A.M. - 6 P.M.

Savories has been a gourmet catering service in Duluth for some time, but it wasn't until the fall of 2001 that its owners opened a retail outlet near Leif Erickson Park in the Plaza Shopping Center. Besides catering for events of any size, Savories offers delicious sandwiches, salads, or complete dinners for individuals or entire families (dinners to go served from 4 P.M. to closing). Sandwiches ($4 to $6) include roast tenderloin, warm pastrami and Swiss, and a New York Reuben. You can get a field green salad for $3 or a caesar topped with lemon chicken for $7. Dinners—which rotate weekly and offer a different meal every day—run anywhere from $8 to $12 and include chicken breast with roasted tomato and kalamata olive sauce served with crispy risotto cakes and a spinach soufflé. They also have lots of baked treats, including specialty desserts such as a triple-layer cheesecake. Pick up some food and a movie at the video store next door for a night on the town in your hotel or living room.

Coco's to Geaux
Downtown, Duluth • 324 W. Superior St. • (218) 740-3039 • M–F 7 A.M. - 5 P.M. (lunch 11 A.M. - 1:30 P.M.)

Coco's to Geaux is the kitchen of chef Arlene Coco-Buscombe, a Louisiana native who derives her cooking style from Creole, Mediterranean, and Asian flavors. Coco-Buscombe's downtown shop in the former Miller's Cafeteria location serves lunch to the downtown business crowd cafeteria style, including soups, sandwiches, a variety of salads, and a random selection of hot meals ranging in price from $5 to $10. The rest of the day it sells premade items (spreads, pasta salads, etc.) from its deli case as well as desserts and specialty coffees. Coco's also offers lunch deliveries. Coco-Buscombe also owns Coco's Catering, which specializes in ethnic foods, and will travel to your cabin or lake home to help you throw a party.

Great Grub to Go

T-Bonz and Terry's Place (home of Pit Stop Pizza) are both neighborhood/sports bars located in Duluth's Lincoln Park neighborhood. They both make great bar grub, but since the smoking ban, they're no longer allowed to serve under their own roofs. Fortunately, their kitchens remain open, and you can order take-out and delivery. Both serve up pizza, burgers, and just about anything that will fit in a deep fryer. The food is good and the portions generous, but don't expect to find many vegetarian options at either location.

T-Bonz Grill & Pizza
Lincoln Park, Duluth • 2531 W. Superior St. • (218) 727-0020 • M–Sun. 11 A.M. - 11 P.M. (food)

T-Bonz specializes in big burgers and pizza. The burgers come in 1/3- and 2/3-pound sizes (except the T-Bonz Triple Cheese, which is a full pound) and are topped with everything from sour cream & onions to ham, mozzarella, and pineapple (The Hawaiian). The pizza is prepared in a traditional brick pizza oven and comes with your choices or in a variety of specials, such as the German Pizza (sausage, ham, kraut, and onions). T-Bonz also serves melts, sandwiches, wraps, and more appetizers than space allows us to list.

Pit Stop (located within Terry's Place)
Lincoln Park • 2232 W. Superior St. • (218) 722-5900 • Sun.–M 11 A.M. - 11 P.M. / T–Th. 11 A.M. - 12 A.M. / F & Sat. 11 A.M. - 1 A.M.

Pit Stop serves everything from pizza to burgers and sandwiches to spaghetti and lasagna. The lunch specials change each week and range from sloppy joes (two of 'em with fries and slaw for under $5) to veal parmesan on a bed of pasta with garlic bread (also under $5). The pizza is cheap and tasty and baked in a brick oven, the way it's supposed to be. Pit Stop delivers to anywhere in Duluth, including hotels. Is that PBS painter Bob "Happy Little Trees" Ross at the Terry's Place bar? Nope, it's just his local look-a-like.

Americana

Buena Vista

Top of the Hillside, Duluth • 1144 Mesaba Ave. • (218) 727-9047 • Every day 7 A.M. - 11 P.M.

It may look like an airport observation tower on the outside, but you'll forgive that as soon as you see the view the Buena Vista's dining room provides—after all, *buena vista* means "good view." Besides great scenery, the Buena offers full breakfast, lunch, and dinner menus. Dinners range from salads and burgers ($6–$8) to pasta, steak, and seafood, including locally-caught walleye and fish from Lake Superior ($8–$17). There's also a full children's menu, including their own "Sky High" pizza, and several vegetarian selections. You can enjoy a beer or a cocktail at the Buena or try something off their limited (but reasonably priced) wine list. Expect a wait on Sunday mornings—the brunch is quite popular. The Buena also has a lounge downstairs and an adjoining hotel.

C.W. Chips

Central Hillside, Duluth • 610 E. 4th St. • (218) 727-9173 • M–Sun. 11 A.M. - 9 P.M.

C.W. Chips, at the site of the former Casa De Roma, is the latest in a string of bars and restaurants owned by Charlie Lemon. The restaurant's many small dining rooms, in fact, have been named for former Lemon establishments, such as the Bellows and Yellow Sub. The décor is a mix of Duluth history (old photos, newer paintings) patriotism (prints of the American flag through history) and Catholicism (photos of Pope John Paul II alongside a three-dimensional rendering of the Last Supper). The food is simple and modestly priced, and it must be good, because this is where a lot of Duluth's Finest take their dinner breaks. Lunches (burgers, sandwiches, etc.) won't cost you more than $7, and dinners (steaks, chicken, fish, pasta) range from $10 to $20. They even have some vegetarian options. Ask to be seated in a booth next to the back window—C.W. Chips provides a pair of binoculars for each window-side booth so diners can enjoy a closer view of the lake.

Americana, continued

Eddie's

Itasca, Superior • 5221 E. 4th St. • (715) 398-0191 • T–Sat. 4 P.M. - 10 P.M. / Sun. 3 P.M. - 8 P.M.

Located next to the railroad yards in Superior's Itasca neighborhood, Eddie's restaurant may be the oldest eatery in Soup Town. When it changed hands a few years ago, the interior became a shrine to the automobile. Model cars line the backs of each booth, antique cans of motor oil weigh down shelves, and authentic auto advertisements cover the walls—so much memorabilia you'll be hard pressed to find a spot where your eyes can rest. The fare is very meat-oriented: steak, chops, chicken, liver & onions, burgers, prime rib, and even a bacon-wrapped turkey tenderloin. They also serve fish and seafood, such as "walleyed" pike. But Eddie's specialty is barbecued ribs, at $17 the most expensive item on the menu (dinners start at $9). Eddie's offers a simple wine list and serves liquor and beer (including brews from Duluth's Lake Superior Brewing Co.). Its smoking section boasts a full bar, which makes for a comfortable place to wait on busy nights.

Hammond Steak House

North End, Superior • 1402 N. 5th St. • (715) 392-3269 • Sun.–Th. 5 P.M. - 9 P.M. / F & Sat. 5 P.M. - 10 P.M.

If you cross from Duluth to Superior on the High Bridge, the first place you encounter is the Hammond Steak House. An old-fashioned supper club like the kind your parents took you to when you were young, the Hammond is home to bread baskets, salad-dressing caddies, and cocktails served in high-ball glasses. The Hammond specializes in Angus beef, prime rib in particular. In fact, an entire menu page is made up of meat photos and a butcher's cow diagram showing various cuts. Besides prime rib and steaks, you'll find chicken, seafood, and ribs ranging in price from $10 to $24 (lobster tail at market price). The décor is a mix of historic harbor photos and foliage—a birch tree dominates one of the dining rooms. The Hammond has a full bar and wine list, and there's a lounge downstairs adjoining a liquor store that claims to offer the cheapest off-sale in town.

Americana, continued

Pickwick
Downtown, Duluth • 508 E. Superior St. • (218) 727-8901 • M–Sat. 11 A.M. - 1 P.M.

Duluth's oldest family-owned restaurant, Pickwick has been a Duluth staple since before it opened its doors in 1914. It actually first opened in 1888 as "The Saloon," and was part of the Fitger's Brewery. Employee Joseph S. Wisocki bought the place in 1918, when Prohibition made saloon ownership a losing proposition, and he turned it into the fine eatery it is today—in fact, his grandsons now run the place. Known for its meat and generous proportions, the Pick's specialties include prime rib and a deep-fried pepper-cheeseburger. The Pick is also known for its atmosphere, including absolutely stunning woodwork. The dining rooms to the rear offer a view of Lake Superior, and its bar is also one of the nicest spots in town to share a quiet drink. Prepare to spend some money: great food, service, and atmosphere add up. Vegetarians and vegans will be better served if they go next door and sup at Fitger's Brewhouse.

Shack Smokehouse & Grille
Billings Park, Superior • 3301 Belknap St. • (715) 392-9836 • M–Sun. 11 A.M. - 9 P.M.

If you're in the mood for big food, you're in the mood for the Shack. They serve up generous portions at reasonable prices in a supper-club-like atmosphere, clean but not too fancy. The furnishings all look rather new and expensive, but look close and you'll see plywood and veneer here and there, and the gold-framed paintings look like they were purchased at Wal-Mart—but that hardly matters once you have a plate of food in front of you. At the Shack you'll find hearty sandwiches (er, Shackwiches, $5 to $7 with fries), meal-sized salads, and lots of meat. Steak, ribs, liver, prime rib, chops, chicken, and plenty of fish and seafood priced from $10 to $18 (and a surf-and-turf for $24). The Shack has a full bar and wine by the glass or bottle. The only questionable item on the menu is the Cuban Chicken sandwich, which the menu says is made with Cajun chicken.

Asian

Cantonese House

Downtown, Duluth • 24 W. 1st St. • (218) 722-0778 • M–Th. 11 A.M. - 10 P.M. / F 'til 12 A.M. / Sat. 3 P.M. - 12 P.M.

Like most of Duluth's many Asian restaurants (the town has an abundance of them), the Cantonese House doesn't look like much on the outside, but walk through its doors and you'll find one of the cleanest, best-appointed eateries in town. The Yung family, which has operated the restaurant for more than 30 years, hails from Canton, so you can count on the recipes having authentic origins. The Cantonese House's menu lists both Cantonese and other popular Chinese dishes ranging in price from $6 to $14 ($4–$6 for lunch) and wonderful family-sized combos that feed up to six people. No buffets here—everything is prepared fresh as it is ordered. And no "Chinese Zodiac" place mats either—even the plates are hand painted, a nice touch. Expect a wait on Friday nights. The Cantonese House serves some American fare but does not serve alcohol.

Chef Yee's

Downtown, Duluth • 319 W. 1st St. • (218) 722-3993 • M–Th. 11 A.M. - 9 P.M. / F 'til 10 P.M. / Sat. 12 P.M. - 10 P.M.

Known among the downtown lunch crowd as a great spot for a quick, inexpensive midday meal, Chef Yee's is home to one of the most popular lunch buffets in town. Between 11 A.M. and 2 P.M., diners plunk down just $5.75 for as many trips through the line as their stomachs can handle (additional lunch specials range from $4 to $4.50). At dinner time, Yee's offers diners a full array of Chinese cuisine, including specialties such as Imperial Beef in Mandarin sauce, Walnut Shrimp with lemon cream sauce, and Chow Champagne, a mix of lobster, bar-becued pork, and chicken sautéed with mixed vegetables. There's also lots of vegetarian fare (like curry tofu or eggplant in garlic sauce), and beer and cocktails are available. Yee's dining room is rather small but very clean and comfy with large booths and tables and mural-covered walls. Limited delivery available.

Asian, continued

Chinese Dragon

Downtown, Duluth • 108 E. Superior St. • (218) 723-4036 • M–F 11 A.M. - 10 P.M. / Sat. 11:30 A.M. - 10 P.M.

For affordable Asian, the Dragon's prices can't be beat—but you'll have to get beyond the décor to enjoy the meal. Its tiny, all-but-windowless dining room off Superior Street is adorned in a mix of Asian clichés and country cabin chic. Paneled walls feature a rustic motif (game birds, deer, a farm house) dominated by large round dragon "welcome" medallions (no less than four of them). But if you came for good, inexpensive food, stop staring at the walls. The Dragon serves both Cantonese and Szechuan dishes and a wide variety of soups—egg drop, won-ton, yecamin, hot & sour, etc.—at prices that can't be beat (lunch tops out at $4.75, dinner at $11.25). The Dragon also has a better Asian spirits selection than other Duluth restaurants, serving everything from sake and plum wine to gekkeikan and wan-fu. It also serves beer.

Chinese Garden

Downtown, Duluth • 231 E. Superior St. • (218) 723-1866 • T–Sat. 11 A.M. - 10 P.M. / Sun. 11:30 A.M. - 10 P.M.

Located within the Hotel Duluth (Greysolon Plaza), the Chinese Garden provides an opportunity for modern diners to enjoy a meal in what was once a premiere hotel (see pages 76 and 217). It's also an opportunity to enjoy some pretty good Cantonese, Mandarin, and Szechuan dishes. The Garden's menu is absolutely vast, and you can choose from something as simple as chow mein to half a roast duck (for only $9.95). The prices stay below $13 for dinners (more for family combos) and $5 for lunch, which includes an entrée, fried rice, soup, and your choice of appetizer. Placing a Chinese restaurant in a Classic-Revival hotel causes some clash in décor, none of which is helped by the blue-and-apricot plaid wallpaper. A dining room filled with beautiful, sturdy wooden tables and chairs and a fireplace decorated with Asian lanterns and wall dividers seems incongruent at first, but becomes charming by the time the meal arrives. Limited delivery available.

Asian, continued

Huie's Chopsticks Inn

Central Hillside, Duluth • 505 E. 4th St. • (218) 727-0820

M–Th. 11 A.M. - 9 P.M. / Fridays 'til 10 P.M. / Sat. 2 P.M. - 10 P.M. / Sundays 4 P.M. - 9 P.M.

If you're still mourning the loss of the Chinese Lantern, it's time to stop your sobbin'. The restaurant may be gone, but its recipes are alive and well and come to life every day in the kitchen of Huie's Chopsticks Inn. Chef Ping Huie—nephew of Joe and cousin of Wing—was the head chef at the Lantern for 20 years until it burned down. He now serves the same great food on the Hillside in a stripped-down, cozier atmosphere than the Lantern's. Ping specializes in cuisine from four different regions: Canton, Mandarin, Shanghai, and Szechuan (Hunan) at reasonable prices (meals up to $18, lunches less than $7). Ping has been talking about retiring, so if you miss the Lantern, you better get to Huie's before it's too late. Limited delivery available.

Jade Fountain

Spirit Valley (West Duluth), Duluth • 305 Central Ave. • (218) 624-4212

M–Th. 11 A.M. - 11 P.M. / Fridays 'til 12 A.M. / Sat. 4 P.M. - 12 A.M. / Sundays 3 P.M. - 10 P.M.

Although Duluth is chock full of Asian eateries, the Jade Fountain alone serves the western side of town. The Fountain's huge menu covers all the Chinese basics and then some—all under $10 unless they involve shrimp or lobster—and includes American fare. Its two dining rooms are decorated with reds and golds typical of Chinese restaurants, but the back dining room's mix of red neon and dark paneling takes some getting used to. The Fountain takes great pride in its bar, featuring cocktails stirred up by its "master mixologists." The Fountain proudly pours ice-cream drinks, after-dinner liqueurs, and house specialties such as a Golden Cadillac, Cucumber Cocktail, Foxy Lady, and French Goddess. Lunch buffet for $6.25 (discounts for seniors and children). Limited delivery available.

Asian, continued

Lan-Chi's

Downtown, Superior • 1320 Belknap St. • (715) 394-4496 • M–Th. 11 A.M. - 10 P.M. / F & Sat. 11 A.M. - 11 P.M. / Sun. 12 P.M. - 10 P.M.

Lan-Chi's serves generous portions of tasty Vietnamese, Chinese (mostly Mandarin and Cantonese), and American food for prices easier to swallow than even the most delicate egg drop soup. Most lunch specials, which include an entrée, fried rice, and an egg roll, cost just $4.95, and most dinners are priced under $10. Another impressive aspect of Lan-Chi's is the décor. Its large, bright dining room is festooned with colorful garlands, window coverings, and Chinese lanterns—and silk flowers await diners at each booth and table. Oddly enough, the walls also display framed arrangements of Minnesota Twins and Milwaukee Brewers baseball cards from days long past. Limited delivery available.

Thai Krathong

Downtown, Duluth • 114 W. 1st St. • (218) 733-9774 • M–Th. 11:30 A.M. - 9 P.M. / Fridays 'til 10 P.M. / Sat. 12 P.M. - 10 P.M.

The only Thai restaurant north of the Twin Cities, Thai Krathong has been a welcome change for Duluth diners since it opened its doors in 2000. The menu contains all you would hope for and expect from a Thai eatery—phad thai, chicken, beef, tofu, and seafood mixed with combinations of chilis, cilantro, mint, ginger, basil, coconut milk, peanut sauce, or red curry—and each entrée comes with steamed jasmine rice. Thai Krathong even offers Tom Yum and Tom Kha, soups so special the restaurant serves them as entrées (Beef Guiteo and Seafood Guiteo served on Saturdays during lunch only). Dinner prices range from $9 to $15. A variety of appetizers are available, as well as beer, wine, and jasmine tea. The dining room décor borders on elegant, as chandeliers, wall sconces, and candles provide soft light that reflects off the white linen table cloths to help create an intimate dining experience.

Indian / Italian (Pizza*)

India Palace

Downtown, Duluth • 319 W. Superior St. • (218) 727-8767 • Dinner: Sun.–Th. 5 P.M. - 9 P.M.; F & Sat. 5 P.M. - 10 P.M. Lunch Buffet: M–F 11:30 A.M. - 2 P.M.

You won't find another Indian restaurant north of the Twin Cities, and you'll find few eateries in Duluth as well appointed as the India Palace. The menu features a wide variety of lamb, chicken, beef, seafood, and vegetarian entrées starting at $10 and running up to $16, including tandoori, rogan, tikka masala, and absolutely exquisite curries. The authentic cuisine is complemented by an elegant yet informal atmosphere created by Indian tapestries hung against brick walls. The wood trim and ceiling beams are painted a creamy pink, very appropriate for an Indian restaurant (pink in India is considered formal, like navy blue in the western world). India Palace also serves wine, imported beers, chai, and authentic Indian desserts. The lunch buffet ($7.50) is outstanding.

The Bulldog Pizza & Grill

Duluth • Mount Royal Shopping Center • (218) 728-3663 • M–Th. 9 A.M. - 10 P.M. / F & Sat. 9 A.M. - 11 P.M. / Sun. 10:30 A.M. - 10 P.M.

In 1986 Ken Wright dropped out of UMD to fill a need for his fellow Bulldogs—an eatery close to the campus with food they could enjoy and afford. Since that time, Ken and his wife Sue have grown The Bulldog into one of Duluth's favorite family restaurants. The Bulldog specializes in pizza and makes both a thick crust and its original, cracker-like thin crust—both cooked in traditional brick pizza ovens. You can order from a selection of traditional toppings or try one of their specialty pizzas, such as barbecued chicken, vegetarian alfredo, Mediterranean pesto pie, or taco. The Bulldog also serves burgers and other hot sandwiches, subs (another one of their specialties), and an assortment of pasta dishes, all for prices from $4.75 to $8.25.

*See also T-Bonz and Pit Stop (both on page 130).

Italian (Pizza)

Sammy's Pizza

Downtown, Duluth · 103 W. 1st St. · (218) 727-8551 · call for hours
Lakeside, Duluth · 4631 E. Superior St. · (218) 525-6604 · call for hours
Spirit Valley (West Duluth), Duluth · 403 N. Central Ave. · (218) 628-2327 · call for hours
Woodland, Duluth · 4011 Woodland Ave. · (218) 724-1277 · call for hours
Downtown, Superior · 1309 Tower Ave. (back of the Elbo Room) · (715) 392-6292 · call for hours

The Perrella family started Sammy's as a small café in Keewatin, Minnesota, in the 1950s before opening as a pizzeria in Hibbing. They have since opened many more stores—most in Duluth—plus shops in Wisconsin and North Dakota. For this, we almost had to omit them from the book, citing our "no chains" criterion. But then we found out that a member of the Perrella family runs the show at every Sammy's location. And besides that, Sammy's Pizza is a tradition in these parts, and they pride themselves on home cooking, fair prices, and good service. A great place for the family and a variety of menu options in stores with seating.

Vintage Italian Pizza

Chester Park, Duluth · 1830 E. 8th St. · (218) 728-4411 · Sun.–Th. 'til 11:30 P.M. / F & Sat. 'til 12:30 A.M.
Downtown, Superior · 1222 Tower Ave. · (715) 392-5555 · Sun.–Th. 'til 11:30 P.M. / F & Sat. 'til 12:30 A.M.

No dining room at V.I.P., just pick-up or delivery. Still, many believe it to be about the best pie in the Twin Ports. Cooked in stone ovens, V.I.P.'s pies come in a variety of styles, so you can get gourmet toppings at pizzeria prices (the most expensive large specialty pizza is just $15). You can order everything from a pepperoni with extra cheese to a "Pizza No. S-1302," which places spinach, ricotta, provolone, mozzeralla, and a touch of dill on a pizza shell brushed with olive oil pesto. Many, many other specialty pies are available, and they all come on traditional, deep dish, or whole wheat crust. Save a little money: order your pie uncooked and bake it at home.

Italian

The Elbo Room

Downtown, Superior • 1309 Tower Ave. • (715) 392-6292 • T–F 11 A.M. - 10 P.M. / Sat. 4 P.M. - 10 P.M.

If you have difficulty making up your mind, give yourself plenty of time to order at the Elbo Room. The menu is absolutely huge and includes *all* your Italian and American favorites. Prices start at $9 for pasta and run to $17 for prime rib. The Elbo Room also offers a fine selection of fish, including salmon, halibut, Lake Superior trout, and mahi mahi. The spaghetti sauce is made with meat, so vegetarians will want to ask for the marinara sauce (it costs more, but it is *much* tastier than the regular). The restaurant's main dining room is decorated with well-rendered fresco-like paintings in an Italian villa theme. Its lounge (a full bar, including a few microbrew selections) and smoking section have richly stained wood panels, deep, comfy booths, and low lighting. The Elbo Room also serves Sammy's Pizza (see page 139).

The Italian Village

Spirit Valley (West Duluth), Duluth • 301 N. Central Ave. • (218) 624–2286 • T–F 10 A.M. - 5:30 P.M. / Sat. 9:30 A.M. - 3:30 P.M.

The Italian Village bills itself as "An Authentic Taste of Italy" and does not disappoint. This quaint little spot is a deli, cappuccino bar, and gourmet shop all in one, featuring homemade and imported goods that are the real thing. In the deli case you'll find homemade Italian sausage (regular and *hot!*), lasagna, and pizza along with a host of imported meats and cheeses like prosciutto, pancetta, parmesan reggiano, and fontanella. The shop's grocery shelves hold imported olive oils, pastas, roasted red peppers, polenta, and other delicioso items. If you stop by on a Saturday morning you can sample a variety of Italian treats that will tempt your palette and your pocketbook. You can also enhance your vocabulary by taking note of the Italian phrase of the week posted in the window.

"Italian"

We've placed the word *Italian* between quotation marks above because although both eateries below call themselves Italian restaurants, we doubt true aficionados of Italian fare would agree. That's not to say the food isn't tasty, but its authenticity as Italian is questionable. We almost placed these two in the "Nightlife" chapters, since the restaurants of both are found within the walls of two great Duluth neighborhood bars.

The Gopher Lounge
Spirit Valley (West Duluth), Duluth • 402 N. Central Ave. • (218) 624-9793 • M–W 8 A.M. - 6 P.M. / Th.–Sat. 'til 8 P.M. / Sun. 'til 3 P.M.

The Gopher officially opens at eight A.M., but according to the waitress, it's "whenever the cook gets here." You'll find the same casual attitude inside the Gopher, a West Duluth fixture. Primarily a bar, the Gopher offers a limited menu, specializing in spaghetti and other Italian fare, including lasagna, rigatoni, and even veal parmesan, all for less than $9. A variety of American items, such as steak, shrimp, and liver & onions, is also available (steak and shrimp combo for $14). The Gopher also has burgers, appetizers, sandwiches, and serves breakfast.

Tappa Keg Inn
Norton Park, Duluth • 7036 Grand Ave. • (218) 624-9881 • M–F 11 A.M. - 11 P.M. / Sat.–Sun. 9 A.M. - 11 P.M.

The name may sound like something thought up by a bunch of drunken frat boys, but the Tappa Keg Inn is one of those little places that regulars don't mind keeping to themselves. Besides the usual bar fare of burgers, sandwiches, and appetizers, the Tappa serves American and Italian dinners (featuring homemade marinara sauce), all for under $11 (most $7 and $8). Aside from steak, chicken, and chops, diners can choose jumbo beef ravioli, fettuccini alfredo, and "Spaghetti Dick's Way," topped with sautéed mushrooms, onions, and green peppers. Its location makes the Tappa Keg Inn the perfect place to fill up after a day of biking the Munger Trail.

Mexican

Hacienda Del Sol

Downtown, Duluth • 319 E. Superior St. • (218) 722-7296 • M–Sat. 11 A.M. - 11 P.M.

Since owner Kevin Deutsch opened its doors in 1982, this tiny café in Old Downtown has been serving up tasty Mexican-style food at rock-bottom prices, and it has long been a local favorite (the only complaint most folks have is that the Hac is closed Sundays). The menu features a variety of tacos, burritos, enchiladas, tostadas, killer nachos, and chile rellenos—and nothing costs more than $10. The staff prepares all the food on site, including the chips and salsa. The mild salsa is mild, and frankly, so is the medium, but the hot—a green sauce—is truly hot. During the summer, the Hac is known for its courtyard, where customers dine among murals featuring Mayan and Aztec themes (but no view of the big lake). The theme continues inside, where you'll find wooden booths and a lunch counter. Currently the Hac serves a wide variety of Mexican and domestic beers, sangria, and an assortment of soft drinks. Plans are underway for a major expansion, including a full liquor license.

Amigo's Mex-Express

Downtown, Superior • 1320 Belknap St. • (715) 395-5225 • M–Th. 11 A.M. - 9 P.M. / F & Sat. 11 A.M. - 3 A.M.

Since the Zona Rosa closed down the Hacienda and Amigo's are the only non-chain Mexican restaurants in the Twin Ports. (Little Angie's in Canal Park and Miller Hill Mall is part of the Grandma's chain and, technically, Southwestern fare.) At Amigo's you'll find no-frills Mexican served up quick. The décor may say fast food, but the abundance of choices makes this little restaurant something more. From tacos to chimichangas to fajitas, the menu fills all your Mexican cravings, and prices range from $1 (basic hardshell or softshell taco) to $7 (chorizo chili rellenos dinner). Lots of appetizer options as well. Parking is tricky, but delivery is available. Since it's open until three in the morning on weekends, add Amigo's to your late-night dining options.

Bakery Goods to Go

European Bakery
Downtown, Duluth • 109 W. 1st St. • (218) 722–2120 • M–Th. 8 A.M. - 5:30 P.M. / F 7:30 A.M. - 5:30 P.M. / Sat. 8 A.M. - 3 P.M.

Besides European baked goods, the European Bakery features a mini-European grocery stocked with items from a variety of European countries. You'll find Hungarian stuffed red peppers, Croatian nougat wafer cookies, and canned mackerel salad along with plenty of good old fashioned American-style bakery fare.

Lakeside Bakery
Lakeside, Duluth • 4509 E. Superior St. • (218) 525-9988 • W–Sat. 6 A.M. - 5:30 P.M.

Bill Gustafson and his father (who turned 90 in 2002) have operated the Lakeside Bakery since the 1950s, and Lakeside residents love the selection of Swedish baked goods, such as kringles flavored with plenty of cardamom and other rolls and cookies. The bakery also makes homemade bread, including Swedish Rye.

Positively 3rd Street Bakery
Hillside, Duluth • 1202 E. 3rd St. • (218) 724-8619 • M–F 8 A.M. - 5:30 P.M. / Sat. 10 A.M. - 4 P.M.

Home of the renowned Thunder Cookie, Positively 3rd Street is an employee-owned co-op that serves up the best organic baked treats around. From granola, bagels, and breads to blueberry bars, muffins, and the biggest and best cookies around, you can count on the folks at 3rd Street to bake with only the best ingredients.

Billings Park Bakery
Billings Park, Superior • 1827 Iowa Ave. • (715) 394-7213 • M–Sat. 6 A.M. - 6 P.M.

This tiny bakery makes all sorts of breads and baked treats, including chocolate bavarian cream strudel. Yum.

Twin Ports Coffee Shops*

Browser's N'eTc. Cafe

Downtown, Duluth • 201 E. Superior St. • (218) 726-0530 • M–F 7:30 A.M. - 12 A.M. / Sat. 9 A.M. - 12 A.M. / Sun. 9 A.M. - 9 P.M.

A full-service coffee house with coffees, teas, chai, and sodas inside the Temple Opera Building, Browser's also has computers with high-speed internet connections and lots of big windows and comfy couches and chairs.

Jitters

Downtown, Duluth • 102 W. Superior St. • (218) 720-6015 • M–Sat. 7 A.M. - 7 P.M. / Sun. 8 A.M. - 5 P.M.

No gimmicks at Jitters, just quality coffee, teas, and chai and a bit to eat on weekdays, including soups, sandwich wraps, and lots of pastries. A great spot for hot cocoa during the Christmas City of the North Parade.

Lakeview Coffee Emporium

Downtown, Duluth • 600 E. Superior St. • (218) 720-4464 • M–Sat. 7 A.M. - 8 P.M. / Sundays 8 A.M. - 6 P.M.

Although it's located in the Fitger's Complex, we had to mention Lakeview because no other coffee shop in Duluth has a view of Lake Superior. All you'd expect from a coffee shop, plus the work of local artists adorns the walls.

Northwoods Coffee & Guitars

Downtown, Superior • 1828 Tower Ave. • (715) 399-0979 • M–F 7 A.M. - 7 P.M. / Sat. 8 A.M. - 5 P.M.

Superior's gourmet coffee and sandwich shop also features guitar sales, repairs, and lessons. Local folk and blues musicians have made it a second home, and you can even join in their regular cribbage tournaments.

*See also Beaner's and At Sarah's Table (both on page 127).

Neighborhood Markets

Bay Side Market

Park Point, Duluth • 1901 Minnesota Ave. • (218) 727-7635 • Daily 7 A.M. - 8 P.M.

Living on Park Point has its trade-offs. The most expensive real estate in town is also about the most inconvenient location, as residents must contend with raised bridges and busy tourist traffic each time they leave the house. That's why the Bay Side Market is one of the best-loved places around. A complete grocery, with fresh produce, meat, dairy, and canned goods, Bay Side even sells gas and meets your other convenience needs.

Little John's 4th Street Market & Deli

Central Hillside, Duluth • 102 E. 4th St. • (218) 727-3811 • 8 A.M. - 11 P.M.

The owner may have a diminutive nickname, but he does things in big style, serving the needs of local residents as the last neighborhood grocer on the Hillside. John's has produce, canned goods, fresh meat and dairy, and a deli with a surprising amount of selections. John's also fills all your convenience store needs, from smokes to movie rentals.

Romano's Grocery

Downtown, Duluth • 231 E. Superior St. • (218) 722-5256 • M–F 7 A.M. - 6 P.M. / Sat. 8 A.M. - 5 P.M.

Romano's Grocery, housed in the first-floor corner of the Hotel Duluth, has served downtown residents for more than 20 years. The tiny store—more a convenience store with produce than a full-fledged grocery—was once a liquor store and, before that, a café. Today, many of its customers arrive via the elevator, as the hotel (now Greysolon Plaza) contains 150 senior apartments.

Specialty Grocers*

First Oriental Grocery (a.k.a. Duluth Oriental Grocery)
Downtown, Duluth • 323 E. Superior St. • (218) 726-0017 • M–Sat. 10 A.M. - 6 P.M.

If you need authentic ingredients for cooking up Asian meals, make your way to the First Oriental Grocery. Inside, you'll find items unavailable anywhere else in town (or the region, we wager). Its shelves are packed tight with everything from special varieties of rice to dried squid, and its selection of teas—especially green teas—is the best in town. Besides food, you can also find rice steamers, tea servers, and other kitchen needs.

Fichtner's Sausage & Meats
Downtown, Duluth • 134 W. 1st St. • (218) 722-2661 • M–F 8:30 A.M. - 5:30 P.M. / Sat. 8 A.M. - 3 P.M.

Fichtner's has been a downtown staple for four decades, three of them at its current location. A long glass case filled with all manner of meat products, including Fichtner's homemade sausages and hams, runs the length of the shop. They also offer a selection of grocery basics, such as dairy products, eggs, bagged chips, soda, barbecue sauces, and bread and buns from the European Bakery. Munch on a giant dill pickle from the big jar on the deli case while you browse the shop, finding everything you need for an impromptu picnic or barbecue.

Whole Foods Co-op
East Hillside, Duluth • 1332 E. 4th St. • (218) 728-0884 • M–F 7 A.M. - 9 P.M. / Sat. & Sun. 8 A.M. - 8 P.M.

Whether you're a vegan, a vegetarian, or just a health-concerned consumer, this complete organic grocery and deli has all sorts of produce and dry and frozen goods to meet your needs. The deli serves up tasty sandwiches, spreads, and homemade soups. The store planned to move before we went to press, so call ahead.

*See also the Italian Village (page 140).

Farmers' Markets

Duluth Farmers' Market
East Hillside, Duluth • Corner of 14th Ave. E. and 3rd St. • (218) 724-9955 • Wed. & Sat., 7 A.M. - Noon

Operated by the Duluth Market Gardeners' Association, the Duluth Farmers' Market gives local farmers of organic and traditionally grown produce a chance to bring their harvest direct to consumers looking for food that hasn't spent a month on a truck. You'll find every kind of vegetable that grows this far north plus plenty of local berries, especially blueberries and raspberries. And there's more than just good food. The market opens each spring the weekend before Mother's Day—when its stalls are filled with annual and perennial bedding plants—and sells produce through the end of October. It reopens for a few weeks in November and December to sell Christmas trees.

UMD Farmers' Market
UMD Campus, Duluth • Outside Kirby Plaza, Kirby Place, UMD • (218) 726-7258 • Wednesdays from 2 P.M. until sold out

Despite its location underneath the University of Minnesota Duluth's Resident Hall Dining Center, the food at the UMD Farmers' Market is fresh, locally produced, and won't add fifteen pounds to your frame during the fist two months of your freshman year. And you don't have to be a UMD student to enjoy it, either—everyone is welcome. The market opens every Wednesday starting in mid-May and runs until the end of September. You'll find organic and traditionally grown vegetables and fruit produced by local farmers and gardeners, most of whom belong to the Sustainable Farmers' Association. Annual and perennial bedding plants and some house plants are also for sale. To find the market, take College Street or St. Marie Street to Kirby Place (formerly Oakland Avenue) and turn onto the UMD campus.

North Shore

New Scenic Café
Scenic 61 • 5461 North Shore Dr. (Scenic Highway 61) • (218) 525-6274 • M–F 11 A.M. - 9 P.M.

The New Scenic might just be the North Shore's worst kept secret. During the summer, expect to wait to be seated—even on a Sunday afternoon. The cost is a bit more than visitors to the area are used to (entrées between $12 and $18, sandwiches $7 to $8), but the cuisine is upscale and many consider it the best around. The menu includes such nonregional delights as cilantro-pesto shrimp with couscous, pan-seared Chilean sea bass with saffron broth, and Indian masala vegetable curry with pineapple. The Scenic also serves a variety of salads and appetizers, including their incredible artichoke slather (mighty tasty, trust us). You'll find a good selection of beer (including Guinness in a nitro can) and a well thought out wine list. The Scenic also serves locally roasted Alakef Coffee. Many vegetarian choices.

Shorecrest Supper Club
Scenic 61 • 5593 North Shore Dr. (Scenic Highway 61) • (218) 525-2286 • Hours changing summer of 2002, so call ahead

The Shorecrest Supper Club is like one of those country supper clubs you find about twenty miles from the family cabin—at once upscale and down-home—except it's on the shore of Lake Superior less than twenty miles from downtown Duluth. In the summer, the Crest opens for breakfast, lunch, and dinner (it closes for a time during the winter months), offering customers American fare that includes plenty of fish and seafood. Trout, broiled walleye, fried fillet of herring, fried shrimp, lobster, and Alaska king crab all grace the menu, but the Crest's specialty is its 16-ounce porterhouse steak. Dinners cost from $9 to $18 (lobster and crab at market prices) and lunches from $5 to $10 (most between $5 and $6). Simple décor—coffee motif tablecloths cover steel and formica tables—and a full bar. Very few vegetarian options.

North Shore, continued

Russ Kendall's Fish House
Knife River, MN • 149 North Shore Dr. (Scenic Highway 61) • (218) 834-5995 • M–Sun. 9 A.M. - 6 P.M.

Russ Kendall's father opened the fish house in 1924 after his truck broke down and he had to sell his smoked fish from the side of the road. Russ bought the place in 1952, and his fish has been a North Shore favorite ever since. Kendall's shop has evolved into a fish house/deli/thrift store/museum hybrid over the years, selling goods that range from picnic supplies (crackers, cheeses, drinks, etc.) to antique postcards from around the world. The back room is a treat for the eye, with paintings, old photos, and bric-a-brac everywhere (some for sale, some not). If the weather isn't cooperating for a picnic, Russ has seating available inside. But it's the fish that keeps people coming in, and Russ specializes in maple-smoked trout, ciscoes, salmon, whitefish, and bluefin. If Russ's place looks busy, his brother Smokey's is just up the road, as is Mel's Fish. Russ's may be the most popular, but folks still argue over whose is best.

Emily's Inn, Deli, & General Store
Knife River, MN • 218 North Shore Dr. (Scenic Highway 61) • (218) 834-5922 • M–Sun. 8 A.M. - 9 P.M. (limited winter hours)

Emily Erickson opened her inn and eatery in 1929 in a building that was once a general store, serving traditional Scandinavian meals that reflected her heritage (Emily emigrated from Norway when she was 12). Her granddaughter Carol now runs the store, which has become increasingly popular over the past few years. Perhaps it's the building's charming authenticity, but it probably has a lot to do with the food. Sandwiches, salads, soups, and desserts grace the menu at Emily's, with prices ranging from $7 to $17. Choices include wild rice cheese soup, Swedish pea soup, smoked fish appetizer, chili with Italian sausage, and grilled Lake Superior trout or salmon. The salads—including wild rice chicken and smoked trout—are especially good. You can even get a meat loaf sandwich, and every Friday from February to October Emily's hosts a fish boil.

North Shore, continued

Judy's Café

Two Harbors, MN • 623 7th Ave. • (218) 834-4802 • M–Sun. 5 A.M. - 8 P.M.

Like Bayfield across the lake, Two Harbors has become a tourist town. Driving down 7th Avenue in Two Harbors, it seems that every other storefront is now home to an antique store or a cleverly named restaurant. Judy's Café opens at five in the morning, so you know they don't cater solely to the tourist crowd. A simple, single-room diner, Judy's makes breakfast all day long, serving local residents and visitors alike. You'll find plenty of options on the menu, from typical diner burgers and sandwiches ($2.50 to $6) to complete dinners such as steak, veal, and walleye ($7 to $10). Judy's also has something you wouldn't expect on a diner menu—Asian stir fry. Try a muffin or a piece of pie—they're homemade, and the selection changes daily. The décor, including industrial tables and chairs, lacks imagination compared to their great tin ceiling.

Northern Lights

Beaver Bay, MN • 1040 Main St. • (218) 226-3102 • M–Sat. 11 A.M. - 9 P.M. / Sun. 9 A.M. - 9 P.M.

If you're looking for a taste of the north woods, look no further than Northern Lights. The menu features regional fish (smoked salmon, pan-fried Lake Superior herring, and excellent fish cakes), big game (smoked elk, barbe-cued bison, caribou pot pie), and fantastic fowl (smoked breast of goose sandwich, smoked pheasant and duck). They also make some of the finest wild rice soup in the region and host a big buffet brunch on Sundays. Lunches run from $6 to $12, dinners $14 to $25 (brunch is under $9), and vegetarian options are increasing. The décor matches the menu—canoes and dog sleds hang from the ceilings, and walls are covered with pelts and mounts of a variety of animals. If you're thirsty, Northern Lights offers over 40 imported and domestic beers, including a fine selection of microbrews in bottles and on tap. During the summer, diners can enjoy a meal from the screen porch/deck or the double-decker bus that is both a beer garden and an ice cream shop.

North Shore, continued

Northwoods Café

Silver Bay, MN • 6 Shopping Center • (218) 226-3699 • M–Sat. 6 A.M. - 7 P.M. / Sun. 6 A.M. - 6 P.M.

Although it is located within a shopping center, Northwoods Café is a true small town diner. Local residents young and old sporting seed caps and Twins hats (or camouflage in the fall) gather each morning to discuss events both local and worldwide—some even have their own tables. Northwoods is a big place, with two dining rooms that can seat up to 150 people, but its customers and décor—comfy booths and prints of outdoor scenes—give it a cozy feeling. Let's put it this way: it's the kind of place where the Tabasco™ never leaves the table. The food is all you would expect, including biscuits & gravy for breakfast. Northwoods serves breakfast (from $2 to $5.25 for a "Stacker": hash browns with bacon or sausage covered in cheese), lunch (burgers and such from $2.50 to $6.75), and complete dinners (steak, fish, chops, chicken from $9 to $13). They also serve beer and wine. Breakfast ends at 11 A.M.

Superior Outlook Grill & Saloon

Milepost 60 on Highway 61 • (218) 226-6492 • M–Sun. 7:30 A.M. - 9:30 P.M. (kitchen closes at 7:30 P.M.)

Located at the intersection of Highway 61 and Highway 1, Superior Outlook is a clean (smoke free!), bright little restaurant with knotty-pine walls covered in wildlife prints and mounted game birds. The menu features everything from appetizers to complete dinners, with lots of sandwiches and burgers in between. Dinners—breaded fish, chicken, lemon-pepper salmon, steak—cost no more than $12, and burgers go for between $3 and $6. The Outlook also serves a good, cheap breakfast, including the Superior breakfast of two eggs, toast, hash browns, and sausage or bacon for under $5. Behind the beautiful polished-wood bar, you'll find a couple of domestic beers on tap plus a good selection of domestics, imports, and microbrews, including Red Hook, Newcastle, and selections from Duluth's Lake Superior Brewing Company.

North Shore, continued

Satellite's Country Inn

Schroeder, MN • Milepost 72, Highway 61 • (218) 663-7574 • M–F 6 A.M. - 9 P.M. / weekend hours unavailable

The only problem with Satellite's Country Inn is the fact that you can easily drive by without noticing it. Satellite's sits on the landward side of the highway in the middle of a sprawling dirt parking lot and assorted outbuildings. The building itself looks more like someone's house; understandable, since it is someone's house, as the décor and layout inside attest. Many North Shore travelers say don't let the looks fool you—try the food before you make any assumptions. Besides a full breakfast menu (some say the best along the shore), Satellite's serves dinners you'd hope for so close to the big lake: Lake Superior herring, walleye, trout, and fish cakes—plus steak, chicken, and ribs—and none of it over $15 (most dinners range from $6 to $12). Oddly enough, Satellite's also sells oil, power steering fluid, brake fluid, and other items for your car. Closed during the winter.

Cross River Café

Schroeder, MN • Milepost 79, Highway 61 • (218) 663-7208 • Sun.–Th. 6 A.M. - 7 P.M. / F & Sat. 6 A.M. - 8 P.M.

Schroeder's Cross River Café is ideally situated for folks partaking in some of our North Shore outdoor adventures, making it a great place to stop for a meal or pick up something for a picnic. It's nine miles from Caribou Falls, a mile from Temperance River's Hidden Falls, and right next to the Cross River and Father Baraga's Cross. Inside the quaint diner you'll find three small dining areas lined with faux log walls. You'll also find a solid menu. Dinners include a fish fry, Chicken Laverne, ocean shrimp, and a good selection of steaks ranging from $8 to $13. Lunches—mostly sandwiches and burgers—run in the $4 to $7 range, and none of the breakfasts cost more than $5. They also have a good selection of appetizers and make all their soups from scratch. Domestic beer and some wines available.

North Shore, continued

The Pie Place
Grand Marais, MN • 2017 W. Highway 61 • (218) 387-1513 • T–Sat. 7:30 A.M. - 8:30 P.M. / Sun. 7:30 A.M. - 8 P.M.

The Pie Place takes pride in preparing everything from scratch—the meals, the pies, the breads, and even the ice cream—for a menu that features what they call "gourmet homecooking." In order to cook with the freshest ingredients, the menu changes weekly, catering to the North Shore's seasonal changes. Past menus have featured pecan waffles with banana syrup for breakfast ($5.95) and a roast beef, mushroom, and brie sandwich for lunch ($6.50). For dinner you can choose from barbecued ribs, coconut chicken, and Thai pork chops. And of course, you don't call your restaurant The Pie Place without offering outstanding pies. Varieties include north woods apple, blackberry cherry walnut, lemon cream cheese, banana cream, sour cream raisin, and a slew of other fruit and cream flavors. Set in a remodeled house, The Pie Place has two dining rooms, one of which ("the porch") looks out over Lake Superior.

Angry Trout
Grand Marais, MN • 416 W. Highway 61 • (218) 387-1265 • Sun.–Th. 11 A.M. - 8:30 P.M. / F & Sat. 11 A.M. - 9 P.M.

Don't worry, we know: it doesn't get much more touristy than the Angry Trout. However, its location and cuisine caused us to make an exception. The restaurant is set *right on* Lake Superior, and it has both dockside and atrium dining, providing natural North Shore atmosphere. And the food is pretty good, too, especially if you're looking for some place fancy after roughing it in the rustic north woods. But be prepared to spend some money, as lunches range from $8 to $10 and dinners from $16 to $18. The Angry Trout serves up a grilled portabella mushroom sandwich, smoked trout salad, grilled Lake Superior catch of the day, grilled shitake mushroom fettuccini, and many other tasty treats. And for those concerned, they even use free-range chicken for their chicken nuggets. The name? Well, the logo image came to the owner in a dream; the name just describes it.

North Shore, continued

Leng's Soda Fountain & Grill
Grand Marais, MN • 5 W. Wisconsin • (218) 387-2648 • M, W, F 8:30 A.M. - 8 P.M. / T, Th, Sat. 11 A.M. - 8 P.M.

Leng's has been slinging burgers and twisting up malts since 1938, when a chocolate sundae cost 30 cents. The prices may have gone up, but not that much—nothing on the menu will run you over $8.50. The menu is all you'd expect (burgers, fries, hot dogs, sandwiches, and all sorts of ice cream treats) with a few surprises, such as a grilled veggie sandwich, but the décor can't be beat. Stools wrap around two large horseshoe-shaped lunch counters, the tables are covered with checkerboard cloths, and black-and-white tiles cover the floor. Memorabilia and artifacts from a variety of eras decorate the place—Elvis, James Dean, Marilyn Monroe, a 1970s-era 7-Up sign, a full-size model of R2-D2 from *Star Wars*, and an old piano and wooden radio all compete for your attention. A great place to take the family. (Closed from 10:30 - 11 A.M. on Monday, Wednesday, and Friday.)

My Sister's Place
Grand Marais, MN • 410 E. Highway 61 • (218) 387-1915 • Sun–Th. 11 A.M. - 9 P.M. / F & Sat. 11 A.M. - 10 P.M.

If this was your sister's place, you'd have one pretty cool sister. This is a family joint, and they lay down the rules right on the menu: "No room for prejudice here; we won't allow it." And if you've had one too many beers, they'll toss ya. If you can handle those guidelines, you're in for a treat. My Sister's Place serves great food among a chaotic melange of decoration, including photos of every set of sisters that has ever dined there. They've covered the ceiling and walls in pelts, washboards, red flannel shirts, license plates, and hornets' nests. Even the barstools are a kitsch touch, hewn from logs. Oh, and they serve some good food as well: burgers, great chili, a fair amount of vegetarian items (like the black bean burger), and the biggest and best selection of hot dogs north of Chicago—and nothing over $8! The bar serves wine and a pretty good variety of beers, including Guinness and a mess of domestic and Canadian brands.

North Shore, continued

Cook County Whole Foods Co-op & Grand Marais Farmers' Market

Grand Marais, MN • Co-op: 20 E. 1st St. • (218) 387-2503 • M–F 10 A.M. - 6 P.M. / Sat. 10 A.M. - 4 P.M.
Farmers' Market: Senior Center Parking Lot • Saturday Mornings from May to September

We wanted to include the Cook County Whole Foods Co-op for those travelers who may be particular about where their food comes from, especially those taking their own food on a hiking, kayaking, or camping excursion. Besides a large variety of organic produce, customers will find organic juices and other beverages and some great trail food. At the time we wrote this, the co-op did not have a deli or much prepared food, but they were considering expanding when they move into their new building on 1st Street (so things may have changed). The Farmers' Market opens every Saturday morning through the summer and offers organic and traditionally produced fruits and vegetables grown locally.

Ryden's Border Store & Café

Grand Portage, MN • Highway 61 • (218) 475-2330 • Summer: M–Sun. 5 A.M. - 10 P.M. / Winter: M–Sun. 7 A.M. - 8 P.M.

Ryden's has just about anything you might need. This hybrid café/gas station/general store/tourist mecca (complete with stuffed jackalopes for sale) is the last commercial enterprise before the Canadian border (it's also a duty free shop for those traveling to Canada). The café has been operating since 1947 and has survived being burned to the ground and forced to relocate due to highway expansion. Great diner fare from a $2 egg-and-toast breakfast to complete dinners for under $8, and the hash browns are absolutely perfect. The café doesn't serve beer, but if you've got a hankerin', you can buy a brew at the store and drink it with your meal. The décor is pretty standard but includes a wonderful mural by artist Jim Korf showing nearby Minnesota Point, Wauswaugoning Bay, Pigeon Bay, the Susie Islands, and Isle Royale—the same view from the Mt. Josephine wayside two miles down the shore.

South Shore

Port Bar & Restaurant

Port Wing, WI • Highway 13 • (715) 774-3731 • M–F 5 P.M. - 8 P.M. / Sat. & Sun. 7 A.M. - 9 P.M.

Split into three rooms, the Port Bar is a combination small town bar and restaurant. The bar itself is all you'd expect from a roadside tavern: simple, utilitarian, and a comfy spot to enjoy a drink (and outside of Summit Porter on tap, a fairly basic choice of beers). The two dining rooms offer unique décor, with a stone fountain complete with goldfish in one and a fireplace made of petrified wood harvested from North Dakota in the other. The Port serves everything from burgers to walleye, but specializes in a pineapple-grilled Alaska salmon. The Sunday breakfast special is prime rib, three eggs, hash browns, and toast for $6.95 ($9.95 with a bloody mary). During the Testicle Festival, held every Father's Day, deep fried Rocky Mountain oysters are the catch of the day. The Port holds a pig boil in August and hosts Wisconsin's largest fish boil on Labor Day.

Fishlipps Bar & Restaurant

Cornucopia, WI • (715) 742-3378 • M–Th. 8 A.M. - 9 P.M. / F & Sat. 'til 10 P.M. / Sat. & Sun. open at 7 A.M.

The first thing you'll notice walking inside Fishlipps is the darkness. Red and black furniture and dim lighting make it feel like perpetual night inside the bar/restaurant, but the food should be enough to brighten your day. Breakfasts run from $3.50 to $8 (a Fishlipps omelette with shrimp, crab, mushrooms, and onions), and the buttermilk pancakes are flavored with vanilla. Lunches offer burgers, sandwiches, and wraps, including a veggie-spinach (one of the few vegetarian options on the menu). The most tempting item is the Crabby Sandwich: Alaska king crab salad, garlic cheese spread, red onion, and tomato on sourdough bread. Dinners include whitefish with potato pancakes, steak, chicken parmesan, and prosciutto and gorgonzola on tomato basil pasta. Fishlipps also serves small pizzas and all sorts of appetizers. Great beer selection.

South Shore, continued

It's a Small World
Washburn, WI • 144 W. Bayfield • (715) 373-5177 • M–Th. 10 A.M. - 8 P.M. / Friday 'til 9 P.M. / Sat. & Sun. open at 8 A.M.

No Disney affiliation here—the name comes from the restaurant's ever-changing menu featuring cuisine from around the world. Whether the menu features French, Italian, Russian, Thai, Greek, Polish, Caribbean, or New Orleans fare, some of the café's favorites are always available, including fajitas, falafel, fish from Lake Superior, and gyros and burger baskets (including vegetarian and shrimp burgers). You can also get a bison burger or 16-ounce sirloin of bison (at $17, the most expensive item on the menu). It's a Small World is also home to the locally famous Oddball Burger. The burger is named after Ray "Oddball" Divine, who originally sold burgers from a stand in downtown Washburn for 20 cents each. But if you could shoot pool and beat Ray in a game of nine ball—"oddball" in some circles—the burger was free. The restaurant's casual atmosphere is a reflection of its attitude—when your meal comes with a salad, they leave a bottle of their homemade dressing on the table.

Good Things A La Cart
Washburn, WI • 331 W. Bayfield • (715) 373-5272 • T–Sat. 11:30 A.M. - 8 P.M.

Good Things is a great thing for those looking for a quick and tasty meal they can take with them. The deli serves up food to go at prices that'll have you coming back. Located across the street from legendary Patsy's Bar in downtown Washburn, Good Things is a tiny deli with no seating available. Owner Jean Lonky serves a variety of hot and cold sandwiches as well as salads and barbecue. The sandwiches will please a variety of tastes and include a grilled brat, kosher beef hot dog, and barbecued beef. The salad selection is phenomenal: garden salads, oriental chicken, chicken caesar, chicken and wild rice, seafood, and tri-colored pasta. But the best value has to be the rib combo: ribs, roll, and choice of baked beans, cole slaw, or potato salad for just $4.49. Wash it all down with Blue Sky sodas, iced coffees (Coffee House Vanilla Mousse), or iced Arizona Teas.

South Shore, continued

Black Cat Coffeehouse

Ashland, WI • 211 Chapple Ave. • (715) 682-3680 • M–Sat. 7 A.M. - 10 P.M. / Sun. 9 A.M. - 5 P.M. • Smoke free

The Black Cat is unique among eateries along the South Shore. Caught somewhere between a tavern and a deli, it has the feel of a place that would be more at home in Portland, Oregon, or Burlington, Vermont. Long and narrow, *Le Chat Noir* comprises two rooms and an outdoor dining patio. Local art covers the walls, and each week the Black Cat brings in a variety of live music. The Black Cat's food sets it apart from the rest of the South Shore. Almost entirely vegetarian (smoked whitefish is available), the menu offers veggie sandwiches and specialty pizzas as well as Greek, taco, garden, and spinach salads—all for under $7.50. Fresh homemade soups, hummus, and a basil-parmesan spread also grace the chalkboard bill of fare. The café has a good selection of bottled beer, including Anchor Steam, Guinness, Bell Stout, and Gray's Oatmeal Stout brewed in Janesville, Wisconsin. Non-beer drinkers can try a Buddy's orange or grape soda, Italian sodas, chai, and specialty coffees.

Golden Glow Café

Ashland, WI • 519 Main St. W. • (715) 682-2838 • M–F 6:30 A.M. - 7 P.M. / Sat.–Sun. 6:30 A.M. - 2 P.M. • Smoke free

If you're looking for a good old-fashioned breakfast or dinner, look no further than the Golden Glow. This clean, spacious diner is home away from home to many local residents but welcomes folks from out of town just the same. You can get just about anything you want at the Glow. Full breakfast options (from oatmeal to steak & eggs) and great diner fare (burgers, sandwiches, walleye, lake trout, country fried steak, liver & onions, etc.) all for no more than $7.25. The house favorite at the Golden Glow is the Golden Burger, which is served on a toasted French round. The Glow serves Brown's Velvet Ice Cream, made locally since 1916 when dairyman Carl John Brown took advantage of nearby French Lake to start an ice business. When he mixed some of that ice with his dairy's own buttermilk and wild berries found nearby, he started making ice cream.

Places to Shop

(fun and curious shops and services)

True North Shopping

As any visitor to the region knows, popular destinations like Bayfield and Duluth's Canal Park are chock full of great places to spend money. There are shops selling gifts, souvenirs, outdoor gear, candy, and anything else you can stick a price tag on. They're a lot of fun to visit and you can't miss 'em. That's why we want to point out some places you might otherwise miss that offer something special: they're locally owned, not part of a chain, and they offer wares and/or atmosphere that make them unique, at least to this area.

We also included listings of shops hobbyists might seek out wherever they go, since we understand what it's like to be passionate about a craft or creative endeavor. Thrift and used book stores were added for those who like to treat shopping as an adventure.

Of course, given our self-imposed geographic boundaries and our desire to focus on lesser-known business-es, we can't mention every last shop in the Twin Ports. But besides highlighting those on the following pages, we can also direct you to business districts where you might discover a gem on your own. You know about Canal Park, you probably know about Fitger's (an exceptional shopping mall east of Canal Park on Superior Street inside the former Fitger's Brewery Complex), but you may not know to check out Superior's East End, which still has an old neighborhood shopping area (on East Fifth Avenue at 22nd Street) featuring lots of clas-sic neon signs. You might not know that Duluth's Superior Street has shopping areas not just downtown, but also at 21st Avenue West and at 44th Avenue East. While you're out in the western side of town, cruise Grand Avenue from about 40th Avenue West through 60th Avenue West and beyond.

This region is fortunate to still have such a variety of locally owned shops. But they need visitors' business in order to thrive. We hope this chapter will encourage you to take some of your dollars out of the canal and away from the mall to where we here in the north truly shop. And if you feel you must buy a souvenir T-shirt, visit Bullseye Silkscreen at 34 East Superior Street; their designs stand head-and-shoulders above the rest.

Environmental Variety

Green Mercantile

Downtown, Duluth • 209 E. Superior St. • (218) 722-1771 • M–Sat. 10 A.M. - 6 P.M.

Green Mercantile isn't just a shop—it's a business with a mission. Its goal is to provide "healthy alternatives to everyday products"—products that are nontoxic, recycled, recyclable, sustainably produced, and that promote fair working conditions and wages. While this definition might sound limiting, Green Mercantile proves it's anything but. The shop offers a wide variety of products including hemp and organic cotton clothing for infants to adults, candles, art supplies, bath and body items, household cleaning supplies, diapers, office supplies, stationery, and much more. The shop also strives to educate consumers about its mission by providing information about how it chooses its wares and the importance of "voting" with your dollars. Visit its website (www.greenmercantile.com) to learn more.

Global Village

Downtown, Duluth • 25 W. Superior St. • (218) 723-1177 • M–F 10 A.M. - 8 P.M. / Sat. 'til 6 P.M. / Sun. 12 P.M. - 5 P.M.

Visitors from the Twin Cities area may be familiar with Global Village since there are two branches in Minneapolis. While the store is not unique to Duluth, it is unique to Minnesota and worth a mention here because it carries a range of items hard to find elsewhere in this region. Global Village comprises two floors of quality imported goods (and some made stateside) including clothing, scarves, hats, jewelry, incense, toys, greeting cards, and a wide selection of home décor items such as candles and candle holders, dishes, pottery, pillows, throws, and rugs. They also have an extensive selection of futons, futon frames, and futon covers. The sheer volume and variety of merchandise from around the world make Global Village a great place to browse, and its second floor is accessible from the Skywalk.

Tobacconists

Butts Smoke Shop

Spirit Valley (West Duluth), Duluth • 5610 Grand Ave. • (218) 628-1502 • M–Sat. 8 A.M. - 7 P.M. / Sun. 10 A.M. - 4 P.M.

Butts Smoke Shop is all about tobacco. The shop focuses on cigars and cigarettes, offering a wide selection of both, as well as chewing tobacco. The shop's large, walk-in humidor houses its imported cigar selection, including varieties from Honduras, Nicaragua, the Dominican Republic, Jamaica, and other warmer climes. Butts's cigarette selection encompasses all the usual domestic selections plus some imports from Canada, France, and other countries.

Duluth Tobacco & Gift

Downtown, Duluth • 11 N. 4th Ave. W. • (218) 722-2229 • M–F 9 A.M. - 5:30 P.M. / Sat. 10 A.M. - 4 P.M.

More than just a place to buy a good cigar, Duluth Tobacco & Gift offers a variety of tobaccos—from cigarettes and pipe tobacco to cigars and snuff—as well as premium coffee and espresso drinks. Call ahead before you stop by—at the time we put this together, the Twin Ports "traditional tobacconists" were considering moving and expanding to include a coffee and wine bar that would be open in the evening.

Lake Superior Smokin' Brews

Downtown, Duluth • 320 E. Superior St. • (218) 724-3491 • M–F 10 A.M. - 6 P.M. / Sat. 11 A.M. - 5 P.M.

Lake Superior Smokin' Brews combines the appreciation of fine cigars with the penchant for fine homemade beer, wine, or even liqueur. You'll find a walk-in humidor protecting the shop's selection of imported cigars plus all the supplies needed to make your own cigar-accompanying beverages.

Music, etc.

The Electric Fetus

Downtown, Duluth • 12 E. Superior St. • (218) 722-9970 • M–F 10 A.M. - 9 P.M. / Sat. 10 A.M. - 8 P.M. / Sun. 11 A.M. - 6 A.M.

Some out-of-town visitors may be acquainted with the Electric Fetus name. The first Electric Fetus opened in 1968 in Minneapolis, followed by locations in St. Cloud and Duluth in 1987. Since the Duluth branch opened, it has become *the* place for music enthusiasts to find whatever they need. Don't let the freaky name scare you—the Fetus (as local residents call it) is a great place to shop for music and a variety of gifts, clothing, and jewelry. The compact disc selection offers both new and used titles and is not to be beat in this area. From the wildly popular to the relatively obscure, the Fetus has it (or will order it on the off chance they don't), and someone on the staff is bound to know exactly what you're looking for. Besides the extensive music selection, the Fetus also offers a wide variety of jewelry, incense, candles, postcards, greeting cards, bath and body products, and novelty toys, along with women's and men's apparel.

Round About Records

Downtown, Duluth • 205 E. Superior St. • (218) 733-0132 • M–F 11 A.M. - 8 P.M. / Sat. 10 A.M. - 9 P.M. / Sun. 12 P.M. - 5 P.M

Most of the merchandise at Round About Records is geared to a fairly young crowd. Round About deals in vinyl records and CDs (new and used), but the focus is on hip-hop, house music, and beat-driven instrumental recordings popular at raves. They also sell video games and urban gear. But what makes Round About truly unique is its dedication to live local music. Every Thursday at 8 P.M. Round About hosts a night of "open mic" and turntables, where DJs and poets and even break dancers show off their stuff. Local graffiti artists have left their work on Round About's walls (Round About sells graffiti art supplies as well), and the store also displays and sells work by local artists.

Curiosity Shops

The Last Place on Earth

Downtown, Duluth • 120 E. Superior St. • (218) 727-1244 • M–Sat. 10 A.M. - 9 P.M. / Sun. 12 A.M. - 6 P.M.

Whenever you walk into a store whose front window states it sells urine cleaner, you know you're in for something different. The Last Place on Earth may be so named because it has things you'll find nowhere else, but some joke that it's the last place on earth at which you'd want anyone to know you shop. Last Place deals in decorative items (posters and stickers celebrating musicians and illegal narcotics), nonfirearm weaponry (knives, martial arts weapons, stun guns, and self-defense gadgets), smoking devices (from simple pipes to elaborate bongs), and even a large assortment of adult movies and "marital aids" (anything you might imagine and some things you probably wouldn't have thought of in a lifetime). If you mention illegal narcotics, they won't sell you any smoking devices. Keep the kids outside: despite a separate section, the adult items are in plain sight.

Tony's Trading Post

Downtown, Duluth • 3 W. Superior St. • (218) 727-3872 • M–Sat. 10 A.M. - 5 P.M. / Sun. 12 P.M. - 4 P.M.

Walking into Tony's Trading Post, you're greeted by the unmistakable aroma of taxidermied critters and "Old Whitey," a huge polar bear who once lived at St. Paul's Como Park Zoo. A notecard explains that when a man trespassed in the bear's habitat, Whitey attacked him, and police were forced to shoot the bear. The man was fined $100. Besides this sad tale, Tony's offers a truly unique environment and selection of animal-related goods, including taxidermied animals of all sizes from North America and Africa, mounted animal heads, pelts, claws, leather, antler lamps and chandeliers, fur hats, and more. The shop also has a variety of American Indian arts and crafts, T-shirts, and military collectibles. A family-owned business for over 30 years, Tony's is a real trading post and will buy, sell, and trade goods with its customers.

Cool Toys for Good Girls & Boys

Explorations
Downtown, Duluth • 201 W. Superior St. • (218) 722-1651 • M–F 9 A.M. - 5:30 P.M. / Sat. 9 A.M. - 5 P.M.

Explorations is to toy stores what PBS is to television. There are no yapping mechanical dogs tethered to the entryway, no Pokemon anything anywhere. Instead, Explorations is filled with toys that will make kids think and have fun at the same time. The store offers developmental toys and games for kids of all ages, along with quality books, toys for infants, and fun stuff like stickers and rocks. Stow the kids in the children's play area while you look around for that perfect gift idea or new family game. If you're not sure what to get, the knowledgeable staff can help you find something appropriate for and popular with any age group. Educators, check out Explorations's selection of quality teaching materials. One more good thing about Explorations: it's directly accessible from the Skywalk.

Toys for Keeps
Downtown, Duluth • 313 W. Superior St. (Skywalk Level) • (218) 720-3568 • M–F 9:30 A.M. - 5 P.M. / Sat. 10 A.M. - 5 P.M. (Extended holiday hours after Thanksgiving)

Toys for Keeps, a specialty toy and gift store, has been in business for 16 years, 4 of those with current owner Cindy McCabe at the helm. McCabe stocks her shop with toys she describes as innovative and engaging and challenging to the child. The shop carries toys for children of all ages from makers like Playmobil, Brio, and Breyer. Toys for Keeps offers a wide selection of plush critters by Gund, Ty, Steiff, and others, as well as a variety of puzzles, craft kits, games, and train sets. One of the shop's most notable features is its gallery of dolls (both playable and collectible) which hosts a selection not likely to be rivaled anywhere else in the region. Free gift wrapping is available, and the shop will prepare items for shipping upon request.

Better Homes & Gardens

Angela's Bella Flora

Downtown, Duluth • 138 W. 1st St. • (218) 279-3444 • M–F 8 A.M. - 6 P.M. / Sat. 9 A.M. - 5 P.M.

Open since 2000, Angela's Bella Flora has made its mark on downtown Duluth with its eye-catching signage and elegantly dressed windows. Just have a glance as you walk past and you'll see this is a place where even Martha would shop. Inside, the shop has a secret garden feel, its shelves filled with high-quality decorative items for the home, such as candles and candle holders, vases, dried flower arrangements, and wreaths. Angela's is also a full–service florist, offering everything from fresh cut flowers and delivery of bouquets to full wedding arrangements. Angela's Bella Flora encourages you to bring the outdoors in and provides everything you need to do it.

Grotto Home & Garden

East End, Duluth • 1434 E. Superior St. • (218) 728-7995 • M–Sat. 10 A.M. - 5 P.M.

Aptly named, Grotto Home & Garden is located in the basement of a quaint corner building many Duluthians and visitors will remember as the home of the Patty Cake Shop—a neighborhood bakery that occupied that spot for decades. While the shop is in a basement, the owners use the lack of natural light to great advantage, employing small lamps throughout to enhance the romantic atmosphere. Entering Grotto Home & Garden you get the feeling you've somehow been transported to a market in Provence. In fact, many of the shop's wares are French in origin, and those that aren't would find themselves at home there. The shop offers dried flowers, cast iron garden items, candles, lamps, French soaps and tea towels, aromatherapeutic household cleaning supplies, and much more. Grotto Home & Garden also creates and delivers unique dried flower arrangements.

Reading Material & Much More

Fragments of History

Downtown, Duluth • 1 W. Superior St. • (218) 786-0707 • M 1 P.M. - 8 P.M. / T.–Fri. 10 A.M. - 6 P.M. / Weekend hours vary

Fragments of History may at first glance seem like just another antique shop, but if you look closer you'll see it's much more. The shop offers an exceptional, well-organized, and neatly displayed selection of rare books (each hardcover is protected by a custom-fitted cellophane wrapper), as well as quality antiques, toys, photographs, prints, autographs, postcards, coins, estate jewelry, and much more. Collectors interested in a specific subject will appreciate owner Terry Roses's binders, organized by subject, filled with postcards and other documents on a variety of topics. If you don't see something you're looking for, be sure to ask—Roses's collection is too extensive to be displayed in the shop alone. Fragments of History also offers appraisal, book search, and estate liquidation services.

The Globe

Downtown, Superior • 1430 Tower Ave. • (715) 392-2090 • Daily 7:30 A.M. - 9 P.M.

Globe News has occupied the same corner space of a historic downtown Superior brick and brownstone building for decades. The building alone, along with the Globe's plentiful old signage, makes it worth a visit. But don't neglect to stop in to check out the variety of wares available inside. As the name suggests, the Globe offers a full selection of periodicals and newspapers for all interests. But the Globe is much more than just an indoor newsstand. You'll also find racks of used paperbacks, bins of used CDs and LPs, as well as a greeting card area and a separate shop-within-a-shop of sports trading cards and other collectible memorabilia. Behind the register you'll find a mini-drugstore offering basics like toothpaste, antacids, batteries and the like—items specially suited for the sailors who frequent the shop.

Used Book Stores*

Amazing Alonzo's Paperback Exchange

Endion, Duluth • 1831 E. Superior St. • (218) 724-3431 • M–F 10 A.M. - 5 P.M. / Sat. 10 A.M. - 4:30 P.M.

Alonzo's offers a wide variety of paperbacks in a variety of genres. Many young adult, romance, western, and mystery series. A few inexpensive hardcovers also available.

Books Bound

East End, Duluth • 2109 E. Superior St. • (218) 722-1419 • M–F 11 A.M. - 6 P.M. / Sat. 10 A.M. - 5 P.M.

Books Bound specializes in used and rare books, especially children's and regional titles. They buy, sell, and restore books and will search for out-of-print titles.

Carlson Used Books & Records

Downtown, Duluth • 206 E. Superior St. • (218) 722-8447 • M–Sun. 10 A.M. - 11 P.M.

Carlson calls itself Duluth's best tourist attraction. With over half a million used books, it's at least the biggest used book store. It also has used records and an extensive "adult" section, so keep an eye on the kids.

Gabriel's Bookstore

Lakeside, Duluth • 4915 E. Superior St. • (218) 525-7542 • M–F 12:30 P.M. - 4:30 P.M. / Sat. 10 A.M. - 3:30 P.M.

Housed in the basement of the former St. Michael's Church school, Gabriel's is a volunteer-run store specializing in rare and used books, from Oscar Wilde first editions to Stephen King, and *old* record albums and maps.

*See also Fragments of History and The Globe (both on page 167).

Used Book Stores, continued

Old Town Antiques & Books
Downtown, Duluth • 102 E. Superior St. • (218) 722-5426 • M–Sat. 10 A.M. - 5 P.M. / Sun. 11 A.M. - 4 P.M.

Old Town Antiques & Books offers used books from several antique and used-book dealers, including North Woods Books. They'll buy your used books, whether you have one rare book or an entire library.

Sunhillow Books
Central Hillside, Duluth • 510 E. 4th St. • (218) 786-9624 • M, W, F 9 A.M. - 7:30 P.M. / T, Th, Sat. 9 A.M. - 5:30 P.M.

Sunhillow is fairly new to the Duluth used book game, but they already have an extensive collection, plus the largest selection of new magazines in town.

Windever Books
Lakeside, Duluth • (218) 525-3781 • By appointment and on the web (domain name not available in time for printing)

Windever specializes in children's and young adult titles but carries a wide variety of genres. Once located downtown, after Internet sales took off, they no longer needed brick-and-mortar space. Search for "Windever."

Second Look Books
Lincoln Park, Duluth • 1925 W. Superior St. • (218) 723-1366 • T–Sat. 9 A.M. - 5 P.M.

A huge collection of used paperbacks (Second Look is also a paperback exchange), including many romance and series titles and a few hardcover and children's titles. Second Look also has tons of used jigsaw puzzles.

Crafts & Hobbies

The Stamping Post

Spirit Valley (West Duluth), Duluth • 5705 Grand Ave. • (218) 624-4722 • M–F 10 A.M. - 5:30 P.M. / T 'til 8 P.M. / Sat. 10 A.M. - 5 P.M.

Stamping, scrap-booking, and paper-making supplies, stickers, wrapping paper, stationery, pens, and more.

Creations Unlimited

Spirit Valley (West Duluth), Duluth • 319 N. Central Ave. • (218) 628-2900 • M–F 10 A.M. - 5 P.M. / Sat. 10 A.M. - 4 P.M.

Quilting supplies: fabric, notions, tools, books, etc.

Fabric Works

Downtown, Superior • 1320 Tower Ave. • (715) 392-7060 • M, T, W, F 9:30 A.M. - 5 P.M. / Th. 'til 8 P.M. / Sat. 10 A.M. - 4 P.M.

Quilting supplies: fabric, notions, tools, books, etc.

Superior Beads

Lakeside, Duluth • 4521 E. Superior St. • (218) 525-7434 • M–F 9:30 A.M. - 5:30 P.M. / Sat. 9:30 A.M. - 5 P.M.

Beading and jewelry-making supplies: Seed beads, delicas, findings, castings, semi-precious stones, etc.

The Bead Palette

Chester Park, Duluth • 1826 E. 8th St. • (218) 728-9332 • M–Th. 12 P.M. - 7 P.M. / Fri. 12 P.M. - 5 P.M. / Sat. 10 A.M. - 5 P.M.

Beading and jewelry-making supplies: Seed beads, charms, vintage beads & buttons, stones, closures, etc.

Crafts & Hobbies, continued

Duluth Leather & Craft
Downtown, Duluth • 22 N. 2nd Ave. W. • (218) 722-9074 • M–F 9 A.M. - 5:30 P.M. / Sat. 9 A.M. - 3 P.M.

Leather-working supplies: Tools, kits, belts, buckles, bead supplies, etc.

Cogwheel
Lakeside, Duluth • 4328 E. Superior St. • (218) 525-6474 • M, T & Th.–Sat. 9 A.M. - 5 P.M. / W 9 A.M. - 9 P.M.

Stained glass supplies and classes, other crafting supplies such as styrofoam forms, wood items, and paints.

Carrs Hobbies
Lincoln Park, Duluth • 2009 W. Superior St. • (218) 722-7129 • M–Sat. 9 A.M. - 5 P.M.

Planes, trains, or automobiles, Carrs is a model-builder's paradise, and the store is full of railroad antiques.

Lester River Fly Shop
Downtown, Duluth • 308 E. Superior St. • (218) 727-1789 • M, T, Th., F 10 A.M. - 7 P.M. / Sat. 9 A.M. - 5 P.M.

One-stop fly fishing paradise, whether you buy 'em or tie 'em yourself. Full fishing outfits and classes available.

Lake Superior Smokin' Brews
Downtown, Duluth • 320 E. Superior St. • (218) 724-3491 • M–F 10 A.M. - 6 P.M. / Sat. 11 A.M. - 5 P.M.

All your home beer-, wine-, and even liqueur-making needs, plus a large assortment of fine cigars.

Laundromats with a Spin

Chester Park Laundromat: Birds & the Great Outdoors

Chester Park/Endion, Duluth • 1328 E. 4th St. • (218) 724-5025 • M–Sun. 6 A.M. - 11 P.M.

Serving Hillside residents and UMD and St. Scholastica students for years, the Chester Park Laundromat might be one of the more unique clothes washing facilities anywhere. Besides your choice of double- and top-loading washers, you can enjoy the sounds of parakeets singing and parrots chatting from within an enclosed aviary. If you get bored with the birds, enjoy Chester Creek, right across the street.

Lincoln Park Wash 'n' Web Laundry: Internet Surfing & Laundry Roulette

Lincoln Park, Duluth • 10 N. 20th Ave. W. • (218) 722-3220 • M–Sun. 8 A.M. - 8 P.M.

If you have a pile of dirty clothes and want to explore the internet, then Lincoln Park Wash 'n' Web has everything you need. The laundromat makes available to its customers five computers hooked up to high-speed internet access—for free! The only catch is that you have to do your laundry at Lincoln Park. You can also play "Laundry Roulette" (the machines are set to randomly allow free loads).

Spirit Valley Laundry: Washing in a Greenhouse

Spirit Valley (West Duluth), Duluth • 232 Central Ave. • (218) 628-3147 • M–F 8 A.M. - 9 P.M. / Sat.–Sun. 8 A.M. - 8 P.M.

The Spirit Valley Laundry facility is impressive. It boasts over 120 washing machines in six different styles (top loaders, side loaders, double loaders) plus extractors and plenty of dryers. The thing is, you hardly notice all the machinery because the place is filled with plants—over 200 the last time anyone bothered to count. The plants help dilute the chemical smells of detergents and fabric softeners, making laundry day a bit more pleasant.

Saunas

Duluth Family Sauna

Downtown, Duluth • 18 N. 1st Ave. E. • (218) 726-1388 • Sun.–Th. 12 P.M. - 10 p.m. / F–Sat. 12 P.M. - 10:30 P.M.

Family-owned since 1922, Duluth Family Sauna is a slice of Minnesota history—one of the state's last vestiges of the days-gone-by tradition of public saunas. The high-ceilinged, ceramic-tiled lobby hints at grander times, but still retains some of its original charm. The establishment's main floor features six individual, private saunas (some constructed of cedar, some tiled), each adjoining a sitting room of sorts. The sitting rooms contain a bed, table, and chair, as well as a TV/VCR and stereo. A stint in a private sauna costs $11 per person, $15 per couple. Duluth Family Sauna's lower floor contains its "men's club," a private club featuring both smoking and non-smoking lounges and a large sauna for patrons to share. You'd be hard pressed to find a more unique way to warm your feet on a chilly winter day in Duluth.

Yoshika Sauna

Lincoln Park, Duluth • 18 N. 21st Ave. W. • (218) 722-5225 • Open 24 hours a day, seven days a week

Note that there is no "family" in the name of this one. We can't tell you much about this place because even though it's open around the clock each and every day of the year, we never made it through the door. We found the Yoshika Sauna's locked door in a small, dark entryway and pushed a grimy buzzer. Shortly thereafter, a young woman slid open a small window and told us that "all the saunas [were] down." However, she told us, we could still get an "erotic message." We passed. Enter at your own risk.

Tattoo Parlors

As any Great Lakes sailor will tell you, there's nothing like a permanent ink stain under your skin to commemorate a weekend in the Twin Ports. How about a begging seagull on your shoulder? A "state bird" mosquito? Perhaps the Aerial Lift Bridge across your chest. Whatever you want, the shops below will be happy to ink you up. But remember, whatever you choose will be with you for *the rest of your life* (unless you undergo laser surgery).

Everlasting Tattoo Studio
Downtown, Duluth • 207 E. Superior St. • (218) 722-6745 • M–Sat. 12 P.M. - 9 P.M.

Featuring the award-winning work of artists Jay and Ritt Graham. Body piercing available.

Superior Tattoo Studio
North End, Superior • 818 Tower Ave. • (715) 392-9004 • T–Sat. 5 P.M. - 12 A.M.

Tattoo artist Zono claims to have the largest selection and lowest prices in the Twin Ports. No piercings.

Tatts by Zapp
Downtown, Duluth • 122 W. 1st St. • (218) 733-9019 • M–Sat. 12 P.M. - 9 P.M. (W closes at 5 P.M.)

Zapp was voted Artist of the Year at the 7th World Tattoo Convention and guarantees all his work.

True Colors Tattoo Studio
East End, Superior • 2301 E. 5th St. • (715) 398-6331 • M–Sun. 6 P.M. - 11 P.M.

Jim, the tattoo artist with no last name, won first place at Lakeview Castle's annual tattoo convention.

Gifts Galore

Mainstreet Gifts

Lakeside, Duluth • 4433 E. Superior St. • (218) 525-3755 • M–F 9:30 A.M. - 5:30 P.M. / Sat. 9:30 A.M. - 5 P.M.

Mainstreet Gifts, located in a quaint corner building of the Lakeside neighborhood, offers a variety of gift items from quality makers. Throughout its two tastefully decorated rooms you'll find Ty Beanie Babies, Burt's Bees bath and body products, Mary Engelbreit decorative items, Department 56 figurines, seasonal décor items, candles, dinnerware, and more.

Rocking Horse Gift Shoppe

Downtown, Superior • 310 Belknap St. • (715) 392-5141 • M–Sat. 10 A.M. - 5 P.M.

Throughout its over ten years in business, Rocking Horse Gift Shoppe has gradually expanded from one room to five rooms full of quality craft and gift items, so come with plenty of time to browse. You'll find framed works, braided rugs, potpourri, wreaths, candles, tea towels, cloth napkins, table runners, Lang calendars, lots of seasonal décor items, and much more.

Lots of Fun

Spirit Valley (West Duluth), Duluth • 5626 Grand Ave. • (218) 624-0977 • M, Sat. 10 A.M. - 4 P.M. / T–F 10 A.M. - 5 P.M.

Lots of Fun features a large selection of craft and gift items covering a variety of styles. Among its offering of decorative items are stained glass window ornaments, framed artwork, handmade doilies, wreaths, swags, candles and candle holders, holiday and seasonal items, and collectibles such as Precious Moments figurines. Lots of Fun also offers useable items such as dinnerware, old-fashioned mixing bowls, coffee mugs, bulk potpourri, kitchen towels, hand-knitted dishcloths, and embellished sweatshirts.

Twin Ports Thrift Stores and Pawn Shops

Duluth

2nd Chance Furniture Outlet
2105 W. Superior St.
(218) 723-1785

2wice But Nice
2509 W. Superior St.
(218) 727-4030

Goodwill
700 Garfield Ave.
(218) 722-3050

St. Vincent DePaul
321 N. Central Ave.
(218) 624-7379

St. Vincent DePaul
109 W. 4th St.
(218) 727-9145

Salvation Army
2101 W. Superior St.
(218) 722-7723

Al's Duluth Pawn & Variety
118 W. 4th St.
(218) 727-3563

The Pawnbroker
701 E. 4th St.
(218) 722-8788

Twin Ports Pawn
18 W. 2nd St.
(218) 726-1716

Superior

Frank's New & Used Furniture
1402 Tower Ave.
(715) 392-6075

Goodwill
1717 Belknap St.
(715) 392-1726

Salvation Army
1621 Broadway St.
(715) 394-5331

Twin Ports Antique Stores (not including Canal Park)

Duluth

Antiques On Superior Street
11 W. Superior St.
(218) 722-7962

Clean Lines
2005 W. Superior St.
Phone number not available

East 4th Street Antiques
928 E. 4th St.
(218) 724-7656

Father Time Antiques
401 W. Superior St.
(218) 722-0629

Memory Lane Antiques
4721 E. Superior St.
(218) 525-7493

Moen's Miscellaneous Salvage
8 N. 2nd Ave. E.
(218) 727-8174 | call ahead

Old Town Antiques & Books
102 E. Superior St.
(218) 722-5426

The Rooster's Nest
101 W. 4th St.
(218) 279-2929

Seaman's Yesterday's Treasures
5617 Grand Ave.
(218) 628-1969

Sunset Antiques
2705 E. 5th St.
(218) 724-8215

A Vintage Attitude
406 W. Superior St.
(218) 279-2839

Woodland Antiques
1535 Woodland Ave.
(218) 728-1996

Superior

Allouez Antiques
4101 E. 2nd St.
(715) 398-0529

Bayside Warehouse
1515 N. 1st St.
(715) 395-9110

Billings Park Antiques
1822 Iowa Ave.
Phone number not available

Curious Goods
1717 Winter St.
(715) 392-7550

Northwind Antiques
2902 Belknap St.
(715) 394-7225

Superior Antique & Art Depot
933 Oakes Ave.
(715) 394-4611

North Shore Antique & Thrift Stores

Two Harbors

Adventure Mall Antiques
Highway 61
(218) 834-9330

Home Sweet Home Antiques
716 7th St.
(218) 834-4017

North Woods Antiques
2777 Highway 61
(218) 834-6456

Second Chance Antiques
127 7th St.
(218) 834-3334

Beaver Bay

Bay Antique Emporium
1008 Main St.
(218) 226-4626

Second Hand Rose
4898 Highway 61
(218) 226-4844

Grand Marais

Lake Superior Collectibles
Highway 61
(218) 387-2200

Rosebush Antiques And Gifts
101 W. Highway 61
(218) 387-1315

South Shore Antique & Thrift Stores

Cornucopia

The Hedgehog Shop
Huron Ave.
(715) 742-3284

Bayfield

Antiques at Twenty North First
20 N. 1st
(715) 779-3909

Bayfield Antique Jewelry
207 Rittenhouse Ave.
(715) 779-5904

Blue Water Antiques
104 Rittenhouse Ave.
(715) 779-2381

Washburn

Washburn Antiques
136 W. Bayfield St.
(715) 373-0926

Wooden Sailor Antiques
18 W. Bayfield St.
(715) 373-2680

Ashland

AP Cameras & Collectibles
Highway 2 (look for signs)
(715) 682-9132

Myott Antique Inn
2016 Lake Shore Dr. E.
(715) 682-5452

Senior Center Bargain Hut
420 Chapple Ave.
(715) 682-8522

Other Notable Shops Along the Shores

Towns along the North and South Shores are filled with all sorts of shops, but as tourism grows, many of them are turning into antique dealers and souvenir stands. We thought we'd mention a few places that remain unique.

Joyne's Department Store
Grand Marais, MN • 205 Wisconsin • (218) 387-2233 • M–Th., Sat. 8 A.M. - 6 P.M. / F 8 A.M. - 7 P.M.

Joyne's has been serving Grand Marais since the 1930s. A few souvenirs, but mostly lots of stuff you need and won't find in all of Grand Marais's ye olde touriste shoppes. Clothes, boots, gear, toiletries—Joyne's has it all.

Cornucopia's "Mini Mall"
Cornucopia, WI • Cornucopia Marina • Hours: According to one shopkeeper, "Some time in the morning 'til around 5 P.M."

Five gift/antique/used book shops in actual former fish processing shacks, worn and weathered with age: Good Earth Shop, What Goes 'Round, River's End, Art & Sol, and Sea Hag Antiques & Gifts.

Ehlers General Store
Cornucopia, WI • (715) 742-3232 • M–Sat. 8 A.M. - 6 P.M. / Sun. 8 A.M. - 1 P.M.

Since 1915 they've had a saying at Ehler's: "If we don't have it, you don't need it" Locals say if Ehler's doesn't have it, they'll get it for you within a week. A *real* general store with everything from fresh produce to motor oil.

Chequamegon Book & Coffee
Washburn, WI • 2 E. Bayfield • (715) 373-2899 • M– Sat. 10 A.M. - 6 P.M. / Sun. 10 A.M. - 5 P.M.

A wonderful used bookstore inside a classic old brownstone, specializing in regional and American Indian titles.

Places to Stay

(locally owned bed & breakfasts,
motels, & campgrounds)

Places to Stay

We held fast to one simple rule in this section: no chain hotels or motels or overgrown tourist resorts. Instead, we've tried to include all the locally owned places we could identify. Since we didn't have time to stay at each location, you'll want to call ahead not only for a reservation but also to find out what each has to offer—many don't have pools or restaurants or continental breakfasts.

Keep in mind that by listing these places to stay, we aren't recommending any of them in particular—we just want you to have an alternative to the nationwide franchises, as they tend to fill up before the smaller, local establishments do. Besides, our goal is to get you to venture away from the typical tourist spots, and that's where most chain motels are found.

We do know a few things about some of the hotels. The Voyageur on Superior Street in Duluth was modeled after a prison and once had secret passages and peepholes (which new owners have remodeled and removed). If you like dogs, stay at the Casa Motel in Duluth, where a black lab spends his days on the motel's front lawn. Duluth's Buena Vista on Skyline Parkway offers guests the best view of any inn in the city. The Androy in Superior and the Seaway in Duluth are for the adventurous—they're not exactly family friendly places (many guests are month-to-month residents). If you're a bicycle enthusiast, stay at the Willard Munger Inn, which has direct access to the Munger trail and bikes to rent. Finally, musicians in town for a gig and looking for a place to crash can call Mark Lindquist at Shaky Ray Records (see page 185).

You'll also want to check the "Events" chapter before planning a visit because some weekends are booked up to a year in advance. For instance, you have to be thinking well ahead of time if you want to stay in Duluth the weekend of Grandma's Marathon or the Bayfront Blues Festival. Bayfield is full on Apple Festival weekend, so you'll want to look to the other towns along the South Shore for somewhere to stay.

Places to Stay in Duluth

Bed & Breakfasts

A. Charles Weiss Inn
1615 E. Superior St.
(218) 724-7016 | 800-525-5243

A.G. Thomson House B&B
2617 E. 3rd St.
(218) 724-3464 | 877-807-8077

Cotton Mansion B&B
2309 E. 1st St.
(218) 724-6405

The Ellery House
28 S. 21st Ave. E.
(218) 724-7639

Firelight Inn On Oregon Creek
2211 E. 3rd St.
(218) 724-0272

Immigrant House
2104 E. Superior St.
(218) 724-3090

Lord Frazer House
2426 E. Superior St.
(218) 728-1889

Manor on the Creek Inn
2215 E. 2nd St.
(218) 728-3189

The Mansion
3600 London Rd.
(218) 724-0739

Mathew S. Burrows 1890 Inn
1632 E. 1st St.
(218) 724-4991

Olcott House B&B
2316 E. 1st St.
(218) 728-1339 | 800-715-1339

PJ's B&B
5757 Bergquist Rd.
(218) 525-2508

Stanford Inn
1415 E. Superior St.
(218) 724-3044

Places to Stay in Duluth, continued

Hotels & Motels

Airliner Motel
5002 Miller Trunk Highway
(218) 729-6628

Allyndale Motel
66th Ave. W. & Cody St.
(218) 628-1061

Buena Vista Motel
1144 Mesaba Ave.
(218) 722-7796

Casa Motel
923 E. Central Entrance
(218) 727-9229

Chalet Motel
1801 London Rd.
(218) 728-4238

Cody Inn
6716 Cody St.
(218) 628-2380

Duluth Motel
4415 Grand Ave.
(218) 628-1008

Edgetown Motel
5150 Miller Trunk Highway
(218) 729-9806

Gardenwood Motel & Cabins
5107 North Shore Dr.
(218) 525-1738

Grand Motel
4312 Grand Ave.
(218) 624-4821

Inn on Gitche Gumee
8517 Congdon Blvd.
(218) 525-4979

Lake Breeze Motel Resort
9000 Congdon Blvd.
(218) 525-6808

Mountain Villas
9525 W. Skyline Pkwy.
(218) 624-5784 | 800-642-6377

Seaway Hotel
2001 W. Superior St.
(218) 722-7476
(also home to month-to-month
residents; not a "family" motel)

Skyline Court Motel
4880 Miller Trunk Highway
(218) 727-1563

Sundown Motel
5310 Thompson Hill Rd.
(218) 628-3613

Voyageur Lakewalk Inn
333 E. Superior St.
(218) 722-3911

Places to Stay in Duluth, continued

Hotels & Motels, cont.

Willard Munger Inn
7408 Grand Ave.
(218) 624-4814

West Duluth Hotel
303 N. Central Ave.
(218) 624-9776

Camping

Buffalo Valley Camping
2586 Guss Rd.
(218) 624-9901

Eagle's Nest Resort
6103 LaVaque Rd.
(218) 721-4147

Indian Point Campground
902 S. 69th Ave. W.
(218) 624-5637

Island Beach Camp Grounds
6640 Fredenberg Lake Rd.
(218) 721-3292

Knife Island Campground
234 Highway 61 W.
(218) 879-6063

River Place Camp & Bait Shop
9902 Hudson Blvd.
(218) 626-1390

Silver Fox Lodge
7495 Boulder Lake Rd.
(218) 721-4840

Spirit Mountain Camp Ground
9500 Spirit Mountain Pl.
(218) 628-8544

Musicians' Crash Pad

If you or your band are in the Twin Ports for a gig and need a place to crash, call Mark Lindquist at Shaky Ray Records. Lindquist, a local writer, musician (Giljunko), and producer, will be happy to put you up:

The Shaky Ray
923 N. 12th Ave. E.
(218) 728-1795
shakyray@aol.com

Places to Stay in Superior

Bed & Breakfasts

Crawford House B&B
2016 Hughitt Ave.
(715) 394-5271

Gull Wing Inn B & B
2302 E. 7th St.
(715) 398-3986

Raspberry Inn
1616 John Ave.
(715) 394-7277

Hotels & Motels

Androy Hotel
1213 Tower Ave.
(715) 394-7731
(also home to month-to-month
residents; not a "family" motel)

Barker's Island Inn
300 Marina Dr.
(715) 392-7152

Bay Motel
306 E. 3rd St.
(715) 392-5166

Budget Uptown Motel
104 E. 5th St.
(715) 394-4449

Driftwood Motel
2200 E. 2nd St.
(715) 398-6661

Lakeview Motel
2821 E. 2nd St.
(715) 398-3589

Manning Motel
3209 Belknap St.
(715) 392-2281

Park Motel
3411 Belknap St.
(715) 392-6226

Prime Rate Inn
110 E. 2nd St.
(715) 392-4873 | 888-515-5040

Shore Line Motel
2302 E. 2nd St.
(715) 398-6688

Places to Stay in Superior, continued

Hotels & Motels, cont.

Sleepy Hollow Motel
7811 E. Highway 2
(715) 398-6989

Stockade Motel
1616 E. 2nd St.
(715) 398-3585

Sunshine Motel
1807 N. 58th St.
(715) 394-7055

Superior Inn
525 Hammond Ave.
(715) 394-7706

Campgrounds

Amnicon Acres Campground
4505 E. Tri Lakes
(715) 399-8443

Manitou Valley Campground
3467 E. Manitou Valley
(715) 399-8469

Places to Stay Along the North Shore

Bed & Breakfasts

Scenic Highway 61

Spinnaker Inn B&B
5427 North Shore Dr.
(218) 525-9292

Two Harbors

Bryan House B&B
123 3rd Ave.
(218) 834-2950

J. Gregers Inn
3320 Highway 61
(218) 226-4614 | 888-226-4614

Lighthouse B&B
Lighthouse Point
(218) 834-4814

Silver Bay

Guest House
299 Outer Dr.
(218) 226-4201

Little Marais

The Stone Hearth Inn B&B
6598 Lakeside Estates Rd.
(218) 226-3020

Grand Marais

Bally's B&B & Boarding House
121 E. 3rd St.
(218) 387-1817 | 888-383-1817

Dream Catcher B&B
2614 County Road 7
(218) 387-2876

MacArthur House B&B
520 W. 2nd St.
(218) 387-1840

Old Shore Beach B&B
1434 Old Shore Rd.
888-387-9707

Pincushion Mountain B&B
968 Gunflint Trail
(218) 387-1276

Poplar Creek Guesthouse
Gunflint Trail
(218) 388-9476 | 800-322-8327

Snuggle Inn B&B
8 7th Ave. W.
(218) 387-2847

Superior Overlook B&B
1620 E. Highway 61
(218) 387-1571 | 800-855-7622

Places to Stay Along the North Shore, continued

Motels, Inns, & Cabins

Scenic Highway 61

Emily's Inn & Deli
218 North Shore Dr.
(218) 834-5922

Heinz Beachway Motel & Cabins
5119 North Shore Dr.
(218) 525-5191

Lakeview Castle Motel
5135 North Shore Dr.
(218) 525-1014

North Shore Cottages
7717 North Shore Dr.
(218) 525-2812

Shorecrest Motel
5593 North Shore Dr.
(218) 525-2286

Two Harbors

Cliff 'n' Shore Motel & Cabins
1810 Silver Cliff Rd.
(218) 834-4675

Flood Bay Motel
1511 Highway 61
(218) 834-4076

**Gooseberry Park Motel
& Lake Cabins**
2778 E. Highway 61
(218) 834-3751 | (218) 834-6087

Grand Superior Lodge
2826 E. Highway 61
(218) 834-3796 | 800-627-9565

Radosevich's Earthwood Inn
933 Stanley Rd.
(218) 834-3847

Silver Cliff Motel
436 A E. Highway 61
(218) 834-4695

Stone Gate Resort
P.O. Box 72
E. Highway 61
(218) 834-3355

Viking Motel
1429 7th Ave.
(218) 834-2645

Voyageur Motel
1227 7th Ave.
(218) 834-3644

Places to Stay Along the North Shore, continued

Motels, Inns, & Cabins, cont.

Beaver Bay

Beaver Bay Inn
Highway 61
(218) 226-4351

Cove Point Lodge
Highway 61
(218) 226-3221

Silver Bay

Mariner Motel
46 Outer Dr.
(218) 226-4488

Northland Trails Guest House
36 Shopping Center
(218) 226-4199

Whispering Pines Motel
5763 Highway 61
(218) 226-4712

Schroeder

Superior Ridge Resort & Motel
Highway 61
(218) 663-7189

Tofte

Bluefin Bay
7192 W. Highway 61
(218) 663-7296

Chateau Leveaux
(218) 663-7223

Gull Harbor Condominiums
6554 W. Highway 61
(218) 663-7205

Lutsen

Caribou Highlands Lodge
371 Ski Hill Rd.
(218) 663-7241 | 800-642-6036

Cascade Lodge
3719 W. Highway 61
(218) 387-1112 | 800-322-9543

Eagle Ridge
565 Ski Hill Rd.
800-686-4669

Lutsen's Mountain Inn
(218) 663-7244

Lutsen Resort & Sea Villas
(218) 663-7212

Solbakken Resort
4874 W. Highway 61
(218) 663-7566

Places to Stay Along the North Shore, continued

Motels, Inns, & Cabins, cont.

Spruce Falls Cabins
4140 W. Highway 61
(218) 387-2558

Thompsonite Beach
2920 W. Highway 61
(218) 387-1532

Grand Marais

Aspen Lodge
310 Highway 61
(218) 387-2500

Devil Track Lodge
205 Fireweed Ln.
(218) 387-9414

East Bay Hotel
(218) 387-2800

Gunflint Motel
101 W. 5th
(218) 387-1454

Harbor Inn
(218) 387-1191 | 800-595-4566

Lund's Motel & Cottages
(218) 387-2155

Naniboujou Lodge
Highway 61
(218) 387-2688

Nelson's Cabins & Motel
(218) 387-1464 | 800-249-1285

Opel's Lakeside Cabins
(218) 387-2754

Outpost Motel
2935 E. Highway 61
(218) 387-1833 | 888-380-1833

Sandgren Motel
Highway 61
(218) 387-2975

Seawall Motel & Cottages
301 W. Highway 61
(218) 387-2095

Shoreline
20 S. Broadway
(218) 387-2633 | 800-247-6020

Trailside Cabins & Motel
1100 W. Highway 61
(218) 387-1550

Wedgewood Motel
1663 E. Highway 61
(218) 387-2944

Grand Portage

Grand Portage Lodge & Casino
(218) 475-2401 | 800-543-1384

Ryden's Border Store & Motel
Highway 61
(218) 475-2330

Places to Stay Along the North Shore, continued

Campgrounds

Scenic Highway 61

Duluth Tent & Trailer Camp
8411 Congdon Blvd.
(Scenic Hwy. 61)
(218) 525-1350

Knife River Campground
196 Scenic Highway 61
(218) 834-5044

Penmarallter Campground
725 Scenic Highway 61
(218) 834-4603

Two Harbors

Big Blaze Camp & Cabins
560 Big Blaze Circle
(218) 834-2512

Burlington Bay Campgrounds
626 Park Rd.
(218) 834-2021

Wagon Wheel Campsite
(218) 834-4901

Schroeder

Lamb's Resort & Campground
Highway 61
(218) 663-7292

Silver Bay

Northern Exposure Campground
5346 Highway 61
(218) 226-3324

Grand Marais

Go-Fer Campground
1201 E. 5th St.
(218) 387-1252

Grand Marais Campground
(218) 387-1712 | 800-998-0959

Gunflint Pines
Gunflint Trail
(218) 388-4454

Okontoe Family Campsites
110 Bow Lake Rd.
(218) 388-2285

Recreation Resource Management
22 Pine Mountain Ct.
(218) 387-2609

Places to Stay Along the South Shore

B & Bs and Cottages

Port Wing

Garden House B & B
9255 Sunnyside Ln.
(715) 774-3705

Holiday Pines Resort
9130 Beach Rd.
(715) 774-3555

Cornucopia

The Fo'c'sle B & B
Highway 13
(715) 742-3337

Lazy Susan's Bed & Brunch
89405 Jack Pine Dr.
(715) 742-3443

Swenson's Cottages
88700 Siskiwit Falls Rd.
(715) 742-3282

Bayfield

Apple Tree Inn B & B
Highway 13
(715) 779-5572

Artesian House
Route 1, Box 218K
(715) 779-3338

Cooper Hill House
33 S. 6th St.
(715) 779-5060

Grey Oak Guest House
105 S. 7th St.
(715) 779-3690

Old Rittenhouse Inn
301 Rittenhouse Ave.
(715) 779-3264

Thimbleberry Inn B & B
15021 Pageant Rd.
(715) 779-5757

Bayfield Inn (Vincent Taylor Lodging)
17 S. 1st St.
(715) 779-5905

Washburn

Pilgrim's Rest
Route 1, Box 39-K
(715) 373-2964

Valhalla View
Route 1, County Trunk C
(715) 373-5321

Ashland

The Residenz B & B
723 Chapple Ave.
(715) 682-2425

Places to Stay Along the South Shore, continued

Hotels & Motels

Port Wing

The Village Inn
Highway 13 & County Trunk C
(715) 742-3941

Herbster

Beach Resort
87460 Bark Point Rd.
(715) 774-3826

Willow Motel
P.O. Box 52
(715) 774-3385

Cornucopia

South Shore Motel
Superior Ave. & Highway 13
(715) 742-3244

Bayfield

Apostle View Inn
Highway 13
(715) 779-3385

Bay Front Inn
15 Front St.
(715) 779-3880

Bayfield Inn
20 Rittenhouse Ave.
(715) 779-3363

Bayfield Waterfront Lodging
308 N. 2nd St.
(715) 779-9747

Brookside Motel
Port Superior Village
(715) 779-5123

Chapman House
100 Rittenhouse Ave.
(715) 779-9576

Dreamcatcher Lodging
Highway 13
(715) 779-5538

Greunke's First Street Inn
17 Rittenhouse Ave.
(715) 779-5480

Harbor's Edge Motel
33 N. Front St.
(715) 779-3962

Isaac Wing House
17 S. 1st St.
(315) 779-3907

Leeward Lodging
308 N. 2nd St.
(715) 779-9747

Pinehurst Inn at Pikes Creek
R.R. 1, Box 222
(715) 779-3676

Places to Stay Along the South Shore, continued

Hotels & Motels, cont.

Seagull Bay Motel
325 S. 7th St.
(715) 779-5558

Silvernail Guest House
249 Rittenhouse Ave.
(715) 779-5575

Winfield Inn
100 Lynde Ave.
(715) 779-3252

Washburn

Redwood Motel & Chalets
26 W. Bayfield St.
(715) 373-5512
Rocky Run

1000 Superior Ave.
(715) 373-2551

Washburn Motel
800 W. Bayfield St.
(715) 373-5580

Ashland

Anderson's Chequamegon Motel
2200 Lake Shore Dr. W.
(715) 682-4658 | 800-727-2776

Ashland Motel
2300 Lake Shore Dr. W.
(715) 682-5503

Bayview Motel
2419 Lake Shore Dr. E.
(715) 682-5253

Bell Motel
407 Lake Shore Dr. E.
(715) 682-4109

Crest Motel
115 Sanborn Ave.
(715) 682-6603

Farm House
R.R. 4, Box 79
(715) 685-9778

Harbor Motel
1206 Lake Shore Dr. W.
(715) 682-5211

Hotel Chequamegon
101 Lake Shore Dr. W.
(715) 682-9095

Lake Aire Inn
101 Lake Shore Dr. E.
(715) 682-4551 | 888-666-2088

Lakeside Motel
1706 Lake Shore Dr. W.
(715) 682-4575

Mission Springs Resort
30175 Mission Springs Rd.
(715) 682-5014

Town Motel
920 Lake Shore Dr. W.
(715) 682-5555

Places to Stay Along the South Shore, continued

Camping & Cabins

Port Wing

Anchor Inn Campground
Highway 13
(715) 774-3658

Deering Tourist Homes
22545 Highway 13
(715) 742-3994

Lake Superior Campground
145 Beach Rd.
(715) 774-3231

Bayfield

**Apostle Islands
Area Campgrounds**
Star Route Rd., Box 8
(715) 779-5524

Buffalo Bay Campground
19550 Campground Rd.
(715) 779-3743

Dalrymple Campground
N. Highway 13
(715) 779-5712

Point Detour Campground
3 miles north of Bayfield on
Highway 13
(715) 779-3743

Washburn

Big Rock Park Campground
3 miles north of Washburn
on County Trunk C
No phone number available

Memorial Park
East end of Washburn
(715) 373-6174

West End Park
West end of Washburn
(715) 373-6174

Apostle Islands

Big Bay State Park
Madeline Island
(715) 747-6425

Big Bay Town Park
Madeline Island
(715) 747-6913

**Apostle Islands National
Lakeshore**
(715) 779-3397
www.nps.gov/apis/camping.htm

Ashland

Kreher Park
2020 6th St.
(715) 682-7061

Shady Oaks Lodge
Rte. 4, Box 18
(715) 682-4659

Annual Events

(festivals, parades, and other
yearly get-togethers)

Annual Events

When you're planning a weekend along the shores of Lake Superior, take events into consideration. There may be some you won't want to miss and some you might want to avoid. For example, a trip to Duluth on the same weekend as the Bayfront Blues Fest or Grandma's Marathon requires some planning, as area hotels are booked a year in advance. You'll find similar difficulties finding accommodations in Bayfield during the Apple Festival. Since many events are held on weekends and costs change from year to year, call for specific dates and prices.

January

Warmer by the Lake
Duluth, MN • January 1 • (218) 723-3337 • FREE

Hayrides, sledding, skating, bonfire, fireworks, free hot chocolate and cookies at Bayfront Park.

Sleigh & Cutter Parade
Duluth, MN • mid January • (715) 378-2392 • FREE

Parade of horse-drawn antique & restored sleighs and bobsleds at Lester Park Golf course; rides available.

Annual Memorial Winter Carnival (a.k.a. "Just for the Halibut")
Duluth, MN • late January • (218) 723-3567 • FREE

Three days of luge rides, lutefisk eating contests, and many other activities in West Duluth.

February

John Beargrease Sled Dog Marathon
Duluth, MN • early February • (218) 722-7631 • FREE

Watching the sled dog teams take off makes for a fun family outing.

Annual Art Show at M & I Bank
Ashland, WI • early February • (715) 682-3422 • FREE

Local art from local artists.

Asaph Whittlesey Showshoe Race
Bayfield, WI • early February • (715) 779-3335 • FREE

All things snowshoe to celebrate the 1870s-era legislator who snowshoed 250 miles to prove a point: races, volleyball, obstacle course, fireworks, cabaret, an Asaph Whittlesey look-alike contest, and more.

February, continued

Run on Water
Bayfield, WI • early February • (715) 779-3335 • FREE

A five-mile foot race over frozen Lake Superior on the "ice road" from Bayfield to Madeline Island and back.

Undergroundhog Day
Duluth, MN • First Saturday • (218) 727-7585

Several local bands play two stages at the historic NorShor Theatre. (Small cover charge.)

Winter Frolic & Showshoe Challenge
Two Harbors, MN • early February • 800-777-7384 • FREE

Pancake breakfast, showshoe race, sliding, snow sculptures, kids' games, and the "Smoosh" race.

Winter Lakefest
Ashland, WI • mid February • 800-284-9484 • FREE

Broomball tournaments, flying kites on the ice, sled dog rides, and more.

Book Across the Bay
Ashland, WI • mid February • 800-284-9484 • FREE

Cross-country skis and snowshoes move the Winter Lakefest (above) from Ashland to Washburn.

March

Annual Spring Carnival
Bayfield, WI • early March • (715) 779-3227 • FREE

Ski and snowboard competition, food, and fun at Mount Ashwaby.

Fun Fair
Duluth, MN • mid March • (218) 726-8564 • $4/person

A three-day indoor expo geared to kids, with rides, food, and music at the DECC auditorium.

Fitger's Bock Fest
Duluth, MN • mid March • (218) 722-8826 • FREE

Two days celebrating spring: music, contests, and bock beer caramelized with a red-hot poker.

April

Northland Folk Festival
Ashland, WI • mid April • (715) 682-1289 • FREE

Folk music, food, and crafts at Northland College.

Smelt Fry
Herbster, WI • late April • (715) 774-3427

Music and deep-fried fishies. (Cost unavailable.)

May

Homegrown Music Festival
Duluth, MN • First weekend • (218) 727-7585 • $10–$15

Up to 40 local and regional acts play for two days and nights at the NorShor Theatre and other venues.

Scandinavian Heritage Day
Ashland, WI • mid May • 800-284-9484 • FREE

Cultural displays, food, music, and dancing at the Bay Area Civic Center.

Big Top Chautauqua Tent Raising Social
Bayfield, WI • mid May • 888-244-8368 • FREE

A social gathering to help hoist the huge canvas. (The Big Top hosts world class folk and bluegrass music from June to September; cost varies with acts.)

Mayflower Festival at Chester Park
Duluth, MN • mid May • (218) 724-9832 • FREE

Music, flower market, kids' activities, craft village, etc.

Horse Extravaganza
Superior, WI • mid May • (715) 399-2928 • $3 per person

Expanded all-breed show, pony club tack sale, demos, equipment vendors, and model horse show at the Head of the Lakes Fairground.

June

Grandma's Marathon
Duluth, MN • mid-June • (218) 727-0947 • charge to see bands

Watch the race and enjoy live music, food, beer, and merchandise at Canal Park.

Testicle Festival
Port Wing, WI (Port Bar) • Father's Day • (715) 774-3731

Deep fried Rocky Mountain oysters are the catch of the day. (Cost unavailable.)

Park Point Rummage Sale
Duluth, MN • June • 800-438-5884 • FREE

The entire neighborhood fills its lawns and driveways with things they no longer want so you can buy them.

Ice Cream Social
Ashland, WI • late June • 800-284-9484 • cost unavailable

Gather on Ashland's courthouse lawn for music, hot dogs, brats, and ice cream, ice cream, ice cream.

Inland Sea Symposium
Bayfield, WI • late June • (715) 373-0760

Much ado about Lake Superior conservation and kayaking. (Cost unavailable.)

June, continued

Voyageur Art Show
Two Harbors, MN • mid June • (218) 834-2366 • FREE

Local art by local artists in a variety of media (no crafts) at the Two Harbors Art Center.

Blessing of the Fleet
Bayfield, WI • mid June • (715) 779-3335 • FREE

The annual tradition of blessing the fishing fleet dates back to Bayfield's early history.

Park Point Music Festival
Duluth, MN • late June • (218) 722-5883 • $12 adults, $6 kids

Mostly local music and food at the Park Point Recreation Facility; children six and under free.

Park Point Art Fair
Duluth, MN • late June • www.parkpoint.org • FREE

Sort of like the Park Point Rummage Sale, but instead of cast-offs, you can buy local art from local artists.

July

Annual Tour of Homes
Duluth, MN • mid July • (218) 724-3168 • $20 per person

Self-guided tours of Duluth's premier homes and gardens, followed by lunch.

Lake Superior Shakespeare Festival
Duluth, MN • July • (218) 590-6333 • call for ticket prices

Shakespeare plays and parodies performed outdoors at Leif Erickson Park.

Head of the Lakes Fair
Superior, WI • last week of July • (715) 394-7848 • $5/$2 kids

Carnival rides, races, and headliner entertainment at the Head of the Lakes fairground. Admission gets you into all the grandstand events.

Patriotic Parade
Ashland, WI • July 4 • 800-284-9484 • FREE

Fifty entries, from high school bands to VFW vets and Shriners—a quintessential Fourth of July parade.

Fourth Fest
Duluth, MN • July 4 • (218) 723-3337 • FREE

Music, food, rides, and what is often the largest fireworks display in the midwest at Bayfront Park.

July, continued

Cornucopia Community Club Fish Fry
Cornucopia, WI • First Sunday in July • (715) 742-3942

A feast of Lake Superior whitefish at Town Hall. (Cost unavailable.)

Heritage Days
Two Harbors, MN • early July • 800-554-2116 • FREE

Ethnic festival with art fair, rides, parade, merchants, sidewalk sales, and water ski show.

Bay Days
Ashland, WI • late July • 800-284-9484 • FREE

Off-road bike race, 10k run, sailboat races, arts & crafts, etc.

Festival of Arts
Bayfield, WI • late July • (715) 779-3335 • FREE

Food, art, and musical variety shows.

Woodies on the Water
Superior, WI • late July • (218) 722-7884 • FREE

Over 50 hand-built or restored wooden boats: canoes, sailboats, kayaks, mahogany runabouts, and power boats at Barker's Island.

Annual Festival of Music & Dance
Duluth, MN • mid July • (218) 727-0570 • FREE

The Ressl Dance company turns the Lakewalk into a long, narrow winding dance floor.

Grand Marais Arts Fair & Festival
Grand Marais, MN • mid July • (218) 387-1284 • FREE

A two-day festival featuring work by two- and three-dimensional artists, strolling musicians, and dancers.

Summer Solstice Celebration
Two Harbors, MN • mid July • (218) 834-4898 • Fundraiser

Bonfire, food, and music on the lawn at the lighthouse in Two Harbors; donations go toward the upkeep and maintenance of the lighthouse.

Two Harbors Folk Fest
Two Harbors, MN • mid July • (218) 834-2600 • $5 - $20

Concerts, workshops, dances, storytelling, artisans, food, and kids' tent at Van Hoven Park and Agate Bay; no alcohol or pets.

Brownstone Days
Washburn, WI • late July • (715) 373-5017 • FREE

A celebration centered on Washburn's many wonderful buildings made of brown Lake Superior sandstone (see page 82).

August

Spirit Valley Days
Duluth, MN • early August • (218) 624-7737 • FREE

Five days of fun in West Duluth: parade, street dance, food, beer garden, etc.

Lion's Club Fisherman's Picnic
Grand Marais, MN • early August • 888-922-5000

Four days of tournaments, fireworks, parade, street dances, raffle, kids' tractor pull, log sawing contest, etc. (Cost unavailable.)

Cornucopia Day
Cornucopia, WI • 2nd Saturday • (715) 742-3211 • FREE

Flea market, food, raffle, parade, fire trucks, kids' activities, and more.

Bayfront Blues Festival
Duluth, MN • early August • www.bayfrontblues.com

It's not all blues, but it's a fest: music, crafts, food, beer, and about 20 renditions of "Mustang Sally." (Prices go up yearly; $25 a day in 2002.)

Duluth International Folk Festival
Duluth, MN • August • (715) 398-5970 • $2/person, $5/family

Ethnic singers, dancers, musicians, exhibits, demonstrations, and food at Leif Erickson Park.

Corn Feed Fund Raiser
Herbster, WI • early August • (715) 774-3411

Music, games, crafts, and lots of food—including plenty of corn on the cob. (Donations accepted.)

Steam Train Days
Two Harbors, MN • mid August • (218) 834-5631 • FREE

Merchants, sidewalk sale, flea market, food, and trains, trains, trains.

Annual Midsummer Organic Food Fest
Duluth, MN • mid August • (218) 728-0884 • FREE

A celebration of organically grown foods and sustainable farming hosted by the Whole Foods Co-op.

Cook County Fair
Grand Marais, MN • mid August • (218) 387-3000

Exhibits, rides, animals, contests, and more.

Lake Superior Fish Boil
Bayfield, WI • late August • (715) 373-0495 • cost unavailable

Come for the fireball of fat, stay for the fish.

Lake County Fair
Two Harbors, MN • late August • (218) 834-8300

Exhibits, rides, horse show, animal barn, pie contest, and refreshments. (Cost unavailable.)

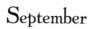

September

Duluth Preservation Alliance House Tour
Duluth, MN • early September • (218) 728-4903 • $15

Tour of five historic Duluth homes. (For a self-guided tour any time of the year, see pages 60–66).

Harvest Festival
Duluth, MN • early September • (218) 727-1414

Youth and family activities, live music, crafters, exhibits, etc. (Cost unavailable.)

Fish Boil & Craft Show
Port Wing, WI • early September • (715) 774-3624

At Port Wing's Port Bar; the regulars claim this is the largest fish boil in Wisconsin. (Cost unavailable.)

Lions Club Fall Festival & Craft Show
Port Wing, WI • early September • (715) 774-3624

Crafts, food, music, and more. (Cost unavailable.)

Barker's Island Sailing Regatta
Superior, WI • early September • 800-826-7010 • FREE

More than 40 boats race in this Lake Superior classic. Picnic follows the race.

Fall Color Car Show
Bayfield, WI • early September • (715) 779-3335

Beautiful fall colors and vintage cars in mint condition. (Cost unavailable.)

Annual Fallfest
Duluth, MN • early-mid September • (218) 724-9832 • $1

Food, crafts, games, music, and more at Chester Park.

Tour of Historic Buildings
Superior, WI • mid September • (715) 392-8449 • $10

Open houses at four historic sites in Superior, starting at the old Post Office.

Hawk Ridge Weekend
Duluth, MN • mid September • (218) 722-4011 • FREE

Watch the hawks come in—and help count them—on their annual migration to Hawk Ridge.

North Shore Inline Skating Marathon
Duluth, MN • mid September • (218) 723-1503 • FREE

With over 4,000 skaters, this is North America's largest inline skating race; spaghetti feed, expo, and festival. Free to watch.

September, continued

Fall Colorama
Superior, WI • mid September • (715) 399-3111 • FREE

Apple cider pressing, leaf printing, tree identification hike, Smokey the Bear, and more. (Pattison Park, 10 miles south of Superior on WI Highway 35).

Spirit of the Lake Fall Fest
Superior, WI • mid September • 800-942-5313 • FREE

One-hundred unit parade with dignitaries, marching and performing groups, bands, floats, horses, classic cars, etc.

Fisherfolk Art Show
Tofte, MN • mid September • (218) 663-7804 • $3, $5/Family

Juried art show with entries in all forms of artistic media portraying fishing in the lives of North Shore people.

Lester River Rendezvous
Duluth, MN • late September • (218) 525-0838

A reenactment of a 1780 voyageur village at Lester Park, with appropriately styled wares and food for sale. Live music, and kids' games. (Cost unavailable.)

October

Marketfest
Ashland, WI • early October • 800-284-9484 • FREE

A celebration of Ashland's shops.

Bayfield Apple Festival
Bayfield, WI • early October • (715) 779-3335 • FREE

Art & craft booths, food vendors, carnival, parade, fun run, live music, and—you guessed it—apples, apples, apples.

Art Show & Fall Flea Market
Cornucopia, WI • early October • (715) 742-3211 • FREE

Local artists and vendors show and sell their works and wares at the beach. (Usually the same weekend as Bayfield's Apple Festival.)

Duluth Art Fair
Duluth, MN • early October • (218) 724-4205 • FREE

Forty regional artists display their work at The Depot.

Scandinavian Festival
Superior, WI • early October • (218) 624-5158 • $2

Rosemaling, arts & crafts fair, demonstrations, and food and refreshments celebrating Scandinavian heritage at the Head of the Lakes Fairground.

October, continued

Whistlestop Festival
Ashland, WI · mid October · 800-284-9484

Marathon, 1/2 marathon, 5k race, 10k race, toddler's race, fish boil & pasta feed, rock 'n' roll fest, and blues 'n' brew fest. (Cost unavailable.)

Grand Marais Birding Festival
Grand Marais, MN · late October · 888-922-5000

Migratory birding field excursions, speakers, presenters, vendors, birding game show, and more. (Cost unavailable.)

Moose Madness
Grand Marais, MN · late October · 888-922-5000

Guided moose-calling excursions, moose T-shirts, desserts, gifts, and general community-wide "mooseness." (Cost unavailable.)

Jack O'Lantern Jamboree
Superior, WI · late October · (715) 996-2261

Pumpkin-carving contest, Halloween folklore, apple cider making, games, chili sampling, etc. (Pattison Park, 10 miles south of Superior on WI Highway 35; cost unavailable.)

Ship of Ghouls
Duluth, MN · mid-late October · (218) 722-5573

The *S.S. William A. Irvin* in Canal Park transforms from an ore boat to a ghost ship, complete with live ghouls and special effects; called "Minnesota's most famous Halloween attraction." (Costs change annually.)

Boo at the Zoo
Duluth, MN · October 31 · 723-3748 · $5 for trick-or-treaters

Trick-or-treating among the animals at the Lake Superior Zoo. (Just $1 for non-trick-or-treating kids.)

The Boogieman Project (a.k.a. "Old Ghosts")
Duluth, MN · Saturday closest to Halloween · (218) 727-7585

Several local bands play two stages at the historic NorShor Theatre. Everyone wears a costume, and the contest has become very competitive. (Small cover charge.)

November

Gales of November
Duluth, MN • early November • (218) 727-2497 • $15 - $60

Speakers on shipwrecks, lighthouses, diving, research, and other Lake Superior topics.

Edmund Fitzgerald Memorial and Beacon Lighting
Split Rock Lighthouse • November 10 • (218) 226-6372

A film about the *Fitzgerald* is screened; lighthouse tours close temporarily at 4:30 P.M. for the ceremony. (Adults $4, children 6–12 $3.)

Christmas Bazaar
Port Wing, WI • late November • (715) 774-3624

Celebrate Christmas in November in the oldest active fishing village in Wisconsin. (Cost unavailable.)

Volunteer Fire Department's Annual Turkey Feed
Cornucopia, WI • late November • (715) 742-3211

A Thanksgiving dinner preview to help raise funds for Corny's Bravest held the Sunday before Turkey Day. (Cost unavailable.)

Christmas City of the North Parade
Duluth, MN • late November • (218) 723-3337 • FREE

Evening holiday parade on Superior Street featuring bands, lighted floats, reindeer, elves, and more dance groups than you'd ever imagine; held the Friday before Thanksgiving.

Washburn's Merry Ol' Christmas
Washburn, WI • late November • (715) 373-5017

An early Christmas among Washburn's historic brownstones. (Cost unavailable.)

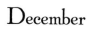

December

Garland City of the North Parade
Ashland, WI · early December · 800-284-9484 · FREE

Holiday parade featuring more than 30 bands, floats, reindeer, elves, and more.

Holiday Craft Show
Bayfield, WI · early December · (715) 779-3335 · FREE

A celebration of locally made holiday crafts.

Santa Lucia Festival
Two Harbors, MN · early December · (218) 834-2969 · FREE

Scandinavians celebrate the life of an Italian saint from the third century A.D. who could not be killed by fire.

Christmas Dinner Concert
Bayfield, WI · mid December · 800-447-4094 · cost unavailable

Dinner and music at the Lakeside Pavilion.

Old Fashioned Christmas Tea
Bayfield, WI · mid December · (715) 373-0495

A holiday tea the way it used to be. (Cost unavailable.)

Holiday Sing Along
Duluth, MN · mid December · (218) 723-3337 · FREE

Christmas carols and hot chocolate at Bayfront Park.

Handel's Messiah Sing Along
Duluth, MN · mid December · (218) 723-6000

Performed by St. Scholastica students at St. Scholastica's Mitchell Auditorium. (Cost unavailable.)

Winter Solstice at Lighthouse Point
Two Harbors, MN · mid December · (218) 834-4898

Bonfire, food, and music on the lawn of the lighthouse in Two Harbors; donations go toward the upkeep and maintenance of the lighthouse.

Zoo Year's Eve
Duluth, MN · December 31 · (218) 723-3748 · FREE

Sliding, skating, zoo visits, and fireworks from 2 P.M. to 5 P.M. at the Lake Superior Zoo.

New Year's Eve Gala
Bayfield, WI · December 31 · (715) 779-3335

Ring in the New Year at the Lakeside Pavilion. (Cost unavailable.)

New Year's Eve at the NorShor
Duluth, MN · December 31 · (218) 727-7585

Several local bands play two stages at the historic NorShor Theatre. Small cover charge.

Local Lore
& Places of Yore
(Twin Ports tales of days gone by)

Local Lore & Places of Yore

The city of Duluth takes its name from French explorer Daniel Greysolon Sieur du Lhut, Gendarme de la Garde du Roi, who grew up outside Lyon, France, and moved to Montreal before exploring the Great Lakes region. (A statue of Sieur du Lhut by sculptor Jacques Lipschitz stands in UMD's Ordean Court.) The explorer met with Ojibwe natives in 1679 at Fond du Lac (French for "bottom of the lake") and tried to persuade them to trade with the French instead of the British. But no Europeans visited the area again until the late 18th century, and it wasn't until 1817 that Englishman John Jacob Astor set up the American Fur Trading Company in Fond du Lac. Different villages and towns developed in the area over the next 100 years—Fond du Lac, Gary, Oneota, Endion, etc.—eventually combining to form the city as it is today.

Duluth has a rich history and has seen more than its share of colorful characters. It has gone from boom to bust to boom again (and again). It was once thought that the city would eclipse Chicago in size and prominence, and at one point it had more millionaires per capita than anywhere else in the U.S. More recently, its economy has struggled but has been bolstered in part by tourism.

We thought we'd use this part of the book to present to readers some of the interesting people and moments in the town's history, along with some notorious events typical visitor guides find inappropriate to discuss. Some of it isn't very pretty, but we think you'll find all of it interesting—it's all part of the story of Duluth.

Part of any city's history is tied to its houses and buildings—monuments to days gone by and examples of the tastes of different times. Unfortunately, many of Duluth's great structures have been lost. And so we have filled the latter pages of this chapter with photos of some of the more remarkable buildings that are no longer standing. We hope reminding the community of what the city has lost will help to save what remains. For, as the *New York Times* stated when Penn Station was levelled in 1963, "We want and deserve tin-can architecture in a tin-horn culture. And we will probably be judged not by the monuments we build but by those we have destroyed."

Dylan Does Duluth

Folk and rock music legend Bob Dylan came into this world at St. Mary's Hospital in Duluth on May 24, 1941, as Robert Zimmerman. He lived with his parents, Abe (a supervisor for Standard Oil Company) and Beatrice, on the second floor of the duplex pictured below and attended Nettleton School. When young Bob was six years old his family moved north to Hibbing, his mother's hometown. (The Duluth house was auctioned off on eBay in the summer of 2001 for $94,600.)

On January 31, 1959, high school senior Zimmerman hitched a ride to Duluth to see Buddy Holly and the Crickets, the Big Bopper, Ritchie Valens, and Dion & the Belmonts play at the National Guard Armory on London Road (see page 78). He had a third-row seat. Two nights later, Holly, the Big Bopper, and Valens gave their final show in Clear Lake, Iowa, and died in a plane crash. In his 1998 Grammy award acceptance speech, Dylan recalled the concert and claimed to have made eye contact with Holly. The Armory is now slated to be demolished and has been placed on the Preservation Alliance of Minnesota's Ten Most Endangered Historic Properties list.

Dylan has played in Duluth twice. His first appearance was at the DECC Arena in the fall of 1998, and he did not acknowledge his hometown in words. During his second appearance, outdoors on July 3, 1999, at Bayfront Park, he pointed up toward his childhood home on the Hillside and joked about an old girlfriend.

Dylan's first digs, 519 East 3rd Street, Duluth.

The Infamous Lynchings

Like any city, Duluth has had some ugly moments in its past, but none more horrible than June 15, 1920. The John Robinson Show Circus was in town the previous day for two performances in West Duluth. Later that night, 18-year-old Duluthian James Sullivan claimed that a black man from the circus held a pistol to his head and forced him to watch four other black circus workers rape Irene Tusken, 19, also from Duluth. It was a lie. A doctor who examined Tusken found no signs of sexual assault, yet he did not report his findings to authorities. Police rounded up a group of black circus workers and eventually held five of them, including Elmer Jackson, Elias Clayton, and material witness Isaac McGhie; all were between 19 and 21 years old.

Though not reported in the newspapers, news of the alleged rape spread through West Duluth, where outraged businessman Louis Dondino began rounding up a mob, causing a chain reaction throughout the community. By 8:40 P.M. a mob of an estimated 10,000 people stormed the downtown jail on Superior Street. By 9:30 they had broken through. After beating and harassing the prisoners, the mob took Jackson and Clayton—and later, McGhie—a block away to the corner of First Street and Second Avenue East. Some tried to stop the mob, including Reverend W. J. Powers, who climbed a light pole to address the crowd. The mob pulled him down and used the same light pole and some rope to kill Jackson, Clayton, and McGhie. The killers then posed for photographs next to their victims before a militia arrived and dispersed the crowd. Later, the photos were sold as postcards. The only punishments given to members of the lynch mob were convictions of rioting, but not murder.

In the 1940s, a St. Louis County Historical Society employee discarded records of the incident, deeming it too unseemly for study by students at the Duluth Normal School (which eventually became UMD).

Duluth is still not free of racial tension, and many local African Americans and American Indians feel they are unfairly treated by police. One group is trying to set things on the right course. An organization has successfully lobbied to establish a memorial to the lynching victims on the very street corner at which they were killed.

The Forgotten Lynching

Before lies and racial prejudice caused the death of three innocent black men, a group of Duluth vigilantes displayed their ignorance by hanging another man for his political beliefs. Actually, they tarred and feathered him first, then they hanged him.

Olli Kinkkonen was an immigrant from Finland and, like many Finns, a Socialist. He refused to join the American Army to fight in World War I and renounced his U.S. citizenship. Some say Kinkkonen considered the war an imperialist conflict, a struggle for economic power, an unjust war. Others say he was simply a peaceful man, a dockworker and logger who wanted no part of war and was mistaken for a more outspoken antiwar Finn. Whatever the case, Kinkkonen had made plans to return to Finland, but he never made it. Historians say it may not matter whether Kinkkonen was against the war, as anti-Finnish sentiment flourished in the area in 1918. What happened to him may have been as much inspired by ethnic bias as by politics.

In September 1918, Kinkkonen was abducted from his boarding house bed by a group calling themselves the Knights of Liberty, vigilantes who labeled those who did not join the army "slackers." The group first phoned then sent a letter to a local newspaper, claiming that they tarred and feathered Kinkkonen as a warning to all slackers. Two weeks after the abduction, Kinkkonen was found hanging by his neck from a tree north of Lester Park, covered in tar and feathers; $410 was found in his shoes. Duluth authorities ruled that Kinkkonen must have committed suicide because he was embarrassed about what had happened to him. His abductors—and probable murderers—were never charged. One local paper, *The Truth*, called the chief of police "unfit for office" and suggested that the *Duluth News-Tribune* knew the truth behind Kinkkonen's hanging.

Kinkkonen was buried in an unmarked grave in the poor section of Duluth's Park Hill Cemetery (two years later, Duluth's three other lynching victims would be buried just a few rows away). In 1993 a Finnish cultural group placed a marker on Kinkkonen's grave. It reads, "Olli Kinkkonen, 1881 to 1918, Victim of Warmongers."

Son-in-Law in the Hallway with a Candlestick

Many a tourist has walked the halls of Glensheen Mansion, the historic home built along London Road next to Lake Superior by Chester Congdon and his wife, Clara. But the tour guides won't discuss how the Congdon's daughter Elisabeth met her fate, nor will they explain other details of the night of June 27, 1977.

But Joe Kimball will. Kimball's book, *Secrets of the Congdon Mansion*, explains in detail the events leading up to the night Elisabeth Congdon and her night nurse, Velma Pietla, were murdered by Roger Caldwell, husband of Elisabeth's adopted daughter Marjorie. It also covers the trial that followed and includes maps of Glensheen, walking you along the murderer's path.

According to Kimball, Caldwell had big problems with finances and alcohol. Caldwell asked the Congdon estate for $800,000 so he and his wife could buy a ranch. After the trustees denied his request, Caldwell claims he hatched a plan to steal a few valuables from the house and sell them. Prosecutors, however, argued he planned to kill Congdon and make it look like she had died in her sleep then collect an inheritance worth millions. Caldwell flew into Minneapolis from Colorado, took the Greyhound to Duluth, and sat in a bar drinking for several hours before taking a cab to Glensheen. He broke into the house, entering through the billiard room off the patio, and made his way upstairs. He was surprised by the night nurse near the stairwell leading to the second floor, struggled with her, and eventually beat her to death with a candlestick. He then entered 83-year-old Elisabeth Congdon's bedroom and smothered her with a satin pillow for four minutes until she died. He took a few pieces of jewelry, a watch, a gold coin, and a car, which he drove to Minneapolis to catch a plane home to Colorado. He claims to have been drunk the entire time he was in Minnesota.

Some say you can still see blood stains on the carpet at the base of the upper set of stairs and along the wall as you climb those stairs (Kimball's book will tell you where to look). The large bedroom just east of the stairwell belonged to Mrs. Congdon—it was in this room that she was murdered.

The Pirates of Park Point

Back in 1889, Minnesota Point—at the time, the village of Park Point—was not nearly as heavily populated as it is today. Few houses stood along the world's largest sand bar, and no roads had been built. It was mostly sand dunes and scrub pine, the perfect place to hide pirate booty.

Park Point's pirates weren't your typical, cutlass-wielding-aaargh-exclaiming-peglegged-hook-handed-eye-patch-wearin'-parrot-totin' buccaneers of the Caribbean, and they hardly plundered ships for gold doubloons and pieces of eight. Duluth's pirates were a band of about six young men who apparently had an aversion to labor and turned to crime on the not-so-high seas to earn their keep.

They built themselves a cave on Park Point at a site close to 39th Street, near what in 1906 would become the Duluth Boat Club's Oatka Boat Club Branch. With open water on both sides, this was a strategic spot for their operation. While they hardly fit the stereotype, their style was not much different than traditional pirates. They plundered various vessels, sawmills, and warehouses.

Apparently, the cave was a temporary lair, and the pirates' goal was to set up permanent housing on the point, as the lumber they stole was used to build a house. Much of that lumber was stolen from the mill of Duluthian R. A. Gray, and Gray had had enough.

When Duluth's buccaneers tried to make off with more of his lumber one night, Gray decided to do something about it. He watched, then pursued the thieves. But the band of ne'er-do-wells had a large sailboat and managed to escape in the Lake Superior darkness.

The patient Mr. Gray eventually found their cave—and his lumber, in use in the unfinished house—and captured the gang after a struggle that history books called a "fierce battle." The half-dozen or so thieves all ended up in the penitentiary.

The Ghost Fleet of Lake Superior

Many a Great Lakes seaman believes Lake Superior is home to a "Ghost Fleet" made up of ships that have disappeared without a trace somewhere between Duluth and Sault Ste. Marie (The Soo). The Ghost Fleet's roster includes, among others, the *Adella Shores*, the *Bannockburn*, and the *Hudson*.

For those who believe in superstitions, the fate of the lumber hooker *Adella Shores* was sealed as she was launched. Built in Gibraltar, Michigan, and towed to Ashland, Wisconsin, before she was finished, the *Adella Shores* was constructed for Ashland mill owner Walter Shores, a leading supporter of the temperance movement in Wisconsin. Rather than have a ship named after his daughter christened with champagne, a bottle of lake water was used to launch the vessel. Mariners considered this very bad luck and an act that doomed the ship. In April 1909, the *Adella Shores* left her home dock in Ashland with a load of lumber. She was never seen again.

The *Bannockburn* also disappeared from Lake Superior, but she has been seen again—in spectral form. The steamer vanished November 21, 1902, while on her way from Port Arthur to The Soo with a load of wheat and 21 men on board. Only a life preserver and an oar were ever found. Still, several sailors claimed to have seen the *Bannockburn* on stormy nights. This has caused many to call the *Bannockburn* the "*Flying Dutchman* of Lake Superior," after the legendary phantom ship that disappeared off the coast of Good Hope.

The *Hudson* was lost near Michigan's Keweenaw Point on September 16, 1901, and like the *Bannockburn,* she has been seen since. Even boarded. As the story goes, a tugboat captain and his mate were near the site on a September 16 in the late 1940s when they spotted a rusty ship covered in brown slime. The tug captain claims to have boarded the vessel to see if it was in distress. In the pilot house he encountered the ragged apparitions of the *Hudson's* helmsman and captain, who explained to him that the ship and its crew were damned to relive the sinking each September 16 and warned him to get off. He leaped from the boat and swam in icy waters to the tug, refusing to explain to his mate what happened to him on board. (And yet somehow we hear the story....)

Bear and Drunk Square Off

Early on a Sunday morning in August of 1929, Arvid Peterson was driving down London Road with a truckload of fish fresh from the North Shore. At 26th Avenue East he noticed a large black bear following his truck. The bear followed him all the way to the corner of Superior Street and Third Avenue East—to the Hotel Duluth (home of the sidewalk compass that inspired this book's name). The bear apparently lost its taste for fish when it smelled the food from the hotel's coffee shop. The bear stood on its hind legs, swung a paw, and smashed through a 15-foot tall plate glass window. It then entered the hotel through the window and ran straight to the coffee shop.

A man described by newspapers as a "local drunk" grabbed a hammer and followed the bear through the broken window. He yelled and waved the hammer, facing the bear in a standoff. All the commotion woke night watchman Albert Nelson. When Nelson saw the bear, he ran to alert the assistant manager, who called police.

Nelson and the drunk occupied the bear, who had been attacking the mezzanine stairway, the inebriated man waving his hammer as the night watchman threw tables and chairs at the bruin. As the battle went on, guests began gathering in the lobby, and the faces of curious passersby filled windows. Soon a crowd had gathered.

Duluth police officers Sergeant Eli Le Bean and Patrolman John Hagen answered the assistant manager's call. Along with others, the officers tried to lasso the bear. After avoiding capture, the bear appeared to be bearing down on Nelson. Sergeant Le Bean raised his rifle and fired once, striking the bear in the head. The bear stood on its hind legs, wobbled for a moment, then fell down the stairs.

The bear's carcass was stuffed, mounted, and displayed in the front window of the hotel for years. Later, the coffee shop became the Black Bear Lounge, which has since closed.

The stuffed bear is on display at Grandma's Saloon & Grill in Canal Park.

Duluth: Home of the Washington Redskins

Many visitors to this area are well aware of the Duluth-Superior Dukes, the semi-pro baseball team that plays in the Northern League and can trace its intermittent history back over 50 years. But not many folks are aware that Duluth was once the home of the Washington Redskins, back when they were known as the Duluth Eskimos.

The Eskimos actually started in 1923 as the Duluth Kelleys, later playing as the Eskimos from 1926 to 1928. They were a traveling team featuring future NFL hall-of-famers Ernie Nevers, Walter Kiesling, and Johnny "Blood" McNally (McNally also played for Green Bay). The Eskimos played against teams such as the Potsville Maroons, the Milwaukee Badgers, and the Canton Bulldogs (as well as the Chicago Bears and the Green Bay Packers).

The 1926 Eskimos, featuring all-American fullback Nevers (a ticket attraction that rivaled Red Grange), were called "The Iron Men of the North." The team played 29 exhibition and league games—28 of them on the road—and Nevers played almost every minute of every game. The team earned a 6-5-3 record that season and played from September until February. Nevers had a good year in 1927. He played professional football, baseball, and basketball that year—the only man ever to do so—scrimmaging with Red Grange and pitching against Babe Ruth.

The Duluth Eskimos folded in 1928, and in 1929 the franchise was sold to New Jersey's Orange Athletic Club. They were renamed the Tornadoes, played one season in East Orange, and moved to Newark in 1930. The NFL then reclaimed the franchise and sold it to a Boston group who renamed it the Braves and, later, the Redskins (when they moved to Fenway Park). The Redskins moved to Washington in 1932. (Eskimos, Braves, Redskins—not the most ethnically sensitive names; and the question remains: what's a Kelley?)

The Duluth team has not been forgotten by all. You can buy Eskimo hats and sweatshirts from Internet retailers, and *Sports Illustrated* writer Rick Reilly coauthored a screenplay centered on the 1927 Eskimos, a comic romance entitled *Leatherheads* (the Eskimos played to a 1-8-0 record that season).

Duluth's Famous Old Soldier

Duluth's Central Hillside was home to Albert Woolsen, the last surviving Union Army soldier of the Civil War. Woolsen lived to be 109 years old. He was born in Watertown, New York, on February 11, 1847, and arrived in Duluth in 1862. At 17, Woolsen joined the Union Army as a "volunteer private." He was assigned to Company C of the First Minnesota Heavy Artillery Regiment, detailed to the drum corps—Albert Woolsen was a drummer boy. He saw no action, but witnessed Sherman's March.

A lifelong Republican, Woolsen cast his first vote for Abraham Lincoln. He was just 17 at the time and voted under a special war clause for members of the armed forces. As the last Union survivor, he was named commander-in-chief of the Grand Army of the Republic.

Woolsen lived most of his life in Duluth at 215 East 5th Street. As he aged—and as other Union veterans died, making him the last—Duluth newspapers annually featured accounts of Woolsen celebrating his birthday; he was often photographed shoveling snow. When he was 105, he recommended the following for a long life: 1. exercise, used judiciously, 2. not worrying over trifles, and 3. due respect for the laws of nature, such as not overeating. "Moderation in all things; that goes for whiskey, women, and food," Woolsen said.

On July 12, 1954—when he was 107 years old—Woolsen wrote a letter that now hangs in an alcove close to City Hall's entrance alongside a plaque, an American flag, and a bust of Woolsen. It reads as follows:

To My Fellow Americans,

On April 9, 1865, the terrible war of rebellion ended; the differences between the Union and the Confederacy were forgotten and the North and South were once again united.

As the last survivor of the Union army, I have seen these United States grow into the greatest nation in the history of mankind.

Our sacrifices were not in vain.

Woolsen died August 2, 1956, at the age of 109 years. A statue of him stands near the end of Canal Park.

Duluth's Not-So-Famous Old Soldier

Colonel Hubert V. Eva, though not as celebrated as Albert Woolsen, was also a last survivor of one of America's wars—one of the war's last battles, to be precise. Unfortunately, it was not a war Eva was exactly proud of. He was the last surviving veteran of the Indian Campaigns.

Often called an "Ex-Indian Fighter" by the press, Eva did not care for the term. In his 29 years in the military, Eva spent about a month involved in conflicts with American Indians. "It was rather foolish," Eva said of the battles. "You don't hunt people like you hunt deer."

Eva was born August 8, 1869, in Penzance, Cornwall (England), and came to Duluth as a lad of 16. In 1889 he enlisted in the Minnesota National Guard. By 1898 he had become a captain and volunteered for service in the Spanish-American war. After that conflict, he fought as part of the 3rd U.S. Regiment during the Leech Lake Indian uprising led by Chippewa Chief Bu-A-May-Geh-Shig, the last Indian conflict in Minnesota in which shots were exchanged. Seven soldiers died and nine were wounded; two Chippewa were wounded. Two years later Eva helped quell an uprising of 500 to 600 Sioux and Chippewa along the Canadian Border. Eva convinced Indian leaders to end the conflict. No shots were fired.

In 1910 Eva found himself in Baudette, Minnesota, leading a detachment to clean up after a major forest fire; he was also involved in helping with the aftermath of other forest fires in the early years of the century. In 1916 Eva served with General Pershing along the Mexican border protecting U.S. citizens against attacks by Pancho Villa and his bandits. During World War I he was stationed in New Mexico, training American troops for combat in Europe. He retired from the military in 1918.

In 1971, at 102 years old, Eva was killed when he and his nurse were struck by a car driven by a UMD student as they crossed Superior Street near 17th Avenue East after attending a dinner at St. Paul's Episcopal Church.

Helter Smelter

During the 1970s and '80s, late April to early May found the shores of Lake Superior lined with drunken revelers waist deep in frigid waters, toting nets, buckets, and even plastic bags in the hope of filling them—and later, their bellies—with smelt. But the smelt no longer run as thick as they once did, and all-night smelting parties at the mouths of the big lake's tributary rivers have ceased.

Smelt (pronounced "shmelt" by many local residents) are small, silver-colored fish native to salt water. People argue over how they got to Lake Superior. Some say that in 1912, live smelt native to the Atlantic Ocean were transported from Green Lake, Maine, to Crystal Lake in Northern Michigan, where they followed drainage systems into Lake Michigan and, eventually, Lake Superior. Others claim smelt are a Pacific Ocean transplant that arrived in Lake Superior after being accidentally introduced to Lake Michigan.

In the 1950s, the sea lamprey (another exotic import from the Atlantic) nearly wiped out Lake Superior's populations of lake herring and trout. In the wake of the lamprey's appetite for their predators, smelt flourished.

By the 1970s, people were hauling away pick-up truck loads of the little fish caught as they gathered at the mouths of rivers to spawn. Folks from out of town arrived in motor homes, set up camp, and netted smelt until they had more than they could possibly handle. Local pizzeria's cashed in by delivering pizza to hungry, inebriated crowds gathered at river mouths. A local Vietnam Veterans' group even staged an annual Smelt Fry, where hundreds would gather for a weekend, eat buckets of deep-fried smelt, drink beer, and enjoy a variety of live bands. The last, dubbed "Helter Smelter," was held at the Douglas County Fairgrounds in Superior in 1984.

Since the sea lamprey population has been controlled and the smelt's predator's populations have risen, the smelt population has declined dramatically, resulting in the decline of the human population's drunken revelry (at least outdoors at night for a few weeks in April and May). Since smelt is an exotic species, there is a debate over what, if anything, should be done to revive its population.

Spirit Little Cedar Tree

The Spirit Little Cedar Tree ("Minido Geezhi-Gans" in Ojibwe, also known disrespectfully as the "Witch Tree" or "Witch's Tree") is a cedar monarch that sprouted from seemingly barren rock on the Hat Point prominence some 400 years ago. For generations the Ojibwe left offerings of tobacco at the tree for safe passage on the big lake. When they encountered Grand Portage, French voyageurs respected the tradition and left offerings of their own.

Now gnarled with age and exposure to the elements, the Spirit Little Cedar Tree has been the subject of countless books and works of art. Reports conflict as to how it came to be called the "Witch Tree." Some say it was dubbed by the voyageurs and other early European explorers; others give credit to Dewey Albinson, one of the many artists drawn to the tree.

Unfortunately, vandals have caused the local band of Grand Portage Ojibwe, who now own the land near Grand Portage where the tree is found, to close off public access to the tree. Over the years, ignorant visitors had carved their initials in the tree or cut away portions of it as souvenirs. If you want to see the Spirit Little Cedar Tree yourself, you have to arrange a tour with a member of the band. For a distant view, you can take the *MV Wenonah* from Grand Portage to Michigan's Isle Royale; it passes by Hat Point to give passengers a view of the tree.

Superior's Berger Hardware

When Berger Hardware opened its doors at 525 Tower Avenue in Superior in 1915, owner Morris Berger's goal was to turn it into the best stocked general goods store around. By the time it closed 70 years down the road, it was not only a hardware store extraordinaire, but an antique store and tourist attraction—a hardware museum.

Berger filled every nook, cranny, and corner of his store with stock purchased from other stores or factories that had gone out of business. The merchandise was stocked haphazardly on high, packed shelves and even hung from the ceiling. Customers who tried to find items on their own were quickly frustrated—only Berger and his son Sam knew where everything was kept.

At Berger customers could find brand new buggy whips, axe handles unloaded by the WPA in the 1930s, and unused milk bottles along with tons of nuts, bolts, and nails. Cases of soldering irons sat adjacent to blacksmith tongs. A home restorer's dream, Berger stocked hinges and doorknobs from days gone by. If you couldn't find something anywhere else, there was a good chance Berger's had it—no matter how old or odd.

Morris Berger ran the hardware store until he died in the late 1970s. Sam took over the helm and kept the doors open another dozen years—until he died at his desk.

In 1994 Jim Kremer bought the store and soon found himself overwhelmed trying to locate merchandise. But that didn't stop people from coming in. According to Kremer, many visitors didn't come to buy anything but just to have a look around. He said that some interested parties had even called ahead to arrange group tours.

In March, 1999, the Berger Hardware inventory was auctioned off. People came from hundreds of miles away to bid on obscurities. Even a group of Amish gentlemen attended to stock up on items, such as buggy parts, they have trouble finding anywhere else. In May of 2001, company officials from Mama Get's, Inc., announced they planned to turn the building into a restaurant. It may well be open by the time you read this.

Duluth's Young at Heart Records

For 41 years beginning in 1956, Richard Wozniak operated the Young at Heart record store ("for the young and the young at heart") at 22 1st Avenue West in downtown Duluth. From the basement to the third floor, Wozniak filled the building with thousands and thousands of 45-, 33-, and 78-rpm vinyl disks—as well as an impressive number of books—creating a mecca for music collectors.

The store takes its name from a 1950s-era Frank Sinatra hit, appropriate enough since the store itself seemed anchored in time. Wozniak decorated with pinks and reds to maintain the "heart" motif. All of the signs were handpainted, as were many of the boxes in which the 45s were kept. Wosniak stocked everything from rock 'n' roll to country and western to jazz to show tunes to classical—just about anything, as long as the lyrics weren't offensive.

More than just a used record shop, Young at Heart was a gathering place for music lovers from all over the map. Vinyl enthusiasts from the Twin Cities to Thunder Bay, from West Duluth to North Dakota came to Wosniak's shop to dig through the endless stacks of wax. Twin Cities weekly newspaper *City Pages* called it "the Babel of vinyl" and encouraged its readers to visit when in Duluth.

Wozniak so loved his store that he practically lived in it during the last few years it was open. He kept several shelves stocked with canned goods and boxed dinners, which he would prepare and eat at the store to avoid leaving for meals.

When Wozniak retired in 1997, relatives put the contents of his store up for sale in order to help finance his retirement. While its doors have closed, the memory of the store will be preserved. The Minnesota Historical Society purchased Young at Heart memorabilia, including its cash register and several hand-decorated 45-rpm record boxes. The Society included these items in an exhibit entitled "Sounds Good to Me: Music in Minnesota" at St. Paul's History Center as an example of mom-and-pop music stores.

Random Radio: Airwave Pirates

In the late 1990s, the airwaves over Duluth's East Hillside were filled with an incredibly eclectic mix of music emanating from Scott Lunt's basement and beamed at 100 watts of power over the radio frequency 93.5 FM.

Random Radio was a "pirate" radio station—that is, a station that operated without an FCC license. The station earned its name three ways. First, the programming (everything from rock to jazz to spoken-word) touched so many different corners, listeners never quite knew what they were in store for. Second, the station operated only when Lunt (a.k.a. "DJ Starfire") or one of his crew had the spare time to be on the air. And third, because of the station's low wattage and its placement on Duluth's Hillside, listeners had only a random chance of picking it up on their radios. It came in best through car stereos, and while Duluthians over the hill couldn't pick it up, listeners along the South Shore in Wisconsin claimed clear reception.

Random Radio's programming included a great deal of local music, such as that of Lunt's own country-inspired group, Father Hennepin. The station also featured live performances by guest musicians, including Duluth's own internationally-recognized Low. Lunt had the foresight to record those appearances, and assembled many of them on a CD entitled "Random Acts of Radio" (the CD is available locally at the Electric Fetus).

But crime doesn't pay (neither does operating a low-watt, commercial-free radio station), and the Feds eventually caught up with Lunt. He received a letter from the FCC listing the laws he was violating and was forced to shut the station down shortly afterward or face stiff fines.

If you want a taste of what Random Radio was like, visit Fitger's Brewhouse in the Fitger's complex on Thursday nights for the Starfire Lounge, where Lunt and his team of DJs spin an eclectic mix of songs old and new, with lots of local music in the mix. And although it's officially off the air, some claim that, just like Lake Superior's ghost ship the *Bannockburn*, on foggy nights when the big lake's waters run rough, you can still hear the efforts of local music lovers drifting over the air at 93.5 FM....

The Aerial Bridge Didn't Always Lift

Duluth's Aerial Lift Bridge—the largest in the world—has become an icon for the city, used in the logos of everything from newspaper websites to food service companies. The original bridge, however, didn't lift. The bridge was built in 1905—a welcome structure to those who lived on Minnesota Point and who had relied upon ferries to cross the canal since it was dug in 1871. (During winter months, a temporary suspension bridge was used.) The 1905 bridge, patterned after a suspended car bridge in Rouen, France, used a gondola to ferry passengers and goods (and, later, streetcars) across the canal. It was called the Aerial Transfer Bridge.

Redesigned in 1930 as a lift bridge, the bridge first lifted for a ship on March 29, 1930, when the *Essayons*, a Corps of Engineers tug, passed through the canal as a test. It has since raised about 400,000 times.

Between 1966 and 1973, tourists were allowed to stay on the bridge as it raised and lowered. Today, police fine those who purposefully trespass on the bridge for rides. At least two tragedies are connected with the bridge.

The original aerial bridge ferried passengers and goods using a gondola.

In 1982, a 19-year-old man from Grand Rapids, Minnesota, grabbed onto the bottom of the bridge; when the bridge was 70 feet above the water, he fell to his death. And on June 10, 1990, a 50-year-old Duluth woman panicked when the bridge's warning bells sounded as she walked across the bridge. She either leaned out to grab a vertical beam or tried to jump, but became caught in the bridge's superstructure. The bridge cut her in half.

To learn more about the bridge, see Thomas Holden's history at www.duluthshippingnews.com/aerialliftbridge.htm.

D. Clint Prescott House

54th Ave. W. & Central Pl. • c. 1888–1948
architect unknown

James Allen Scott, author of *Duluth's Legacy Volume 1: Architecture*, calls the Prescott House "The best costumed participant in [Duluth's] Mardi Gras of prosperity" and says that "nowhere on the house could the observer find a moment of visual rest." Iron executive D. Clint Prescott's Queen Anne-style home was indeed a treat for the eyes. Again, the eloquent Mr. Scott describes it beautifully: "[The] three-story house was a carnival of dormers and gables, porches, and verandas, carvings and spindles, chimneys and towers, bargeboards and lattices, and gaily dressed lightning rods."

Prescott worked for the Marinette Iron Works Company, which relocated to Duluth from Marinette, Wisconsin, in 1890. He moved his family to Chicago before the end of the century, and the house took on a series of owners and later became a hospital before it was eventually abandoned. Like many empty mansions, rumors of hauntings persisted until the house was destroyed in 1948.

The Duluth Preservation Alliance uses a drawing of the D. Clint Prescott House as its logo.

Hartley House

1305 Superior St. • 1889–1954 • Oliver G. Traphagen, architect

You'd be hard pressed to spend any amount of time in Duluth without bearing witness to the mark left by Guilford and Caroline E. Hartley. That Tudor Revival building rising above the Lakewalk east of the Portland Malt Shop? That's their office building. The Kitchi Gammi Club? Mr. Hartley played a principal role in its construction (note the similarity between the Kitch and the Hartley's office building). Hartley Park? Well, you get the picture. A

businessman with eclectic interests, Guilford Hartley focused on industry, politics, cattle, agriculture, transportation, and the press (he owned one of Duluth's early newspapers). He also helped found Northland Country Club.

In 1889 he and his wife, Caroline, had Oliver Traphagen design a house one block from what is now the Rose Garden and Leif Erickson Park. The Romanesque mansion stood nearly four stories tall and included a carriage house. The house became the first in Duluth to be wired for electricity and the first to have a telephone. Chester Creek ran along its eastern edge.

The lots upon which the house once stood are now home to a Walgreens and its parking lot.

First Methodist Episcopal Church

215 N. 3rd Ave. W. • 1892–1966 • architect unknown

Built for $120,000 in 1892, the Gothic red sandstone First Methodist Episcopal Church seated 2,200 parishioners when all its galleries were open. All of its windows were stained glass, and paintings adorned the interior walls. Its chimes were the first to be installed in Duluth. The ten bells, the largest of which weighed 1,200 pounds, played in two keys and were the gift of Thomas and George Martin, who paid $10,000 for them in 1921. The chimes rang each day at noon, before Sunday services, and on national holidays and other special occasions.

Because most of its parishioners had moved away from the downtown area, the church closed its doors after its last service on November 6, 1966. It was replaced by the Pietro Belluschi-designed First United Methodist Church at Skyline Parkway and Central Entrance (also known as the "Coppertop Church," see page 53).

The church also held a historic pipe organ made by the Austin firm of Hartford, Connecticut. The organ, a gift from a parishioner, had 1,500 pipes and was originally water driven. The instrument was dismantled before the church was torn down. Its cathedral chimes and stops were transplanted into the new church's organ.

Duluth Curling Club

1330 London Rd. • 1912–1984 • Frederick G. German, architect

Curling is a shuffleboard-like sport played on a sheet of ice with brooms and rocks with handles—Scottish bocce ball, if you will. Local residents have participated in organized curling since Christmas Day of 1891, when the Duluth Curling Club was born on a $400 rink at 3rd Avenue East and Superior Street. (By the way, Superior's Raymond "Bud" Somerville led the U.S. Olympic curling team to a bronze medal in 1992; he was 55 years old.)

Built in 1912, the Duluth Curling Club eclipsed all other curling facilities in sheer number of rinks with 12. Ice skaters and hockey players used rinks on the second floor and in the summer the space was used for roller skating.

In 1984 the curling club caught fire and was demolished just before work on the I-35 extension began. The lot on which it stood is now a parking lot next to the Rose Garden. Today, the Curling Club plays its matches at its facility inside the Duluth Entertainment and Convention Center.

The Duluth Boat Club

You can't live next to the largest body of fresh water in the world without finding plenty of ways to have fun with it, and from early on Duluthians found recreation on the great lake. In 1886 eleven local men got together to form the Duluth Boat Club and soon built a clubhouse at 7th Avenue West along the St. Louis Bay (pictured below). Eventually a second club house had to be built at 10th Street on the bay side of Minnesota Point.

According to the current Duluth Boat Club, the old club "offered rowing, sailing, canoeing, swimming, tennis, and other sports [and] also hosted lavish banquets, festivals and dances." At its peak the club had 1,400 members and became the hub of social activities for Duluth's elite.

Over the years the Boat Club produced 20 national rowing championship teams led by coach James Ten Eyck, Jr., and in 1916 played host to the national championships. But by 1926 Eyck had left and automobiles were all the rage. Starving for funds, the club closed its doors.

Duluth was without a boating organization until 1956, when the Duluth Rowing Club was formed. The current club credits its growing youth program to its members' volunteer mentoring and dedication.

The Duluth Rowing Club changed its name to the Duluth Boat Club in the fall of 1999. Members have proposed building a $2 million to $2.5 million facility at 14th Street and St. Louis Avenue. The new facility would be youth-oriented, handicapped-accessible, and affordable, setting it apart from the exclusive Boat Club of years gone by.

Duluth Incline Railway & Pavilion

7th Ave. W. • Railway: 1891–1939 | Pavilion: 1891–1901 • Traphagen & Fitzpatrick, pavilion architects

The Incline Railway was a system of steam engines and cables that pulled tram cars up and down two sets of elevated tracks on what is now 7th Avenue West to get commuters from their homes at the top of the hill down to Superior Street and their jobs downtown. On weekends and evenings, residents hopped on the Incline for a ride up to its expansive pavilion. There, Duluthians enjoyed dances, vaudeville performances, or dined in one of its restaurants. Others picnicked outdoors or took a ride in a hot-air balloon.

Unfortunately, in 1901 a fire began in the pavilion and destroyed it. The fire spread to the power station, and the heat melted the railway's cables, releasing a flam-

ing trolley car that raced toward Superior Street, crashed through the railway's depot gates, crossed Superior Street, and came to a halt in the railyards near the Union Depot. No one was injured.

The Incline served the city until Labor Day, 1939. It was dismantled and sold as scrap.

Original Cascade Park

4th St. below Mesaba Ave. • 1895–1975

The City of Duluth didn't always run roughshod over its natural beauty in order to make a few developers rich. As far back as 1890, the city was purchasing land to reserve as parks. Cascade Park, a 3.19-acre space complete with a creek and waterfalls, was part of the first wave of park development. In 1895 the city added a sand-stone pavilion and bell tower at the heart of the park, giving it a whimsical, castle-like atmosphere.

Clark House Creek ran through the park and right through the pavilion, its waterfall cascading through an opening on the building's lakeview facade. Unfortunately, the bell tower was destroyed during a storm in 1897. Portions of the creek were altered to flow underground as the area surrounding the park developed

Only two-and-a-half acres of Cascade Park survive. When Mesaba Avenue was widened in 1975 to accommodate traffic heading toward the Duluth Heights neighborhood and the mall, part of the park was sacrificed. Its sandstone structures were destroyed and the remainder of the creek was forced underground. The city then rebuilt the bell tower, though in a different design than the original.

Top of the Temple Opera Building

201 E. Superior St. • 1889–c. 1940
Charles McMillen & E.S. Stebbins, architects

When the Masonic Temple Opera Block opened its doors in 1889, it housed the first Duluth Public Library, a Masonic lodge, an opera house, and business offices. The six-story building was designed in the Moorish Romanesque style complete with an onion-shaped dome at its top. But when Guilford Hartley bought the building, things changed.

In 1910 Hartley financed the construction of the Orpheum Theatre, a vaudeville house designed by J.E.O. Pridemore and built at the back of the opera house, replacing the ornate 2nd Avenue East entrance and facade with an awning and Classic Revival pillars. Hartley later had the top three floors and the dome of the Temple Opera Building removed.

The Orpheum closed in the 1930s. In 1941 the building was dramatically converted into the NorShor Theatre, an art deco movie house (see page 100). Portions of the Orpheum are actually still inside the structure of the NorShor, whose entrance is on Superior Street. When first built, the NorShor featured a tower of lights that reached 65 feet in the air. (Some say Hartley had the Temple Opera Building altered to make the tower more visible, but he died in 1922). The Temple Opera Building currently houses office space and Browser's N'eTc., an Internet coffee shop run by a Hartley descendant.

Lyceum Theatre

Superior St. at 5th Ave. W. • 1891–1966 • Traphagen & Fitzpatrick, architects

When the Lyceum Theatre opened for business in July of 1891, it was proudly hailed as the "handsomest and costliest building in the Northwest." The building stood six stories high in a style the *Duluth Daily Tribune* called "reposeful and majestic Romanesque" and contained an auditorium surrounded by business offices. Its facade was a treat for the eyes.

The Lyceum featured a triple-arched, two-story entryway on Superior Street complete with stone lions to guard the entry and the ornate carvings of Duluth's master stone artisan, Norwegian immigrant O. George Thrana (Thrana's work still graces many of Duluth's old buildings). The Lyceum seated 1,500 and its stage was the second largest in the Northwest.

Opera divas, actors, and vaudevillians trod its stage's boards for 30 years before it was converted to a movie theater. It operated until November 1960, and in January 1966 was destroyed to make room for KDLH-TV's studios. You can still see some remains of the Lyceum: its stairway's stone lions, appropriately enough, have found a home at the Lake Superior Zoo, and the drama and comedy masks that flanked its entrance now grace the Duluth Playhouse Theater.

The Lyceum Theatre's ornate, two-story Superior Street entrance.

U.S. Government Building

431 W. 1st St. • 1894–1934 • Traphagen & Fitzpatrick, architects

Another fine example of the many stone Romanesque Revival buildings that once flourished throughout Duluth, the U.S. Government Building's square stone tower reached five stories into the sky. The building stood at 5th Avenue West and 1st Street, across the street from what is now the home of the *Duluth News-Tribune*. The heavy stone structure was often called the Post Office building, because it also held Duluth's central post office.

When it was dismantled in 1934, its arched doorway was supposed to go to Leif Erickson Park to act as a gateway to the park (if it did indeed move to the park, it is no longer there). A single nine-ton piece of stone featuring a carved eagle was also removed and was to be given to the Naval Reserve Station on Minnesota Point, but it was too heavy. Workers dismantling the building found a bottle; in the bottle was a cloth with the message "goodby, Friends." It was dated November 11, 1892, and signed by "James Peterson, 14th Ave. E. and Charles Bowman, 465 23rd W."

Appendix
(credits, bibliography, and index)

Photo & Illustration Credits

All illustrations, maps, and photos by Tony Dierckins, except:

The illustration of the Spirit Little Cedar Tree (page 222) was drawn by Kent Aldrich of The Nomadic Press.

The image of the Aerial Transfer Bridge (page 226) is from a postcard c. 1905; publisher unknown.

The image of Old Cascade Park (page 233) is from the private postcard collection of Bob Swanfeld.

The image of the Duluth Union Depot (page 73) is from a postcard originally published by A. Gallagher.

The photo of the Squaw Bay caves (page 49) is courtesy of Joe Taatjes.

The following photos appear courtesy of the Northeast Minnesota Historical Center, Duluth, Minnesota: Morgan Park Goodfellowship Club (page 79), Hartley House (page 228), First Methodist Episcopal Church (page 229), Duluth Incline Railway Pavilion (page 232), Temple Opera Building (page 234), Lyceum Theatre (page 235), U.S. Government Building (page 236).

The NEMHC photos of the D. Clint Prescott home (page 227) and the Duluth Boat Club (page 231) were originally published in the 1890 edition of *Duluth Illustrated* (J.P. Craig, publisher).

The NEMHC photos of the Duluth Incline Railway (page 232) and the Duluth Curling Club (page 230) are Hugh McKenzie photographs.

Bibliography

Books & Pamphlets

Aubut, Sheldon T. and Maryanne C. Norton. *Images of America: Duluth, Minnesota*. Arcadia Publishing, Chicago, IL: 2001.

Buchanon, James. *The Twin Ports: A Guide to Duluth and Superior*. Nodin Press, Minneapolis, MN: 1992.

El-Hai, Jack. *Lost Minnesota: Stories of Vanished Places*. University of Minnesota Press, Minneapolis, MN: 2000.

Fedo, Michael. *The Lynchings in Duluth*. Minnesota Historical Society Press, St. Paul, MN: 2000.

Harnish, Sue, et. al. *Mission Creek Nature Trail* (pamphlet). Junior League of Duluth, Duluth, MN: 1975.

Hertzel, Laurie, ed. *Boomtown Landmarks*. Pfeifer-Hamilton Publishers, Duluth, MN: 1992.

Kimball, Joe. *Secrets of the Congdon Mansion*. JayKay Publishing, Minneapolis, MN: 1985.

MacDonald, Dora Mary. *This is Duluth*. Paradigm Press, Ashland, WI: 1999.

Morgan Park/Smithville Community Club 1994 Calendar. Morgan Park/Smithville Community Club, Duluth, MN: 1994.

Nash, Anedith and Robert Silberman. *Morgan Park: Continuity and Change in a Company Town*. Publisher and publication date unknown.

Perich, Shawn. *The North Shore: A Four Season Guide to Minnesota's Favorite Destination*. Pfeifer-Hamilton Publishers, Duluth, MN: 1992.

Powell, Mrs. Thomas. *Congdon Creek Park* (pamphlet). Junior League of Duluth. Duluth, MN: publication date unknown.

Bibliography, continued

More Books

Scott, James Allen. *Duluth's Legacy: Volume 1, Architecture*. City of Duluth, Duluth, MN: 1974.

Simonowicz, Nina. *Nina's North Shore Guide*. University of Minnesota Press, Minneapolis, MN: 1999.

Stonehouse, Frederick. *Haunted Lakes*. Lake Superior Port Cities, Inc., Duluth, MN: 1997.

Tierney, Carol. *Chester Creek Nature Trail* (pamphlet). Junior League of Duluth. Duluth, MN: 1974.

Newspapers

The Duluth News-Tribune (Duluth, MN)

The Duluth Herald (Duluth, MN; no longer in publication)

Ripsaw (Duluth, MN)

The Truth (Duluth, MN; no longer in publication)

Websites*

Eichten, Gary, et al. *Minnesota Public Radio Online*. http://www.mpr.org/index_main.shtml

Thomas, Thomas R. "Duluth's Aerial Lift Bridges." *Duluth Shipping News*. http://www.duluthshippingnews.com/aerialliftbridge.htm

Lundgren, Paul and Brad Nelson, eds. *Ripsaw Online*. http://www.ripsawnews.com

Ryan, Mark. *The History of Seven Bridges Road*. http://www.geocities.com/SoHo/Lofts/4839/SevenBridges/

*See also the websites listed on page 14.

Index

Index, continued

Index, continued

Index, continued

Index, continued

Index, continued

Help Us Out!

Because this book had to go to the printer long before it could be placed in stores, we realize that some of the information may have changed—some shops and restaurants may have moved, changed their business hours, or even closed. We also realize we may have overlooked some places worthy of mention. If you find something has changed or that we've left out one of your favorite places, let us know and we'll work it into the next edition.

We'd also like to add to our "Outdoor Adventures," "Annual Events," and "Local Lore" sections (or any other part of the book, for that matter), so if you know of anything that might be appropriate, please tell us about it.

Just e-mail us at truenorth@x-communication.org.

Check Online for Updates

As we continue to expand and update *True North* for future editions, we will post any information that changes from the entries in this edition on our publisher's website in order to keep you current. Simply visit the X-communication website at www.x-communication.org and follow the links to the *True North* home page.

About the Authors

St. Paul native **Tony Dierckins** first moved to Duluth in 1984 to attend the University of Minnesota Duluth. He has moved away twice but was drawn back each time, making the city his permanent home in 1996. Dierckins has taught writing and graphic design at UMD and has coauthored over a dozen books, including *The Mosquito Book, The WD-40 Book,* and the *Duct Tape* books and calendars. He also created the CoasterBook series published by Running Press.

Kerry Elliott was born in Kaukauna, Wisconsin, and grew up in Duluth. She too moved away but was drawn back to make her home in Duluth. Elliott analyzes numbers and data for Maurices, Inc., at its corporate headquarters in downtown Duluth and writes feature articles and film reviews for the *Ripsaw*, a regional weekly arts & entertainment paper. This is her first book.